Praise for *Wide and Deep*

2015 New England Society Book Award—Contemporary Nonfiction Book of the Year

2015 New England Outdoor Writers Award—Book of the Year

2015 Outdoor Writers Association of America—Book of the Year

"When readers do keep writers company, we're introduced to characters seen through their eyes. With luck, by the end of a book, we remember them well. That happens in *Wide and Deep*. Author Randy Spencer paddles clients and readers through deep woods and waters filled with smallmouth bass, pickerel and perch, landlocked salmon, moody moose, a tattletale raven, mostly while seated in a pampered canoe that's almost an animate partner. His descriptions are rich and measured, detailed but not overwrought; while I've never visited this country, I suspect I'll find it familiar when I do."

—Seth Norman, *Fly Rod and Reel Magazine*

"Reading *Wide and Deep* quickens the pulse of anyone who loves dawn on the water, a filling campfire lunch, or sunset on a far shore. The great strength of *Wide and Deep* lies in its power to endure. Like fishing season itself, the power of Spencer's stories is that they can come around again and again. Read ten or twenty years hence, they will reveal the same truths as they do today . . . Spencer is a gifted storyteller. Lucky anglers will read and understand *Wide and Deep*. Really lucky anglers will someday share a canoe with him."

—Colonel J. C. Allard, the *Outdoor Gazette*

"Delivers a set of tales that will leave readers entertained, and leave his fellow outdoor writers saying, 'Wow. Wish I'd written that.' . . . Spencer spins yarns with the well-practiced skill of a natural storyteller. Years spent in a canoe, turning strangers into friends, one story at a time, will do that to you."

—John Holyoke, *Banger Daily News*

Other books from Randy Spencer:

Where Cool Waters Flow: Four Seasons with a Master Maine Guide

WIDE
AND
DEEP

Tales and Recollections from a Master Maine Fishing Guide

RANDY SPENCER

Skyhorse Publishing

Skyhorse Publishing books may be purchased in bulk at special discounts for sales promotion, corporate gifts, fund-raising, or educational purposes. Special editions can also be created to specifications. For details, contact the Special Sales Department, Skyhorse Publishing, 307 West 36th Street, 11th Floor, New York, NY 10018 or info@ skyhorsepublishing.com.

Skyhorse® and Skyhorse Publishing® are registered trademarks of Skyhorse Publishing, Inc.®, a Delaware corporation.

www.skyhorsepublishing.com

10 9 8 7 6 5 4 3 2 1

Library of Congress Cataloging-in-Publication Data is available on file.

Paperback ISBN: 978-1-5107-1432-8
Ebook ISBN: 978-1-62873-998-5
Previous Hardcover ISBN: 978-1-62873-639-7

Printed in the United States of America

Cover photography: F. Carl Mahoney
Back cover art: Courtesy of Randy Spencer
All photographs are courtesy of Randy Spencer unless otherwise noted.
Cover design by Brian Peterson
Editing: Barbara J. Barr, Impeccably Edited, La Jolla, CA

*Dedicated to the memory of Henry P. Spencer,
Henry J. Spencer, and Kerwin A. Spencer Sr.,
all legends of the spring in my fishing pedigree.*

PROLOGUE

Every fishing family has a legend. If you're born into one of these families, you become part of that legend. In my case, my one living grandfather at the time of my birth, his son—my father—and both maternal and paternal uncles fished. In due course, so did all my cousins and both of my brothers. All the women in the family fished faithfully, too, if perhaps without the same frequency. While growing up, it didn't seem as if fishing was something you decided to do or not to do. It was like going to school, only better. Or riding a bike. Or swimming. Not to fish, in my family, would have been like not living.

My grandfather, Henry P. Spencer, fished for brook trout into his late eighties. Then, after having one of the very first pacemakers put into his chest at Yale New Haven Hospital in the early 1960s, he resumed fishing. Some of my earliest memories are of him taking me in "the old jalopy" (the term the legend gave to his even-then-old Model A Ford) to a secluded brook not four feet wide in some stretches. He wore hip boots, fished with a short bamboo fly rod of no distinction, and carried a creel slung over his right shoulder, resting on his left hip. He fished slowly. Very slowly. He taught me the importance of shadows on the water, and how to avoid casting any when you're trout fishing. Fish fear shadows.

He fished with "angle worms" dug from his garden. Often, he impaled two with his hook so that four ends would dangle tantalizingly as the bait floated downstream beneath the riffles. I learned from him how to watch the line to see when a trout had picked up the bait. It would first straighten, then move in one direction or another. After waiting so long that it was sometimes painful, it was time to set the hook. For me, nothing has ever been more beautiful to behold than the living color of speckled, squaretail trout in my grandfather's hand. He would pick up some wet moss along the stream bank to line the bottom of his creel with before laying the fish in.

Fishing conversations with anyone in my family, extended family included, were commonplace. To talk fishing, to read about fishing in *Field & Stream* or *Outdoor Life*, to go to bait and tackle shops— all of this was routine. The vacations we took were fishing vacations. The outings we shared with family were fishing outings. People who didn't fish were exotic to me. I didn't understand how someone could be a normal person and know nothing about fish. It seemed the same as denying the existence of water.

That's what I was born into, the legend I joined. It has since lengthened and deepened with my own experiences, and now with those of my son. Maybe I should call it a fishing pedigree. As I guide, I love to hear about someone else's fishing pedigree, where it has taken them, how it has played into other aspects of their life.

You can't help your background, and that's mine. Sometimes, people turn away from their pedigree, sending a shockwave through the family. They may need to do so for various reasons, and they may even pull it off without adverse effects. That's not what happened here. Looking up through the branches of my family tree, it's a wonder more fishing guides didn't fall from those limbs.

These days, I hear from a lot of young people who are interested in becoming guides. I find myself thinking, "What's the rush?" It would probably dismay them to know that I advocate living a rich, full life *before* becoming a guide. Butcher, baker, candlestick maker—it will all come in handy if, in maturity, you do decide to become a working guide. The more varied the experiences under your belt, the better. That's because what a fishing relationship between a sport and a guide amounts to is an ongoing conversation—sometimes for days on end, sometimes for years. The more you can bring to that conversation, the more fruitful it will be, and the longer it will last. Then you may hear along the way, as some guides do, that the company you offer is just as valued as the company you keep.

There is one credential, however, that is compulsory. It trumps a lifetime of fishing. It overshadows being a gifted teacher. It even eclipses a detailed knowledge of all the waters of your guiding region. That credential is the ability to listen, honestly and well. It has been said that the whole world awaits a good listener, and there is no enactment of that aphorism more powerfully compelling than guided fishing. No psychiatrist's couch, no confessional, no dimly lit boudoir evokes more truth than two souls floating, and fishing, together.

These stories, saved up from lots of listening, are arranged for the most part as they happened. If they had passed through my canoe and out of my reach due to my own preoccupation or inattentiveness, it would've been one of my life's great losses. It was my intention here to give them the care and attention they deserve.

Life and death situations do arise in guiding, and the first story you'll read here was the most significant and difficult in my career so far. I was fortunate to have the counsel of someone much older to help me through it, someone who metes out his wisdom generously from an off-the-grid, rustic cabin deep in the Maine woods.

In fact, many of the stories that follow derive from my experiences with older sports. This is no surprise to me, as I have been drawn to the elderly since childhood. Those I write about here have made a more advanced stage of life far less daunting to me. I might even say that they're the ones doing the guiding. With their long view backward, and their clear-eyed view of the present, they make the waters I must navigate far less murky.

A Cry for Help

There's no way to fully prepare for a real emergency. They blindside you every time. As a full-time fishing guide, I'd been around my share.

Like the time two fishermen rented an aluminum boat and motored out to the middle of West Grand Lake in late September. The salmon season stays open there until October 15, and they were rigged to troll. It's a good time for that. The lakes have "turned over" by that time. The water temperature has dropped drastically, and the sport fish (landlocked salmon) have come up closer to the surface following the thermocline. While that may be predictable, the wind and weather in the middle of a 15,000–acre lake isn't. That late afternoon, a wind came up. It didn't seem like much, but with the right combination of events, it doesn't take much.

The two men were traveling into the wind when a wave hit the bow and threw them both off balance. Off balance enough to land in the lake. The boat kept going, pilotless, with the personal flotation devices on the floor. It was found by guides later, up against a distant shore, motor still running. One of the men swam nearly two miles in frigid water to shore, walked another quarter of a mile, and stumbled into a camp. His buddy, a Philadelphia police officer, was not so lucky. His body surfaced in Farm Cove, several miles from the scene, the following December.

Not long after that, in the middle of the same lake on a rough day, I came upon a "party boat," the colloquial name given to those pontoon-platform vessels that have grown increasingly popular in recent years. There was no one aboard. This was enough to alarm me, as well as the two clients I was guiding that day. The boat was outfitted with a large outboard and a smaller "kicker" motor beside it for trolling or for backup if the primary power source failed. It looked like that was what had happened. The only trouble was that the kicker motor was hanging upside down in the lake from its safety chain. Only the most horrible scenario now presented itself from the visible evidence: The kicker motor had failed, too, and in attempts to work on it in rough water, the operator had gone over and drowned.

Using the extra eyes of my sports, Curtis and Tammy Sue Willey of Manchester, Connecticut, I searched the entire area before making all the necessary calls. The news that night was better than any birthday cake I've ever had. The owners of the party boat, who were also camp owners on the lake, were safely at home in New Hampshire. The boat had simply slipped its mooring! The kicker motor had then jostled itself loose. If only every emergency could end that way. If only.

Everything about the early season that year had seemed normal. The ice had gone out May 1, and I was at my post in the stern seat of my Grand Laker canoe by May 16. My first clients were none other than the "Stalwarts," my nickname for four guys who went to college together in the 1950s and, despite their age, are willing to brave brutal salmon weather each spring. Landlocked salmon—they're the biggest draw in May for the guiding commerce of Grand Lake Stream, Maine. It's a good start to the season for me, reconvening with sports who have become friends, sharing in the joy of every one of their catches. I made a fish chowder for them on that first day, just as I always do. Mike Fastoso, now deceased, had caught a fine togue (the Native word for lake trout) on a Governor Aiken tandem streamer fly. We took one look at that fish flopping in the net and pronounced it perfect for the chowder pot. By the end of our three days on the water, I'd found the stride that was to last me until early October. Or so I thought.

Right after the "Stalwarts" came Rob and Rebecca Lekowski, whom I've guided for over ten years. They represent my model fishing couple, the one I talk about most to other sports. The one word I've never heard pass their lips with regard to fishing adventures is "No." We have ranged so far off beaten paths and well-traveled waterways, it's just possible we've fished once or twice where no lines have been cast before. We keep the details of these experiences to ourselves, knowing that shared secrets form the most lasting bonds.

June, the fastest thirty days of the year for local fishing guides, was off to a great start with the McCandlish brothers, Charlie and Tom from Raleigh and Richmond, respectively. After five years of fishing together, the underlying competitiveness that the brothers carry onto the water has been transformed into an ongoing dialogue that sounds like a professional comedy routine. I act as mediator. It's a role I play to the fullest, coming from a family of brothers myself. I had finished up three days with Charlie and Tom and said good-byes that would've been sadder had they not included vows all around to resume the dialogue the following year. I also gave private thanks that the tone of my season had gotten off on very high notes, thanks to these first three parties.

It was an uncharacteristically warm evening for early June. From where I dropped off the McCandlish brothers, I had only to haul canoe and trailer past The Pine Tree Store, hang a left, and cross the only traffic bridge in Grand Lake Stream. As I did, dozens of mayflies struck my windshield. The Hendrickson hatch! Sure enough, when I glanced upstream to the Dam Pool, several fly fishers were hard at it, fishing this blizzard of mayflies, which in turn were inspiring salmon to dimple the surface like large raindrops. One more left turn onto Tough End Road, and I'd soon be home.

Tough End Road runs parallel to the stream for several hundred yards. Then the stream veers off and continues its three-mile run to Big Lake. There are several classic salmon pools in this first section. The second pool is named the Hatchery Pool since it begins where the last in a line of roofed, salmon-breeding raceways ends. Here, the stream flow takes a nearly 90-degree left turn. My canoe garage was straight uphill from the Pool, about 250 yards away.

The chores at the beginning and end of a guided fishing day lengthen that day by about an hour. I emptied the canoe, hung the all-weather runner carpet up to dry, used the wet-dry vac between all the ash ribs, then wiped the whole canoe out with a chamois cloth. I filled my gas tank for the outboard, then did a final inspection of the canoe, inside and out.

Satisfied, I was on my way across the lawn to the house when I heard a shout from the stream. Nothing unusual there. From that vantage, if the wind is right, I can hear not only the stream, but fly fishers conversing as well. For years, I've listened to the jubilant calls of lucky anglers who've just hooked into a salmon in the Hatchery Pool. Having experienced this myself, it can be an involuntary reaction to the force of the pullback, or to the tail walk that dazzles you no matter how many times you've seen it. Having seen the Hendrickson hatch when I crossed the bridge, I had no doubt there'd be good fishing tonight.

The shouts continued as I made my way across the yard and up onto the deck off the front door of the house. I smiled to think this must be somebody's fish of a lifetime. Then, in the midst of all the yelling, just as I opened my front door, one of those shouts sounded enough like the word "Help" to stop me in my tracks. I let go of the door and started moving across my front yard toward the stream.

A neighbor's lawn sloped from the high ground next to Tough End Road all the way down to the sharp, leftward sweep of the Hatchery Pool. As I neared that rise, another, this time unmistakable, cry of "Help!" set me on a dead run. As I ran, I could make out a man standing in the deep water in the center of the pool. He was unnaturally hunched over. Now I was running as fast as I could without tumbling down the hill. Wearing typical guiding attire— khaki pants, chamois shirt, and L.L. Bean boots—I hit the water in full stride only to see, coming from upstream, fellow guide John Shamel. He'd apparently heard what I'd heard and had responded the same way at the same time.

By now, we could both see that it was not one man, but two, each appearing to be in his late fifties. The hunched-over man was holding another man by the armpits. He'd been standing there in the deep water and fast current since the very first shouts that I'd mistaken for the caterwauls of angling success. He was clearly played out.

Simultaneously, John and I grabbed the fallen, huskily built man who appeared to be unconscious and hauled him to the nearest shore—the one I'd come from. The exhausted man followed. We laid the very pale, limp, waders-clad man down gently, face up on the muddy, grassy bank. John worked to undo the waders' belt while I loosened the man's collar and swept his mouth and throat with my index finger. We each took his pulse. It was faint, weak, irregular.

Since I was nearest to the man's head, I positioned myself on my knees and began CPR. Luckily, my training came back to me, except that this was no classroom dummy. It hit me like a paddle blade across the forehead that just a moment ago I was thinking about what I might cook for supper, and now, I was involved in someone's life-and-death struggle. Everything was happening too fast.

The protocol had recently changed from fifteen compressions to thirty before giving a rescue breath. I called out the number of each compression, so as not to lose count. After each set, I cleared the airway again and blew in. The man who had been holding him in the stream started calling out, "C'mon Tyke. C'mon buddy." Only then did I realize that they knew each other and were probably friends, brothers, business associates, or relatives fishing together. Somehow that kicked up the adrenaline even more. After several compression sets, John moved up to relieve me. By that time, Sammy Sprague, brother of my old friend the late Sonny Sprague, had arrived ready to help. He said the Rescue Squad had been called and was on its way.

The pace never slackened. We all took turns, each doing three to four sets of compressions while one of the other two took Tyke's pulse, a pulse that was now undetectable. After multiple rounds each, only the faces told the truth that no one would speak. It was a time for denying the truth and pressing on. No one stopped. There was never an interruption in the rhythm of compressions and breaths. We only heard the more and more fervent pleas of "Tyke! C'mon Tyke!" from the man kneeling beside us in the mud.

We had been working on Tyke for forty-five minutes, working even after the EMTs had applied the defibrillator paddles several times. I was back in position by the fallen fisherman's head to begin another set when I felt a hand on my shoulder. I went to work just the same and then heard a voice I recognized as that of EMT Robin Harriman, speaking my name. Without turning around I kept on compressing, and then she said it again. I ignored her, but this time she put her other hand under my arm as though to lift me. She spoke my name one more time, only more softly this time. When I turned toward her, all she said was, "He's gone, Randy."

Robin has had to say these words many times in similar situations. She knew how to say them convincingly, leaving no room for doubt. With those words, my own weight seemed to double, driving my knees deeper into the mud. I slumped there for some length of time—it could have been seconds or minutes. When I looked up, I saw John and Sammy standing to either side of the body wearing expressions that mirrored what I felt: that we had been powerless; that nothing we'd done had mattered in the end.

Then I looked at the man on the ground beside the deceased. I had never seen anyone so bereft. I stood up and said, "I'm sorry," and the statement sounded so absurd, I wished I could grab it out of the air and jam it back down my throat. I made my way through the people who had gathered on shore behind us, some of whom patted me on the back. Each pat intensified my self-loathing. I slogged up the hill and crossed the street to my house, now completely shrouded in darkness.

Collapsing on my deck in soaked clothing, I watched lights flashing from rescue and game warden vehicles as each jockeyed into position at the top of the hill. Now a larger crowd had formed. Overcome with thirst, I went into the kitchen, pulled a beer out of the fridge, and gulped it down much too quickly. My head was swimming. Back in the deck chair, it must have been the beer that allowed messages from different muscle groups to make their way to my brain. I suddenly felt as if I had just pushed a truck up to the top of the hill on Tough End Road. My heart rate tripped into tachycardia. I watched the crowd gradually thin out, and finally saw the gurney loaded into the ambulance. I put my face in my hands. Time stopped. When I looked up, my clothes were almost dry, and the moon had risen.

It wasn't the face of death that kept flashing before my eyes. It was the face of the other man, the one on the ground next to the deceased. His cries of "C'mon Tyke" still rang in my ears. We'd all been thrown together in a moment of crisis and then things went from bad to worse. When I finally got up, my clothes were as good as dry. I went in, patted my face with water at the kitchen sink, toweled off, put on the same fishing hat I'd worn guiding all day, then went out and started the truck. I drove down Tough End Road, over the bridge, and stopped at The Pine Tree Store, knowing that Kurt and Kathy Cressey would be the most likely to know where the two men were staying. Most of the fishing licenses of visiting sports are purchased at the store. Grand Lake Steam is so small a town, Kurt and Kathy would by now have heard not only the whole Hatchery Pool tragedy, but also who was involved and who the victim was.

I barely got the door open when Kathy pulled me into a hug. "I'm so sorry," she said, and I had to swallow hard to keep down what wanted to come flooding out. She knew who the two fishermen were and where they were staying. She knew it was Tyke that had died. She was gracious as always, ready to talk or listen. I thanked her, but excused myself and headed down Water Street.

At 6 a.m. the next morning, my phone rang. I'd been awake most of the night thinking about my visit to the cabin on Water Street, where Tyke and his friend Joe were staying. The call was from the sporting lodge that had hired me for the next three days. My sports' flight from Cleveland the previous evening had been delayed because of a summer storm system that had roared through the Midwest. After several delays, the flight was canceled. The airline was making good on their tickets, but my group decided to move their trip to September.

This was not good news. I was counting on my guiding work to jolt me out of my gloom. A second cup of coffee seemed only to intensify the anxiety that had settled over me. To make matters worse, when I walked from the house to the garage I heard an imaginary voice calling for help again, and that was the last straw.

I saw no point in sticking around when to do so would inevitably mean encountering well-meaning townsfolk. I recalled a song lyric that perfectly describes Grand Lake Stream. The first line of the Kieran Kane song called "In A Town This Size" is:

> *In a town this size*
> *there's no place to hide*
> *everywhere you go*
> *you meet someone you know . . .*

If, today, I were to take my habitual morning walk, as I do every morning of the off-season, I would meet my friends and neighbors. If I stopped by the store, they'd be there, too. The problem was not them—it was me. Whatever these thoughts were, they were overtaking me like an avalanche. I needed to be alone with them.

I was aware that something inside me had changed, or moved. Something like this had never happened to me before. But if there were one person who might help me make sense of it all it was Drummond Humchuck, and seeing him meant making a quiet exit from town.

Township Unknown, a name I use for a place that has no official name, has a population of one. It encompasses, as far as I can tell, not the usual thirty-six square miles of an unorganized township, but an area equal only to the space taken up by Drummond Humchuck's estate.

I use the term estate lightly; and yet, there it is, a self-contained, working plantation, the products of which are fish and game; birch, beech, and ash for both work and warmth; spruce, cedar, and fir for the protection of wintering mammals; and cranberries, blueberries, and blackberries for Drummond's larder. There are beechnuts, too, and even the occasional acorn. Oaks are not as prolific here at the forty-fifth latitude as they are points south.

I use the word plantation lightly too, but Township Unknown is a unique one in that it sustains itself with just one caretaker. Drummond Humchuck does take from it what supports his existence, but what he gives back more than compensates. He culls fallen hardwoods for his firewood, thereby opening up space for new understory to make a start. This in turn provides browse for deer, moose, and other mammals, and cover for upland game birds. He thins the wild berry crops annually (aided by black bears), a practice just as beneficial in the wild as on domestic fruit farms. Growth and production are greatly enhanced as plants stay healthier and heartier. Drummond harvests only the fish and game he can use. He treats the woods and waters close to this cabin as a kind of Eden, which will provide for him so long as he does not bite into the apple of waste.

That's my friend: eighty-something, clear-eyed and fit, full of wit and humor: a woods sage if ever one walked this earth. We sit on birch twig chairs of his own making, but I feel as if I sit at his feet, soaking up every story, every tangent he travels, every lesson he doesn't know he's teaching me.

My sworn oath is to respect and protect his one wish—to leave him to his privacy. He has no interest in fishbowl examinations of a life he believes to be very ordinary, and he certainly has no interest in celebrity.*

But there is something about the private and the intentionally hidden that can't help but pique our curiosity. I can't count the number of times I've been asked to spill the beans on Drummond's actual whereabouts. "Prove that he exists," they say, eager to solve the mystery. "For all we know, you could have just made him up!"

Perhaps oddly, I'm just as content to let readers consider my friend unreal. Surely some of them reject out of hand the possibility that someone in this day and age who has a home might not have an address. Or a bank account. Or a tax return. These good folks, who

---

* Even so, when I told him that after the publication of my first book, *Where Cool Waters Flow*, most of the mail I received was about him, he blushed, and then suddenly grew more animated. Who among us doesn't love praise?

sometimes label themselves "realists" or "healthy skeptics," would indeed need proof that such a person exists by way of a full disclosure of Drummond Humchuck's exact whereabouts. My apologies to them.

I write about Drummond with the full faith and support of those who already know that within a reasonable distance from the home of any Maine resident lives a Drummond Humchuck. It could be a cabin on any old family plot. It might be a mobile home picked up in a fire sale and moved to the end of some overgrown woods road. These places rarely have power or plumbing. Forty-two percent of Maine is unorganized territory comprising huge tracts of wilderness—twelve million acres to be exact. Who's to say how many recluses, on the fringe and off the grid, inhabit them? Before knowing Drummond, I had long heard the legend of Roy Flint, the "hermit of Mount Katahdin." The idea that he lived in a cabin at the foot of the mountain and received groceries from sympathetic bush pilots was certainly an alluring one. I confess—I doubted he was real. Then I met his granddaughter at a book signing in Boothbay Harbor. She confirmed both his existence and his legend.

I'm indebted to those readers who require no proof, especially since that proof might compromise the unique life Drummond leads. It may be that at some point in their own lives, they knew someone like my friend. For others, he may represent a life unlived, an experiment never undertaken.

When I read those letters, I couldn't help but wish that those readers knew more. In a way, I felt as if I had slighted them. The text of that book took up so many other aspects of life in Grand Lake Stream that the constraints of space dictated only a smattering of anecdotes from Drummond Humchuck's deep woods existence. In a sense, that did him an injustice. His life is no more comprised of anecdotes than anyone else's is. It's a full life, a complete life with a past, a present, and a future, though it's true that Drummond lives in the present more than most.

I recall one conversation in which I had referred several times to "the future," as in planning for the future, or preparing for the future.

I faintly recall having been visited by a life insurance salesman just before this time. It was a concept quite foreign to Drummond. Finally, after listening all the way through as he always does, he blew out a cloud of red willow smoke from his whittled, homemade pipe and said, "This future yer talkin' 'bout chum . . . when is it?" My mind went blank. I looked at my friend, dumbfounded. I thought, everyone knows when the future is, don't they?

"I heard about it a few times before," Drummond continued, "so I begun checkin' every day to see if it was here yet. And ya know what chum? Every time I checked, it was still now."

I was flummoxed. There's no use arguing against an unprovable premise or a pearl of wisdom from so pure a source. In practice, Drummond does plan for tomorrow, but that activity occurs now, so he's still living in the present. By his reckoning, tomorrow is really just another aspect of today. So today, he'll cut a little firewood for tomorrow. And today, he'll use a bar of soap cut from a batch he made a year ago to last him until today. In the most practical sense possible, past, present, and future are living harmoniously in Drummond Humchuck, today!

Some of those letters I received about Drummond were detailed and inquisitive. One sport of mine from Chapel Hill, North Carolina, wrote to inquire specifically after Drummond's health, his diet, and whether he suffered any of the usual setbacks that would be expected in someone his age. I have long contemplated, for selfish reasons mostly, how age doesn't steal from Drummond Humchuck the way it does from most people. Everyone knows that age robs agility, lucidity, strength, stamina, resilience, equilibrium, and perhaps most of all, confidence. If I could crack the code as to how Drummond maintains these as well as he does, then maybe I could also avoid these setbacks in the next thirty years. Apart from the sheer enjoyment of Drummond's company, I'm always studying him.

Of the many things Drummond is apparently exempt from, there is one that fascinates me more than anything else. It's not one of the obvious things. It's not that fish and game laws as I know them don't apply to him. It's not that his is the one plot of ground in all this country that seems to have no tax on it. It's not that the "normal" stresses of our world—bills, bosses, deadlines, traffic, politics, governments—have no reality for him. It's how he manages to cope with the weight of time.

After all, there he is, alone, hours from the nearest equivalent of civilization, for that's what Grand Lake Stream is. You still have to travel considerably from there to get to the goods and services part of civilization. For Drummond, as with all of us, there are twenty-four hours to contend with each day. Most people will rest from six to eight hours out of that twenty-four. If he rests eight, that still leaves sixteen with no one to talk to, no radio, no TV, no computer, none of the distractions that we consider essential.

I've heard it described by other elderly people as the problem of time. Time, they've told me, is a double-edged sword, one that wounds in two ways. On the one hand, a backward glance is a shocking revelation of how quickly time has passed. "It seems like only yesterday the kids graduated from high school, and now my *grandchildren* are in high school!" One of my senior sports said this to me one day as we drifted with the current on the St. Croix River. "And yet, time in the present moves so slowly," he went on. "How cruel, how unfair that the biggest, most meaningful things in life occurred when time was moving too fast to fully savor them. Now, when time has slowed to one long, laborious plod, nothing happens!"

Unfair indeed. Drummond is twenty years older than a good many people I know who have already adopted this mode of thinking, and I've never observed one sign to indicate that he is vulnerable on this score. I can only point to the obvious: What lightens the weight of time for Drummond Humchuck is a busy, meaningful present.

When a daily allotment of energy must be used for sustenance and survival, there is no need for distractions. In Drummond's world, distractions are detractors. That distractions have become desirable in our world is a conversation I've avoided with my friend. What Drummond turns to in the hours he is not fishing, hunting, trapping, repairing snowshoes, rendering fat, smoking meats, making soap, or chopping wood, is his brand of home entertainment: whittling and whistling. I have written at some length about Drummond's Popsicle-stick masterworks. First in columns for the *Downeast Times*, then in *Where Cool Waters Flow*, I described these respectfully intricate and detailed likenesses of historical landmarks and monuments. What I did not recount was his accompaniment while he works.

People who first met Drummond in the pages of that small-town newspaper, the *Downeast Times*, will recall that he wasn't always a hermit. There was a life prior to Township Unknown, though not one he has ever seen fit to discuss. I have privately speculated that a life very rich in other ways preceded the one I observe now. His music is all the proof I need.

The first time I heard Drummond whistle was from a distance down the trail leading away from his cabin. I had just departed after staying the entire afternoon on one of my annual spring visits. It stopped me in my tracks. At first, I thought I was hearing spring birds, exulting in the retreating snows. Then, the unmistakable melody of "Froggy Went A-Courtin'" emerged between trills and arpeggios. These were no bird sounds I'd ever heard! What's more, it was the version of "Froggy" made famous by Tex Ritter, a talent that would have been known, via radio, to a young Drummond Humchuck. I turned around, faced the cabin, and stood there in the trail for the balance of the impromptu concert. When Drummond got to the part corresponding to the lyric, "Where will the wedding supper be? . . . Way down yonder in a hollow tree," he must've done some kind of hambone percussion with his pipe on the doorjamb to emulate the hollow tree. I laughed out loud. Here was yet another dimension to Drummond Humchuck that I now had to consider—a possible key to my friend before I knew him. Consider it I would, and on my next visit, I was determined to find a way to take it up with him.

As fate would have it, in the interim a program about auditory memory aired on Maine Public Radio. I learned that people stricken with deafness may continue to "hear" sounds that come not from without, but from within. It might be likened to phantom pain in which a person "feels" a limb that's no longer there. The ear, being understimulated in deafness, begins to receive a kind of counterfeit stimulation from the brain, which is answering the call from the understimulated cochlea nerve. It may receive whole songs note for note, symphonies, speeches, wind, or any other sound sample from the noisy universe. These are not imagined sounds. They are actually being "heard" as the brain fills the auditory void with pulses of remembered vibrations. Likewise, people of hearing—and this is where Drummond Humchuck comes in—who, for a variety of reasons, undergo protracted periods of silence may experience a similar phenomenon. In other words, the auditory sense might be understimulated by too much quiet.

And so, the deer hunter who has been sitting for hours on a windless morning begins to hear footfalls. They come from the recesses of the brain but are indistinguishable from the recesses of the forest. Out there on the periphery where real or imagined is a toss-up, a large buck is approaching—according to the understimulated ear of the hunter. The hunter's spine straightens. His fingers move from gunstock to trigger guard. The only trouble is, the sound stays at the same distance—just far enough away to deny the listener details that would confirm its reality, but close enough to keep doubt (and readiness) at a pitch.

Drummond Humchuck, who certainly lives amid a rumpus of natural sounds, must also be, at times, sound deprived. Unlike our world, his does not include the din of telecommunication. No beeps, blips, buzzers, or synthesized ringtones interrupt the contemplative quiet he inhabits. No chimes ding from laptops booting up, no endless drivel emanates from a TV that will blunt a brain for an affordable monthly fee.

In periods of auditory hunger, Drummond's brain serves up a rich diet of musical material stored there from his life before Township Unknown—a life still unknown to me. His instrument of choice when he wants to accompany these gifts from his personal auditory angel is a whistle. Not the penny whistle. Not a slide whistle. Not a storm whistle, or a dog whistle. His is the kind that can be moistened with a swipe of the tongue. He has apparently, over his long lifetime, developed tricks and airy twitterings that must serve to delight him to no end, for he rarely has an audience.

My next visit that year was in the fall after a full guiding season. When I arrived, Drummond was sitting in the doorway, smoking his red willow pipe as usual. Of course, tea for two was ready.

"Heard you whistling when I was leaving in the spring," I said.

"That so?" Drummond replied.

"Yup. Where'd you learn how to do that?"

"Whistle? Everybody knows how to whistle, don't they?"

"Not like that. And where'd you ever hear, "Froggy Went A-Courtin'"?

"Yessah!" he exclaimed, slapping his knee. "Been tryin' to remember the name a that for years."

"OK, but where'd you hear it in the first place?" I persisted.

"Radio, I'd imagine," he answered, just as matter-of-factly as if there were one playing in the cabin behind him.

"Tex Ritter?" I chanced.

"Yessah!" Drummond said, smiling broadly. "Tex Rittah. Thanks, chum."

Since that time, I've heard Drummond give spine-tingling renditions of "Camptown Races" by Stephen Foster, "Red River Valley" in the style popularized by Marty Robbins, and "Dance of the Sugar Plum Fairy" from Tchaikovsky's *The Nutcracker*. It is something beyond spellbinding to hear music articulated by body parts alone. Teeth, gums, tongue, tonsils, lips—all are conscripted into service when Drummond performs. The result is not just something you'd recognize as *The Nutcracker*, for example. It's an interpretation, expanding the work far beyond the boundaries given it by its composer. I have never been so entertained, and yet, these productions have been staged in my presence only rarely. Drummond must be in a certain frame of mind, one that I wish I could kindle at will, for I have a suspicion that I have heard only the smallest part of his repertoire. What else can he perform? The "Orange Blossom Special"? "Ode to Joy" from Beethoven's Ninth Symphony? Almost nothing would surprise me now.

When Drummond completes a composition, we both sit in silence the way Native Americans do at a postmortem vigil waiting for the soul of the deceased to leave the body. It's as though we must wait for the music to settle over us, to hit its mark. Only after this informal ceremony are we able to resume conversation, make more tea, and continue with whatever we were doing before the opus began.

I give so broad an account of my friend in the woods so that it might be understood why I would seek his companionship in a time of personal crisis. People turn to priests, prophets, shamans, and soothsayers at such times. Without pulpit, parish, or adoring flock, and only the primeval forest of Township Unknown for a cathedral, Drummond Humchuck is all those things to me, and more. In the past, I had brought many a lesser problem to my friend than the one I was about to burden him with this time.

Despite my best efforts, I've never been able to catch Drummond off guard on my arrival. How he always knows I'm coming remains a mystery, but if ever there were a time I might get the drop on my friend, this might have been it. This trip was far out of my routine. Only a few weeks previously, I'd made my annual spring visit right after the ice went out of West Grand Lake. As far as he knew, I wouldn't be due to show up again until fall, at the end of my guiding season.

But regardless of when I arrive or how spur-of-the-moment my visit is, I always come bearing gifts. It's not because Drummond doesn't get out much: He's in circulation more than anyone his age I know. It's just that "getting out" for Drummond means traipsing an area of perhaps four square miles around his cabin. It means harvesting fiddleheads in spring along trout streams where elms used to grow. It means gathering cranberries in vermilion heaths after the first frost. It means trapping eels, beaver, and muskrat as the seasons progress from fall to spring, and then collecting raspberries, blueberries, and blackberries in summer.

None of these things would be on a checklist of items Drummond needs. What he needs are nails, tape, tacks, glue, toothpicks, Vaseline, Cloverine, Bag Balm, string, aluminum foil, and Popsicle sticks. Since I had brought most of those on my recent trip, I went around the house and shop gathering things up, then brought anything I could think of that might come in handy in Drummond Humchuck's hermitage.

Visiting Drummond is a two-and-a-half-hour undertaking—one way. The smallest fraction of it is on paved road. The roads, such as they are, then steadily deteriorate from dirt, to skidder or twitch trail, and finally to hash-marked, angular paths through thick woods, crossing several streams and a couple of logans along the way. I was just plain lost and embarrassed when I stumbled into Drummond's world that first time, eleven years ago. I had been "chasing a big buck rather than waiting for him"—that was the first nugget of woods wisdom bestowed on me by the man whose cabin appeared before me like an apparition. He was teetering on a chair in the doorway smoking a pipe, looking like a vision of Rip Van Winkle or Gandalf the Grey. These days, neither Drummond nor I regard that incident as an accident.

I made hash marks on trees on the way out because I knew I had just had one of the most important "chance" meetings in my life. There was no question I'd be back. Those marks are old and faded now. It's more a case of "woods memory" that gets me in and out of Township Unknown these days. People who work in the woods—guides, hunters, and trappers—are familiar with woods memory. You come to know a huge plot of ground the way urbanites know a city block. Your mind's eye says, "There's that boulder perched precariously out on the edge of that outcropping." "There's that hemlock tree, three-and-a-half feet through at the base." And "There's that fallen pine that went down during that god-awful blow three years back." So goes the process of recognition and orientation for the woods-savvy traveler. It should be said, too, that woods memory can vanish with one good snowstorm.

After setting out, I went back home three times for things I had laid out and then forgot for being so preoccupied. The night of the Hatchery Pool incident was still playing before my mind's eye as though on a continuous loop.

To make matters a little bit worse, when I had driven to my first turnoff from hardtop to gravel, I saw, in my rearview mirror, a vehicle behind me closing the gap fast. This was not good. In a sporting destination like Grand Lake Stream, seeing someone who is known to be a guide turning down some nondescript woods road is an alluring curiosity. What secrets are hidden there? Could it be a trout stream that he keeps to himself? Could it be a covert of grouse or a likely layover of migrating woodcock? Has he been scouting some majestically antlered whitetail to be stalked in the fall when the regular firearms season opens? In the summertime, this same phenomenon is called green canoe syndrome. When fishermen new to the area see guides' canoes, they sometimes follow them as a sort of free fish finder. In the present case, I surely wasn't interested in someone tracking me to Township Unknown. My suspicions were allayed when the follower, impatient with my deliberate granny pace, gunned past me and disappeared on the straightaway ahead.

At last, I could undertake my journey in peace. As I set out from my truck, pack basket loaded to the hilt, I was already smiling at the prospect of my friend's sixth sense failing him this time. I also noticed that I was feeling more like myself now.

I've learned, from nearly a dozen years of making this trek, the most likely spots to see a moose or a deer. Bobcat and bear, on the other hand, are much less predictable. And that most wily of all cats, the cougar, who sometimes guards an area up to four hundred square miles, can show up anywhere, any time. He doesn't show up at all, according to the Maine fisheries and wildlife department and the department of tourism. We officially don't have cougars in Maine. As a cautionary note, if I were a novice woods wanderer, I'd check with guides, loggers, and trappers to see how their information compares with that of the desk jockeys in Augusta before heading off to parts unknown in the Maine woods.

That first blush of feeling better was soon dampened by blood—my own. Early June may be known for many wonderful things in Maine, but black flies aren't on that list. They'll drive a bull moose out of the deep woods to seek refuge in the open, or to immerse himself in water. A moose will do anything to escape those vampires of the north woods, which, like the fabled vampires of Transylvania, actually bite their victims—unlike mosquitoes. They drill first, then suck blood. Ahead of me was the deepest of woods, and without fly dope, a person would soon look something like that mass of meat byproducts known as scrapple before getting very far. Luckily, I keep some Deep Woods Off! in the bottom of my pack basket year-round.

I rummaged through the basket, found it and sprayed on a good coating, then tried to hike just under the sweat threshold. Sweat acts like a hormone lure to black flies, mosquitoes, and no-see-ums. So does anxiety. This may explain the immunity that some of the older guides seem to have to blooms of black flies in the spring. I once saw Val Moore seated between two sports on the bench outside The Pine Tree Store. The two clients each looked like Pigpen from *Peanuts* with dark clouds of black flies suspended over their heads. Val was unfazed and unmolested by the voracious hordes preying on his customers to either side of him. The key? They were frazzled, while Val was cool and calm.

Believe it or not, it was still possible on the third of June to see the odd patch of snow hidden in dark hollows beneath hemlock trees. Even a shard or two of ice hung from roots over little rivulets far back in the woods. It's these things that bring home the truth of how short the summer really is at this latitude. Occasionally, I'd see one of my old hash marks, now blending into the bark around it.

In one of these musings, a cat crossed the trail perhaps forty yards in front of me, looking at me unperturbed as it sauntered. This was no cougar or bobcat. It lacked the long, sleek tail of the former and the bobbed nub of the latter. This was a fisher cat. Low-walking like a ground sloth, with an elongated snout, russet fur, and a medium-sized, bushy tail, this is one tough customer. It is believed that fisher populations fluctuate with porcupine populations. The fisher seems to be the one animal that can easily overcome the quills and kill this spiny prey. A hunter may find a porcupine dead on its back, ripped open from soup to nuts, with all the entrails gone. It's the work of a fisher cat like the one that had just crossed in front of me. They tend to be retiring around humans, but I wouldn't push it, just the same.

I crossed three small flowages where in spring, muskrats abound. Though I didn't happen to mark any, Drummond would surely have set traps along these flowages. It is difficult to find people today with a taste for muskrat, but the elders from the tribe still prize the meat, and so does Drummond. The fur is, of course, valuable to the trapper who trades. Drummond has his own uses for it. He still uses basswood stretchers of his own making after skinning his catch, something almost unknown to present-day trappers—nearly all use the more modern wire stretchers. He likes spring trapping because it yields the white, globe-shaped glands from the animal, which will later allow Drummond to make his own muskrat lure. Commercial trappers sell these along with the fur.

With so much to take in on my trek, the time went by quickly. A doe with two spotted fawns allowed me to come within twenty yards before bolting. A snapping turtle the size of a washer drum had furrowed its way up out of a deadwater to lay its eggs in hoped-for safety. The odds are tough—those eggs are preferred in the diets of snakes, otters, eagles, ospreys, ravens, hawks, and owls. I gave the monster mom a wide berth, but still she gave me an open-mouthed hiss that made the hackles on the back of my neck stand up.

Finally, in contrast to the canopy that had darkened the trail most of the way, I saw up ahead a bright, sunny opening signifying Drummond's dooryard. I slowed my gait and stepped as quietly as I could, trying to avoid breaking a twig. When possible, I kept a large pine or hemlock between the opening and me to maximize my chances of a surprise. I smelled the wood smoke before I saw it; but once I got close, I could see it spiraling up from the stovepipe. It could mean that sensing my arrival, he'd stoked the stove for tea.

But seeing him nowhere, this didn't thwart me. What did was the voice behind me.

"Howdy, Chum. Tea's on." I nearly jumped out of my pack basket straps. Once I collected myself, I could see how delighted Drummond was, both to see me and to have gotten the best of me when I was so obviously trying to sneak up on him. He was carrying a dead muskrat in one hand and a conibear trap in the other. "I see ya pass a while ago back there," he said as he gave an approving look at my full pack basket and then walked ahead of me.

I blew out a sigh of exasperation and followed. He hung the muskrat and the trap on nails in the woodshed before heading inside. Sure enough, there were two blue enamel cups on the cookstove's warmer shelf, and the teapot on a back burner. While he poured, I unloaded the pack basket. Handing me my tea, he appraised every item with an approving nod.

When he came to the aluminum foil he said, "This'll be good for keepin' them rat glands. Thanks Chum."

"Don't mention it Drum," I replied.

"So what happened?" Drummond said, matter-of-factly, as he was sitting down.

"Whadaya mean what happened?"

"What happened?" Drummond fixed a stare on me while pulling his pipe out of his shirt pocket, a sure sign he was ready to sit for a while. "That there teapot's fulla black alder. Good for loosnin' the tongue, and I'm all ears."

I shuddered at what an open book I was to Drummond Humchuck. He waited patiently, puffing on red willow, the smoke encircling his head, and then following the stovepipe up to the ceiling.

Now that it was time to speak, a tidal wave of anxiety from the last twenty-four hours swept over me all at once. I tested the heat of the black alder tea on my lips; looked up at Drummond's reassuring expression; and then, after several fumbled starts, began.

I was in the best of places to tell my story, because I was telling it to the person who taught me the art of listening. Drummond remained attentive throughout, waiting patiently through painful pauses in the most difficult parts. When I told of reaching the river and seeing the unconscious man held up from behind by his armpits, a dark shadow overtook my friend's face. It remained there to the story's sad conclusion, but began to recede when I started to talk about Joe Verlicco.

He was the loneliest man in the world the night he welcomed me into his cabin on Water Street, after Kathy Cressey had told me where to find him. Our handshake quickly collapsed into a hug. His grief quaked and heaved in his chest. After several minutes, we sat down on the porch facing the stream, one pool below the now fateful Hatchery Pool.

"He was my best friend," Joe said, and that alone explained so much. It explained the supplications he called out continuously as we worked on Tyke. He wanted Tyke to hear those pleas and call him back to life. It explained the face of the man I saw when I so pathetically uttered the words, "I'm sorry" earlier that night. That look burned a hole in my heart, I told Drummond. It was what brought me to his cabin.

"It was his heart," Joe went on. "Some kind of embolism or hemorrhage. It had to be. Something wasn't right with Tyke today, but he was stubborn and he was going to fish, come hell or high water."

We introduced ourselves with full names and I asked Joe for Tyke's real name. "Mike," he said. "Mike Aniolowski. Some of us called him Tyke, some didn't. I think his father had tagged him with that nickname." Joe explained that both he and Tyke were sixty-two years old, and both were born and raised in Quincy, Massachusetts, where they still lived. I had undershot their ages by several years. I told Joe that I knew it would sound strange, but I wondered if sometime down the road he might send me a picture of Tyke so that I might know him as he was in life. I didn't want my lasting impression of him to be the one from earlier that evening.

That request set Joe on a roll. Suddenly, he was channeling the early 1960s. Tyke, he told me, had grown up in the Germantown section of Quincy in "the projects," as Joe called them. These were affordable housing neighborhoods built primarily for returning World War II vets. It was a hardscrabble, hardworking, blue-collar beginning for Tyke, raised in a family of five children. Joe grew up a half a mile away. They each belonged to neighborhood gangs, though without the modern connotations of that word. The gangs played each other in sandlot sports as well as in hockey. Tyke was trim and muscular in junior high, where he held the record for most sit-ups. Three hundred! Joe smiled recalling this, and now, Drummond smiled to hear it.

The best friends graduated from high school in 1963, and stayed around town the following year. By then, the Vietnam War was gathering steam, and both boys decided to enlist rather than wait to be drafted. They did so on the same day. Joe joined the Navy, Mike the Marines. Both received orders after boot camp to ship out for Southeast Asia. Joe and Tyke were fortunate, both surviving that war in one piece.

Back home as civilians in Quincy, they joined the Quincy Fire Department on the same day. It was a natural progression for Tyke, whose father Chester "Chet" Aniolowski was a career Quincy firefighter. Both Joe and Tyke, who had just discharged their duties in their respective services, would now embark on careers of public service. Joe's sadness seemed to lift as he talked about this friendship, which for these two men had a life of its own apart from their individual lives and families.

In their early years as firefighters, they began a fishing tradition. Discovering the peace and tranquility of Grand Lake Stream, Maine, was the perfect counterpoint to fighting flames in office buildings, car fires, or homes and trying to get everyone out alive. A typical day at work could bring any measure of horrors, but this fishing vacation was a time for healing, a time when their friendship flourished. Both men opened up to the sport, learning the finer points, taking up fly tying, traveling to different destinations to test their skills at other times of the year. Grand Lake Stream grew into something necessary for their health and well-being, a new mainstay and keel to their friendship. Eventually, they added a fall trip, as so many do, since the fall salmon fishing can be every bit as good as the spring fishing.

Joe and Tyke developed a relationship with a local lodge owner who, in later years, rented them a property of his own, right on the stream—the very cabin in which Joe regaled me now with tales of Tyke. He told of the many friendships they'd formed on the river, people they looked forward to seeing again each time they returned. They traded fly tying patterns with these new friends, also tips and tricks, and corresponded with some of them the rest of the year. The more time passed, the more invested they became in this fixed part of their friendship and their lives. Joe and Tyke built up a shared chronicle of fishing memories in thirty-three years of coming to Grand Lake Stream.

As Joe's account moved closer to the present, I saw sadness steal over him again. I wished we could linger longer in the past. Joe and Tyke served out full careers in the QFD and both recently retired. That brought us up to today, the saddest day of Joe Verlicco's life.

"I can't stop asking myself how it was that I was two minutes late from saving him from floating into the deep water in the middle of the river, and yet I was there early enough to hold him for a couple of minutes and talk to him before he slipped away. Just before all that, I'd been headed down to fish the pool below the Hatchery Pool," Joe said, gesturing toward it from the porch where we sat. "For some odd reason, at the last minute, I decided to turn around and come back to fish with Tyke. How was it, at the height of spring fishing, that there wasn't another soul in that pool? That's unheard of!"

I told Joe I'd been playing through all of the "if only's" myself. If only I'd gotten home earlier, and if only I'd finished my canoe chores sooner. If only, instead of chalking up all the shouting to someone's lucky night on the stream, I'd run over to check out what the commotion was about. If only I'd pressed harder while performing CPR, or worked faster—"

For two perfect strangers, we found comfort in hearing each other's clumsy attempts to work through the grief. Each consoled the other that there was no fault or blame—neither one, for his own part, believing it.

"I'm not sure I'll be back here," Joe said as I stood up to go. "I have to sort this all out."

"I hope when you do, you will come back," I said. "After what you've told me about Tyke, I think he'd want you to."

"Oh—" Joe began as I opened the screen door.

"Yes, Joe?"

"A little while before this happened, Tyke landed and released a beautiful landlocked salmon." We both stood in the doorway for a few seconds picturing that.

Drummond, I could see, was picturing it too, but only now did I notice that both eyes were red and brimming with tears. He was reaching for my cup even before I stopped talking. He poured more tea, then stoked the cookstove. For a long time he stared up into the rafters that ran from the eaves up to a ridge pole, which in turn ran the length of his cabin. I assumed we were observing another ritual, letting the story settle.

"Mihku's father and me built this place after the war. He peeled and skun every one a them poles with a draw knife." Drummond continued looking up, admiring the full length of each log as though they'd all been hewn and set in place yesterday.

In one breath, he had given me more of a window into his life than he had in all the eleven years I'd known him. I did know about Mihku, a Passamaquoddy eel trapper. Learning, six years earlier, of his annual visits to Township Unknown confirmed what I'd long suspected—that I wasn't the only one who brought supplies to Drummond.

I had learned of him through unabashed nosiness. Curiosity over Drummond's lifestyle had overpowered me—and my manners. I'd always marveled at how Drummond seemed to usually have what he needed. It is admittedly a Spartan existence, even by backwoods standards, but it still requires supplies. What I carried in on my seasonal visits would not make up a fraction of what it would actually take to live through the year, even as Drummond lives. So, on that one visit six years previous, I got up the courage to just come out and ask about it.

Drummond opened up as though he'd been wondering what took me so long to ask. Years before—he didn't say how many—Drummond

was tending his eel sluice one autumn morning before dawn. It had
stormed all night and the morning was as still as could be after the
night's violence had passed. It had been a good night for eeling. As
usual, he netted his catch into a holding box with floats attached to
both sides. He then hitched up lines to these floats so that he could
paddle the catch box downstream a short ways to deeper water. One
full holding box would provide more than enough eels for Drummond's
personal needs for a year. He preserves the meat, renders the fat, and
dries all the skins.

On that morning after the storm, as he was going about his
business transferring eels from catch box to holding box, he had a
strange feeling that he was being watched. He ignored it for a while,
but it continued right through the process of tying off the lines in
order to tow the screened box downstream. Finally, he stopped and
looked up, scanning all the tree branches. When he'd had this feeling
before, it had turned out to be a raven, a barred owl, or a bald eagle
waiting, hoping to get a share of the eel harvest.*

But there were no birds of prey lurking about. At least Drummond couldn't see any. Even so, instead of subsiding, the sensation
intensified. Finally, Drummond stopped paddling and just drifted.
He sat motionless, staring forward from his canoe until finally,
through a thick mist hanging over the stream, Drummond made out

---

* I can vouch for how keenly the presence of a predator can be felt. So can George
Gamerdinger of Port of Spain, Trinidad. When I guided him salmon fishing
on Grand Lake Stream, he was jumpy all morning. George, who worked for
the United Nations, had been stationed all over the world and had fly-fished
in many exotic places. That morning, each time he presented his fly, he would
quickly look back over his shoulder, first on one side, then the other. He kept
this up all morning. At lunch I asked him if everything was all right. He said
yes, but wanted to know why I had asked. I said I'd been observing his habit
of checking behind after each cast, and he said, "Oh, that." He explained that
it was a habit he'd gotten into out of necessity when he worked in Nairobi,
Kenya. "The lions would watch you from the banks of the rivers as you fished.
You could feel their eyes on you!" I've always prized the Mrs. Simpson trout fly
George brought me from a fly shop in Nairobi. He also brought home to me
the idea of feeling a predator observing you.

a shape. In such poor light, it could've been anything: the trunk of a fallen tree, or a floating dri-ki (driftwood) sculpture broken away from shore. As the current slowly moved Drummond's canoe closer, goose bumps rose on his neck. When the object before him came into view, it hovered there like a mirror image of himself—a canoe with a man in it! A shudder shot up his spine. This was Township Unknown—his home, his domain. That someone could get this close to him undetected sent a bolt of adrenaline through his veins. Beads of sweat, even on that crisp morning, welled up on his brow.

Drummond took a paddle stroke forward and the man answered with one paddle stroke of his own. It was the response of a seasoned outdoorsman and a gesture known to all old guides, showing no ill intention. This continued, one stroke after another, until both canoes came into clear view of one another. Drummond now saw that the surprise visitor was Native. He was paddling a bark canoe of the authentic kind, not one of the knockoffs sometimes seen at theme events. His attire, too, was authentic—fringed sleeves and leggings with a beaded breastwork. He had long, jet-black hair parted in the middle with braids that fell far below his collarbones. It was hard to tell his age—a common challenge with many Natives who tend to remain youthful-looking well up in years. Only the lines of the man's face might have hinted of late middle age, Drummond guessed.

This meeting was productive, inaugurating a business partnership between Drummond and Mihku that has continued to this day. No money is exchanged. Drummond sets his sluice every fall as usual, and with each trip to tend it, he moves eels into his catch box kept in a deadwater just downstream of the trap. It never fills to overflowing, because Mihku comes to remove them to an invention of his called a rowing pen.

Crafts fitting this description were used as early as the 1860s to transport hatchery-grown salmon to stocking destinations. They looked like dories that had been sunk up to the gunwales on purpose. The boat's interior was sectioned into cages. To prevent fish from jumping to freedom, a canvas was spread over a ridgepole and secured to the gunwales, giving the whole contraption the appearance of a floating tent. Though called rowing pens, there were no oars or oarsmen on these crafts. The oarsmen were in the lead boat, which did the towing. Sometimes, two or three pens were strung in a train behind the towing dory.

Mihku's method may have come first for all we know, since his people were here first and they certainly could've figured out a way to move live fish. His rig might better be called a paddling pen since he paddles rather than rows to tow the eel barge downstream. Several times through the fall, he makes these trips to move Drummond's catch to his own pen downstream. That's their arrangement. Drummond keeps only enough eels for his personal needs—one full holding box—and in return for the rest of his harvest, he receives an annual delivery that comes with Mihku on his last trip of the season. It is a cache of supplies that lasts Drummond a full year. It may include blankets, footwear, socks and undergarments, hardware, wheel cheese, flour, large cans of cherries or other fruit preserves, sugar, salt, any spices Drummond doesn't already collect on his own, medical supplies, and so on. It's all on the list that Drummond leaves wrapped in cellophane and nailed to the pen when it's about to make its last trip of the season.

In ten minutes, Drummond had revealed more about his life in Township Unknown than he had in eleven years. Up to this point in our relationship—six years ago—Drummond had never mentioned Mihku, let alone Mihku's father.

It's all smooth going from the deadwater below Drummond's eel sluice to Mihku's destination, which must still be in Township Unknown. All Drummond would say is that Mihku meets up with a truck from New York. It is outfitted with a pump, aerators, refrigeration, and a scale. The eels that come out of Mihku's paddling pen by the netful are weighed, then deposited in tanks designed for travel. Mihku is paid based on weight, and the transaction ends with a handshake and a pledge to meet in the same place at the same time the following year. Those eels find a robust market awaiting them in New York City.

Mihku presumably splits his profits between what he must pay for Drummond's cache and himself. He doesn't seem to be concerned about whether one partner is making out better than the other. Knowing now that Mihku's father was a friend to Drummond, I had to consider the possibility that Drummond knew Mihku as a boy. It would explain a lot. If true, it might mean that once Drummond got close enough that morning in the mist, he might actually have recognized Mihku. It would also explain why Drummond was so willing to enter into the arrangement in the first place—he was trusting the son of an old friend.

When I submitted columns about Drummond to the *Down East Times* for almost eight years, people wrote to the paper's address in Calais, Maine, on the Canadian border, pressing for information on his whereabouts. As often as I could, I repeated in writing that my permission to write about him was contingent on an agreement to protect his privacy. Still, there are those who cannot let this rest. They will reason from these accounts that there's a way into Township Unknown by water—the route Mihku takes—and of course they're right. They'll reason too that somewhere, that flowage, or stream, or trickle, crosses a road or else the eel truck couldn't net the catch from Mihku's paddling pen. Again, they'd be right. So, they could well extrapolate, all they'd have to do is find a flowage or stream where eels run in the fall, a stream that somewhere crosses some kind of road, and they'd have a leg up on discovering Township Unknown!

To that intrepid soul who embarks on this quest, my most heartfelt "Good luck" goes with you. But please consider this: If there are 30,000 lakes and ponds in the state of Maine, there are certainly 80,000 flowages and streams. Eels run in every one of them, and most of them cross some kind of road at some point. Drummond and Mihku, sleep well. Your partnership and your pact are secure.

Remembering how forthcoming Drummond had been in telling how he'd met up with Mihku, I wondered if this mention of Mihku's father meant that he was now ready to reveal more. I decided to chance it.

"Mihku's father was your friend, Drum?"

"Oh yes. The very best."

"And where is he now?"

"He's showin' your Tyke where the salmon are in heaven."

"Moses Wihwahsin."

When Drummond pronounced the name of Mihku's father, it came out like a song. I'd come to love the cadences, accents, and intonations of the Passamaquoddy tongue through my off-season archival work for the tribe. From my familiarity with the dialect, Drummond was correct in putting the accent on the first and last syllables with the middle one, "wah," subdued. The English tendency would be to make this the strongest syllable, but it ends up, like so many Native words, sounding melodic when spoken as intended.

Moses is a common name within the tribe. Mihku is a common word, but more likely a nickname than a birth name. It means "the squirrel" and, like so many other animals, it is commemorated in different imagery and symbolism in tribal lore and custom. Even today, a sign ravaged by time and weather for *Mihku Lodge and Resort Cottages* can be seen on the shores of Lewey Lake in Indian Township.

Drummond omitted how and when he and Moses met, but I'd long suspected that my friend had some Native lineage. I wondered now whether he might have been raised within the tribe. I knew better than to stop him for explanations. I gathered from the very first that fishing, hunting, and trapping formed the foundation of their friendship. Perhaps they'd met in the woods on a trapline, or maybe baiting bear. As my friend talked, I guessed at these details to fill in gaps for myself.

Moses was older than Drummond by enough of a margin to be a mentor to him. Growing up, he'd been taught by tribal elders who, in their day, depended on fish, game, and furs for survival. In Drummond, Moses found an eager student. Moses taught him the prints and pawings of every animal native to that country. Drummond learned what seasons to harvest certain species in to avoid "off flavors" in their flesh, and how not to interfere with breeding cycles. He learned where to find trout in the heat of summer when they had long since abandoned their spring haunts. He learned how to snare roosting game birds at night, a form of poaching so antiquated now, the books on appropriate punishment for such practices have dry-rotted in courthouse basements.

Thanks to Moses, young Drummond became the beneficiary of old medicine still practiced in the tribe at that time. It was hinted that Moses' father may have been a shaman who taught his son to be his own apothecary. Among many other things, Moses taught Drummond how to harvest the tulip-like blossoms of the poplar tree in spring in order to make a truly remarkable elixir.

On one spring visit before my guiding season began, I noticed bottles of a dark liquid on the table in Drummond's cabin. He called it something that sounded like "bogwani," though I'm at a loss as to what that might mean in Passamaquoddy, if it's a Passamaquoddy word at all. I do know what it means to cuts, lesions, and other abrasions. He explained to me that using alcohol probably provided by Mihku, he extracted the oil from poplar blossoms. After a regime of boiling, simmering, skimming, straining, and cooling, he bottled the healing brew.

That spring, he gave me a small amount of bogwani to take home. I kept it in my canoe dry bag, knowing that the time would come when I could test it on some injury incurred in the line of duty. It came in the form of an open, gushing puncture wound resulting from the treble hook of a Jitterbug lure. It had been lodged deeply in the mandibles of a sizable smallmouth bass. Just at the point when I had the leverage I needed to back it out, the fish bounded out of my hands, over the side, and into the lake, leaving the hook buried deeply in the meat just below my thumb joint.

With the horror-stricken eyes of two sports on me, I pointed to an eagle soaring overhead. When they looked up, I muckled onto the Jitterbug barbs with my Leatherman tool and yanked. A bandana tourniquet got me through the morning, but then the trouble began. Remembering Drummond's remedy at lunch, I retrieved the vial from my canoe bag and applied it liberally to the jagged hole in my hand. The bleeding was immediately stanched. Then, for the next two days I watched in amazement as the wound completely resolved, leaving no scar. This was an injury that would've warranted several stitches and antibiotics had I gone to the ER.

Later, when I looked up "extract of poplar" it led, after a circuitous journey through mythological, herbal, and arborist literature, to the compound benzoin, used since biblical times for a variety of curative purposes.

Moses, through his connection to the elders in the tribe, was not so far removed from a time when prowess as a hunter/gatherer ensured the pick of wives, respected status, and security. Drummond allowed that in the early years of their friendship, Moses married and fatherhood soon followed. Mihku was the fruit of that union. Here, I filled in another gap for myself. The lad must have shown uncommon vim, scurrying busily about like Mihku, the squirrel.

Now Moses had more than just himself to provide for, so he worked as a team with Drummond, his younger companion and student. Two men hunting, two men trapping, two men cutting wood far more than doubles the yield.

Drummond's zeal for learning flattered Moses, inspiring him to teach his charge everything he knew. From my own relationship to Drummond, I concluded that the best mentors must have once been mentored themselves.

Another gap in the story I had to guess at was how their area of operations became the place I know as Township Unknown. They seemed to have had it to themselves, since it was somehow always overlooked by logging crews. In Maine's millions of acres of forestable land, no logging means no roads, and in Township Unknown there are no roads. What I'm used to every place else is second growth, or regenerational forest, with logging roads everywhere. There is no comparison between that and a virgin, or primeval, forest. It is well-documented that old-growth forests tend to be home to both endangered animals and plants, havens for life that cannot be sustained where excessive logging goes on.

Though small, it truly may have been a forgotten tract when first the National Geodetic Survey, and then the US Geological Survey cartographers and surveyors came through. Later, one mistake could have been compounded by another: lands being drawn up as Reservation lands did not include the tract, since it was nonexistent on previous maps and surveys. In any event, if it doesn't exist, no one cares about it, and from any map I've ever been able to get my hands on, including old topo's from the 1950s, it doesn't exist. So, based on that one happy accident, on that one happenstance intersection of folly and fortune, Moses Wihwahsin and Drummond Humchuck decided to build a lodge.

Moses came from the last generation of Passamaquoddies in possession of the skills to build longhouses. That name gave way to the name "lodge," and we call them cabins now. These buildings were the genesis of the great heritage of Maine sporting lodges.

It only helped when Teddy Roosevelt romanticized this style of camp at the Chicago World's Fair in 1893, though it was by no means new then. The whole country knew that Honest Abe was born in just such a cabin in Kentucky in 1809. Crosscut saw, double-bitted axe, hatchet, drawknife, and adze comprised the carpentry kit of a lodge builder. Mortise and tenon joinery caught on in some corners of Maine, but Moses' logs were scooped and fitted at the ends in the traditional way, so that once they were laid into place, they weren't coming loose. I was looking at just such a structure when I admired Drummond's cabin from inside and out. Only now had it come to light that four hands had built it, not two, as I had always assumed.

I thought we would move on in Drummond's eye-opening account from the building of the cabin to more recent history. Instead, that same darkness I'd seen earlier now moved across my friend's complexion. I studied Drummond's face. The stove hissed and the teapot lid jiggled.

Tragedy parted these two friends before they'd finished building the cabin that was to serve as the base of operations for their partnership. Moses and Drummond were working the eel harvest. The cabin was close enough to completion that they'd been staying in it until a stormy autumn night on the dark of the moon sent them to the eel sluice. On such a night, it was bound to be a big haul.

They kept a bark canoe overturned next to their makeshift eeling shack, which they'd built on the bank near the sluice. The eels were running so thick that night that Moses and Drummond took turns netting them from sluice to catch box every few hours. While one worked, the other dozed in the shack on an army cot, beside a kerosene lamp on a stump. The eels kept coming. Neither man got much sleep. The woods were loud with wind, and there were occasional bolts of lightning followed by crashes of thunder.

On one shift toward morning, as Drummond slipped in and out of sleep in the shack, he heard a tremendous crack. It sounded less like thunder than a tree breaking under the force of the wind. He bounded off the bunk and threw open the door, just in time to see a shaft of chain lightning illuminate the stream. There, just below the sluice, a mature maple tree, which had been leaning ominously across the stream, had let go, probably because the torrents had loosened the tree's root webbing on the bank. The sound Drummond had heard was the tree slamming down on the bark canoe with Moses in it.

Drummond vaulted out onto the sluiceway, then jumped downstream into chest-high water. Only Moses' face and one arm were showing. The rest of him was under the tree. Drummond took him by the one arm and pulled with a strength only fear and adrenaline can produce in a man, and yet Moses didn't budge. He was pinned fast to the muddy bottom.

The problem was that some of the tree's root webbing had not let go of the bank. If Drummond ran to the shack to look for a tool to help free him, Moses would surely drown in Drummond's absence under the tree's quickly increasing weight. If Drummond stayed, he could only hold Moses' head up enough to allow him to breathe, and hope that as the tree creaked and cracked and settled further, it would free his friend. The idea of Moses—Drummond's mentor—being helpless must have carried a special charge of terror.

After a long pause, and even then with great difficulty, Drummond told me that at the last of it, Moses kept repeating, "It's OK" until those words came out as air and bubbles. It was over as fast as it began. When the tree fully let go, it did not free Moses. He expired to the screams and cries of his younger friend and pupil who tried, even long after Moses drowned, to pull him out.

Drummond stopped here. This time it was I that jumped up to get the teapot. I didn't know what else to do since Drummond's chin had begun to quiver and his eyes had filled up with tears, as had mine.

"It's OK, chum. Just ain't told it out loud like that for a long time."

Now I took a whole new look at Drummond's cabin. I, too, gazed up into the rafters and wall ties and saw the handiwork of Moses Wihwahsin. In the Drummond I knew, there was much of Moses. It had cost Drummond something to relive that terrible night for my sake. It was perhaps his greatest burden in life. I would not ask more of him, even though a hundred questions bubbled in my mind.

In the meantime, I realized that the weight and anxiety I'd brought with me had vanished. Just exactly how Drummond had worked that magic, I would have to figure out with time. It was late. In fact, I had never stayed so late since that very first time when I'd walked into this world eleven years earlier like a man entering a foreign land.

"You OK, Drum?"

"Sure, chum. You better hit the trail."

"Thanks, friend," I said as I put my arms through the pack basket straps and reached out to shake his hand. He gave me his usual vise grip.

"Nawgh, it's me thankin' you, chum. Got a full season ahead?"

"Yup. And you know what that means."

"Don't worry 'bout me, chum. I'll be on the lookout for ya in the fall."

I laughed at that, knowing that he'd hardly have to be on the lookout. Not with that sixth sense, or telepathy, of his. I waved behind me; yelled, "Thanks!" one more time; and headed down the trail, knowing it would soon be dark enough to dust off those celestial navigational skills Drummond had long ago taught me.

When I'd gotten roughly to the place where Drummond had surprised me on my way in, I heard the first measures of a song. I stopped and turned around to face the sound. From Drummond's chair in the cabin doorway, one of the most melancholy of early American melodies reached my ears in whistling vibrato. It was "Near the Lake A Long Time Ago" which opens with the lines:

> *Near the lake where drooped the willow,*
> *Long time ago!*
> *Where the rock threw back the billow,*
> *Brighter than snow . . .*

With those notes, I thought of Moses Wihwahsin, and Mike Aniolowski, or Tyke. I thought how each had left this life in the arms of his best friend, doing what he wanted most to be doing, in a place he loved. I thought how the best vigil any survivor could observe was to live the life a friend like that would want you to live. I knew that Drummond was doing that. Now I hoped that Joe Verlicco could, too.

THE SURFACE WORLD

When I returned home from Township Unknown just before midnight, the phone message machine was flashing "1," and just that fast, my two remaining days off evaporated. That's because it was June, the money month. In June around here, if you've got a guide's license and you're willing to work, you will. The message was from a lodge owner who'd heard through a social network, faster than any invented so far, that I'd had a cancellation. It was the Grand Lake Stream grapevine, which has two main stems: the Post Office and The Pine Tree Store. In a town this size, the grapevine is completely interconnected. It's for that reason that you can dial a wrong number in Grand Lake Stream and talk for forty-five minutes.

It was to be a solo job, meaning I'd have only one sport for the two days. Suddenly and surprisingly, I felt up to jumping back into the game, and I realized that that's what Drummond had done for me. By sharing a parable from his own long life, he had shown me what a thin membrane exists between the here and gone. Moses had said, "It's OK," to Drummond with his final breath. I spent a lot of time pondering what that could possibly mean between men who were so fully committed to living solely in the present. But instead of having some great epiphany, I found myself living in the moment, focused on the immediate task in front of me. My trip to Township Unknown had done all I could ask of it: plant me squarely in the now.

My client's name was Caleb. From the moment he stepped into my canoe, he was continually scanning the horizon in every direction.

It's understandable, and quite common. He had never been to this part of Maine, where every blink of his eye revealed a world brand new to him. A stiff southeast wind had whipped up the lake so that spray was coming over the gunwales, and though Caleb was pitching in his seat, he seemed unfazed as he took everything in.

In the morning when you're traveling with a first-time client who is facing you from the bow seat in the canoe, you inevitably try to guess their line of work. It will come out eventually in the course of the day, but it's possible to acquire a fairly good batting average in the game of guessing occupations. Is he a contractor? It might show up in his gait and bearing. A job foreman might speak at a volume a decibel or two louder than normal as their work environment demands. A surgeon or anesthesiologist, on the other hand, is usually quiet-spoken. Professors may be professorial, even in a canoe in the middle of nowhere with a complete stranger. If all these stereotypes fail, as they so often do, sometimes the eyes hold the prize, or maybe the diction. Failing that, too, a close look at someone's hands can be very telltale.

On all counts, I was coming up bust with Caleb. His was by no means a bland face. On the contrary, it was intense: a face that focused on you and you alone. His eyes were dark blue, framed by heavy, long eyebrows and deep indentations of crow's feet at the corners. His clean-shaven face was dark from a robust growth of beard that would surely be sprouting by midday. His lips were thin. This was a challenging case with no obvious clues. And yet, that incessant scanning of the lake, the tree line, and the horizon seemed to be saying something about Caleb. Many people do this, just not so intensely. He definitely seemed used to being on the water. That was clear from his comfort level on a very unfriendly lake that morning.

Try as I might, I couldn't crack Caleb's code. I determined to look for my opening as soon after we stopped as possible. I'd say something benign like, "So, are you on vacation, Caleb?" and hope for a full disclosure. The fact that he was well-equipped to fly-fish might've been helpful information once upon a time, but therein lies one of today's most fallible stereotypes. At least up to and through the Eisenhower administration, if you found a fly fisherman on a river, he was, by most definitions of the day, a gentleman. Most of those definitions spoke to station in life, especially among "the professions." Today, the backhoe operator and house painter may both be fly fishermen. Their dentist or lawyer may be an avid basser, fond of fast boats and beguiling lures that win them trophies or cash in competitions.

Caleb took a Sage nine-foot, five-weight rod out of its case and attached a Pflueger Medalist 1496 reel to the butt section. He threaded the rod with line one weight heavier than the rod weight for faster casting action. His leaders were his own, tied with blood knots in descending strengths down to a 4x tippet. This was clearly not his first day at the fly-fishing game. When I complimented his choice of fly rods, he told me it was the rod he used for trout fishing on the Little Red River in Arkansas.

"Is that where you're from, Caleb?"

"Yeah, Little Rock," and right then, a hidden chamber of his voice opened up, one that hinted of collards and okra and chicken-fried steak. "I get back there as often as I can to visit the folks and to fish," and "fish" came out, "feeush." He must've heard it too, since the door of that chamber quickly closed.

Wind gusts were trying to organize into a gale. To give Caleb a fighting chance on the fly rod, I had to find a relatively quiet cove or lee shoreline. The lake I'd chosen allowed good opportunities because of its many islands.

Despite our first real exchange, Caleb seemed in no hurry to fully identify himself. He was content to be taking in the scenery while presenting a beaded olive wooly bugger. It was a good choice on that dour day to go below the surface and show this universally accepted pattern to deeper fish. Caleb allowed that up until today, the only kind of bass he'd ever fished for were—and he no sooner got the word "largemouths" out of his own mouth when he had his first fish on. "Wow, these smallmouths really pack a punch, don't they?" No matter what species you're after, a pullback is a pullback, and it's exciting. It put the first wide grin of the day on Caleb's face. It was now clear that all he needed was to be put over fish. His skills were obvious, but my batting average for career guessing had tanked. The suspense was killing me.

"So, Caleb, what line of work are you in?"

"Oh, I'm a submarine commander." He fixed his gaze on me as if trying to read my mind. He might've read: "I've fished with a lot of interesting people before, but I never would've come up with that one! No wonder he's always scanning the horizon! No wonder he's unimpressed by pitching up and down in a Grand Laker!" Then I realized he was waiting for some kind of reaction.

"Sorry, you're the first one I've ever met." Caleb smiled and unfurled for another cast. He deftly stripped line between thumb and forefinger until a pullback yanked the line out of his hand. When he found the line with his left hand, it was too late. The fish had come unbuttoned. "Huh," he said. "That'll teach me to pay attention."

On guided fishing days, it's good to get cats out of the bag that spur conversation. Now, I was nosy to know anything he'd tell me about his life at sea. I learned first that it's quite typical for submarine commanders to be rotated between sea and land assignments. Most often for Caleb, it was three years at sea, two on terra firma. He was currently stationed in Memphis, his last sub hitch having been *The Pacific* out of Pearl Harbor. Caleb spends six months at a time underwater. No sunlight. Just a very tight-knit group of officers and enlisted men who come to know each other extremely well.

Before that assignment, his first as a commander, he was navigator on a submarine working the Indian Ocean. He saw Hong Kong, Singapore, Thailand, and other ports of call along the way. He began to use the expression *the surface world* as if it needed no explanation. I finally realized that it meant the world I live in, not the one he and his kind inhabit so much of the time. For Caleb, there was a clear distinction between the two. Once out to sea, nuclear submarines rarely surface.

"Quite often we're traveling at PD," he said.

"PD?" He has to continually be reminded he's talking to someone from the surface world. He apologized and told me it stood for periscope depth. Once Caleb had landed several smallmouths, including two he picked out for lunch, he slipped easily into talking about his life at sea. He explained that the workday is extremely busy on a sub. It's all about surveillance, or collecting scientific data, or ecological research. He also said he wouldn't be able to discuss a lot of the work they do. The fishing was good that gusty morning and I had a good fisherman aboard, so good that my impatience to hear more was almost palpable. While I didn't want to overdo it, I reasoned, how often do I get a nuclear submarine commander in my canoe?

I wondered out loud about hurricanes, tsunamis, and other potentially catastrophic weather events at sea. How deep do you need to go to be safe from these things? He told me that whatever is happening to the surface world, it is not felt at the normal running depth of a sub, which is three hundred to six hundred feet. "There is no sensation whatsoever of the weather going on topside. At PD though, you can feel everything."

Once, while "running," as he put it, in the north Pacific, Caleb said he heard an eerie sound. Day after day, this sound kept haunting him, especially since it was not being picked up by any of the onboard high-tech instruments. There were walls of steel separating him and his crew from bone-crushing pressure outside the hull, and yet this sound was getting through. As commander, he concealed the unsettling effect it was having on him. After several days of living on edge because of the persistent sound, its source was discovered. A whale, perhaps traveling the same route as the sub as though "schooling with it, was droning its plaintive mating call. "It's a sound you'd never forget," Caleb told me.

At lunch, still scanning the horizon, only now from his picnic-table perch, Caleb talked about the *Connecticut* and its mission to run up under the ice cap all the way to the North Pole. I interrupted to ask how submarines were named, and it led to the subject of boat naming in general. The story of any boat might begin with why the names of most shipping and sailing vessels are feminine. Whether it's the *Queen Mary* or the aluminum runabout parked on the trailer in the yard, it's usually a she. The British Royal Navy and Lloyd's List of London have officially used the feminine for all British shipping since 1734. Before that, we know that boats have been considered female since the earliest Egyptians. They were built resembling certain feminine attributes and were thought to bring crews good luck. Throughout literature, symbolism, and psychology, the sea is referred to in the feminine, just like the earth and the moon. A contradiction in vessel-naming traditions seems to be submarines. American cruiser subs, Caleb told me, tend to be named after cities in the United States, while attack subs are usually named after states. His term for subs was "fishes."

He told of instruments on the *Connecticut* that measure the thickness of the ice above. When all the sub's coordinates said they were exactly at the North Pole, the ice device read only a thin sheet overhead. So they surfaced. By thin, Caleb meant two to three feet—thin by polar ice cap standards. The upward force and propulsion of the submarine exploded the ice cap like a rocket from below. Even so, the polar bears standing by to witness what must have seemed the apocalypse weren't impressed enough to leave. The sailors snapped pictures of them loitering all around the submarine deck.

I learned that it was submarines on missions just like this one that first detected the movements of enormous schools of Atlantic salmon migrating from Greenland to the Canadian Maritimes and New England. It happened before their numbers were ravaged from the 1970s to the 1990s by deep- and midlevel trawling. Caleb said that much of the earliest scientific data collected on these migrations was owed to submarines.

During the afternoon of our second day together, I could see that in some sense, Caleb was always onboard his sub. His representations of his undersea life and work revealed a proprietary relationship to it. On land assignments, when he was in the surface world and his crew was out with another commander, it was a kind of violation to him, like a general forsaking his troops. Things wouldn't be exactly right with him until he returned to his command.

On those two days of fishing in the Grand Lakes region, he said he felt a reprieve from that anxiety. Maybe it was just being out on the water. Maybe it was the fishing. Fly-fishing a freshwater lake, he confessed, is one of the things he likes most about the surface world. The intensity of his gaze never changed while we were together, but frequent smiles softened the severity of the lines in his complexion. I made my confession, too. That first morning, I'd been trying to psych out what he did for a living, something I'm usually pretty good at. I'd come up with a fat zero. Caleb laughed. "It's an unusual line of work."

On my way home after dropping Caleb off, I thought about what had just happened. I work in a town with less population than half a city block. I return one phone call and end up the captive audience of a nuclear submarine commander. I might've been his guide, but in truth, I was his beneficiary. In that time, I got to know someone who undoubtedly could steel himself for situations unimaginable to me, but whose easy, soft-spoken manner inspired me. It surprised me too, but I came away with the feeling that with Caleb on duty at the helm of his fish, probing the depths of his world, I could somehow rest easier here in mine.

GRAND FALLS FLOWAGE

In June 1993, not far from where the St. Croix River scrawls an international border between the United States and Canada, two canoes maneuver into a place known to the paddlers as "Charlie's honey hole." Moments later, an urn comes out, some words break the morning silence, and then a film of gray ash expands on the water's surface around the canoes.

Thirty years earlier, the man whose ashes are being committed, Charlie Lipscomb of Dallas, Texas, had unknowingly inaugurated a family saga on the fabled fishery known as Grand Falls Flowage, a tradition that would go on for two generations beyond him. When he died, no one had any questions about what to do with his remains.

The Flowage had an earlier name. Long before a white man ever thought of yoking its attributes to industry, its Native name was Kennebasis, and of course, it was a toponym. It means "river that weaves through many marshes." There are Natives today who still use the name Kennebasis when referring to the bay and its backwaters. It covers a span of around five miles, running southwest to northeast until it joins the east branch of the St. Croix River and forms the international border.

Just before that confluence, Kennebasis drops thirty feet over Grand Falls. There, just below those falls, lies rock-hard evidence of the continental split 250 million years ago, when Eurasia was still joined to North America as a supercontinent, Pangaea. According to rock and mineral evidence, the base of Grand Falls lies along the fault line of that epochal divide. For years, geologists have made long journeys to chip away at those ledges.

Charlie Lipscomb may not have known any of this. His mission was to bass fish in waters that appealed to him in ways only he understood. Was it because most of the fisheries in Texas where he grew up were man made, just like this one? Later, his brother and other family members would come to understand Charlie's abiding love for these new waters in Maine.

After all, in the grand scheme of the other lakes of the region, these were indeed new waters. They did not exist fifty years earlier. Grand Falls Flowage is one of the few man-made fisheries in the state of Maine.

In 1912, the St. Croix Paper Company secured the rights from the state and a handful of local landowners to flood four thousand acres with construction of the Grand Falls Dam. It would help power a paper mill downstream. The transition from historic Kennebasis to Grand Falls Flowage would create a new fishery, even if neither the fish perfectly suited to the new habitat nor Charlie Lipscomb had arrived yet.

Remnants of what was flooded—stumps, piers, and cribworks— remained, providing structure, shelter, and even spawning opportunities for smallmouth bass. By 1965, just fifty years after its construction, the new face of Kennebasis—Grand Falls Flowage— was a sport-friendly fishing destination that helped inspire an advertising campaign that labeled Princeton, Maine as "A Sportsman's Paradise."

The stage was perfectly set for Charlie Lipscomb's debut appearance that year. Veteran local guides Paul Slipp and his brother-in-law, Hovey Gould, were assigned to Charlie's party of five. After two slow days of fishing out of a lake camp west of the Flowage, Hovey suggested they head for "the river." That decision, and that day, began a Lipscomb family love affair that has lasted half a century.

"Charlie came from New York City, but only because he was working there," yelled Paul Slipp through his phone from his Florida residence. The combination of the phone connection and Paul's 95-year-old ears made our conversation more like a shouting match.

"Charlie was really from Texas, but was working in the insurance business in New York. He was a man who never talked about his work. That was the last thing on his mind when he was fishing."

Paul's guiding sensibilities were immediately evident to me. "Charlie could cast anywhere he wanted and catch fish. He had a good sense of where bass should be. He would take turns going with Hovey and me. If Charlie told Hovey where they should go first thing in the morning (always his honey hole), Hovey would argue in favor of other places. But if Charlie said nothing when they first went out, Hovey always took him straight to his honey hole." Paul Slipp chuckled at this peculiarity of his late brother-in-law.

Such things are the quirks and nettles of long-term guide/sport relationships. When these relationships become friendships, the lines are sometimes blurred as to who's guiding whom. On one point, Charlie and the two guides agreed: this business of always going to the river was not setting well with the owner of the lake camp where they were staying. Charlie explored other options and found Margie Plaistead of Plaistead's Camps close by in Princeton. It would be his home twice a year on spring and fall fishing trips until Margie sold the camps. He then moved to The Lakeside Inn on Lewey Lake, the last lake before the watershed narrows into the Flowage.

"He had cancer practically the whole time I knew him," Paul said. "He'd be better some years, worse others, but it never stopped him. Didn't he love the river, and especially that honey hole!"

Paul Slipp shouted one more thing into the phone before we hung up. "He (Charlie) was one of the best fisherman I ever knew. Maybe the best."

Charlie invited his brother Forrest from Dallas to fish with the group when they were staying at The Lakeside, and with that invitation, a new era of Lipscomb pilgrimages dawned, one that continues to this day. Forrest, who named one of his sons after Charlie, was soon on the biannual plan too, fishing with Charlie right up to his final year.

By then, Hovey Gould was long dead, and the Lipscomb party was learning that few guides possessed knowledge of the river to compare with that of Native guides. It was during this period that Ray Sockabasin, Albert Dana, and Ray's brother David, all tribal guides, began to guide the group that now included Forrest's two sons, Jay and Charles.

The guide called into service to replace retired or deceased legends knows that those shoes can't be filled. Under such an onus, the new guy arrives as an imposter. The clients must adjust their expectations downward, knowing that the best that's possible with the person who presumes to guide them now that their heroes are gone, will be well below the bar already set.

Forrest Lipscomb dispelled most of those fears within minutes. He made no pronouncements, issued no inviolable edicts, drew no lines in the sand. He settled comfortably into the bow seat of my canoe for the first time in June 2004 as though he'd been there before. When my keel kissed one of the ten thousand drowned tree stumps, he only smiled and said, "That's the Flowage!"

I was to learn, my first morning with Forrest, what a qualifier was, the hard way. The Lipscomb tradition begun by Charlie decades earlier included a friendly family competition. Bass weighing in at two pounds or greater were qualifiers. The most qualifiers caught by any contestant won the kitty contributed to by all present on the trip. It might be Forrest; his eldest son, Jay; next oldest, Charles; or a friend they brought along. Friendly competitions that involve money carry a charge, I soon learned. Qualifiers were important. The guy you're guiding would probably like to win.

When Forrest took the scale we would use out of its leather case, the stakes of the game were suddenly heightened, at least in my mind. This was no Fisherman's De-Liar. It was a finely balanced brass instrument, a prized relic of earlier times still wearing the marks of mandibles, teeth, and scales from qualifiers of old.

Before I had even killed the outboard and grabbed my prized paddle (made for me by David Sockabasin), we were in the game. Forrest had landed a surface lure so close to a showing stump that the feeling of an imminent fish strike was palpable.

Then, everything blew up. The eruption and its loud report on that quiet morning let us both know that this fish might be not just a qualifier, but a nullifier—surely no one else would land a fish of this length and girth. Forrest played the heavy bass expertly up to the canoe. A lucky swing with the rubber mesh net landed the monster at my feet, where it spat out the lure and glared at me through red-rimmed retinas.

Full of anticipation, Forrest passed me the heirloom brass scale. I hooked the trophy under a gill plate, hoisted away, and before my eyes could focus on a reading, the smallmouth with the big mouth slapped its tail one way, its head the other, and threw the scale over the side of the canoe. As I lurched futilely to intercept it, nearly capsizing the canoe, the prize game fish leapt out of my now-loosened grasp and went over the opposite side, nullifying the catch, the weight, and snatching defeat from the jaws of victory.

I heard Hovey, Hubert, Albert, and Charlie Lipscomb all laughing from some celestial balcony. "Oh, don't worry about it," Forrest said, but I began to poke at the muddy bottom with my paddle blade, hoping I might feel the clink of metal. Back and forth, around and around in circles I went, poking, probing, just not clinking. When Forrest said, "Don't worry about it," a third time, I knew it meant we should get back in the game.

The morning's brisk action of several qualifiers and many sub-qualifiers helped allay my fear that this would be my last outing with the Lipscomb party. This was the first of five days we'd spend together. Why, I badgered myself, couldn't I have saved my klutzy performance for the last day instead of firing all my guns on the first? Little did I know then that I was packing even more ammunition.

It was a good day to be fishing. The cold front that would accompany the Lipscomb party for the next few days had not yet arrived, but had sent a low-pressure messenger ahead. The fish responded as they usually do, with a frenetic feed. Forrest switched between the three rods he had rigged for different baits. The Acadia rod was his favorite for rubber and plastic lures. He used a non-stretch line so his response from a pullback would telescope directly to the hook rather than bend and stretch first. In likely bass haunts, he fired to hotspots, and then turned his head as though listening as he worked the lure along the bottom. When he felt that certain vibration, he waited another few seconds, and then came up hard with both hands.

Luckily, the afternoon's fishing stayed busy enough to keep that brass heirloom off our minds. Much is forgiven with good fishing, and so, while I didn't feel redeemed, I felt hopeful—at least until I stepped out of the canoe back at the boat launch. Forrest had already gotten up on the dock, grabbed the painter (bow line), and then knelt down to hold the canoe. As I swung my right foot up, the toe of my L.L.Bean boot caught the Acadia rod lying across the canoe thwarts. The rod wedged itself between canoe and dock while I was in midstep. As soon as the canoe was relieved of my weight, it rocked once more and snapped the Acadia in two. Forrest sighed, smiled once again, and said, "Well, it's only a rod." I looked up once more, imagining the toothy grins of the legends looking on.

Bad starts like that either spell the end, or they become fodder for fond and funny memories. Back at The Lakeside, I wouldn't have been surprised to hear a benediction from Forrest, or a, "We want to thank you for your services" type of send-off. Instead, he reached for my hand, with the same smile he'd worn all day, and said, "See you in the morning."

These days, at least once a trip, we relive that bad start with a belly laugh. Then, it's back in the game to catch qualifiers to win the kitty. That game now includes Will, Jay's son, the third generation of Lipscombs to ply the waters of Kennebasis. Ray Sockabasin is still on the job, able to retell his own bad start stories from days gone by, and share some of the quirks of his old guiding comrades, including Albert Dana—who wasn't particularly adept in his late years at backing up a boat trailer. That didn't bar him from entry in the Lipscomb Pantheon of celebrated guides they've known.

The Lipscomb family has embraced the entire history of Grand Falls Flowage since it became a bass fishery in the mid-1960s. It is a family whose diaries and photo albums include faces of, and friendships with, guides now long gone. It is a story that began with a man discovering the new fishery, and then inviting his brother into that story. Thanks to that brother, the story can be told today even as it continues to unfold.

I know that Charlie crosses Forrest's mind more often than he lets on. When it happens, his smile widens and deepens. Now, at 89, he is seeing a past I can't see. And beyond that is a past no one alive can see. It is the old Kennebasis and those ancient rocks below the Falls. When I'm with Forrest on those special mornings, I remember the words of another fisherman who, also in his late years, was meditating on the memory of his own brother. . .

> Eventually, all things merge into one, and a river runs through it. The river was cut by the world's great flood and runs over rocks from the basement of time. On some of the rocks are timeless raindrops. Under the rocks are the words, and some of the words are theirs.
> I am haunted by waters.

> —*A River Runs Through It* by Norman Maclean

Finnan Haddie

A tradition faithfully honored each year by the Lipscomb party is a banquet-style lunch featuring finnan haddie, a recipe that has been passed down to each guide in the family's three-generation fishing history.

For so modest a meal, finnan haddie's past, dating to the mid-1600s, is full of controversy. Different regions of Scotland, such as Findon, near Aberdeenshire, and the River Findhorn, in Moray, would claim all the glory for this culinary mainstay, but it was a glory that couldn't be contained. London pubs were touting finnan haddie by the 1830s, and of course from there, this fish recipe would swim to foreign shores.

The key is cold smoked haddock, and if the smoker stays true to finnan haddie's heritage, only green hardwoods and peat are used. Peat leaves its signature smokiness not only on cold smoked haddock, but on some of Scotland's finest single malt scotches. To serve one of them with finnan haddie is a complement, and a compliment.

Cold smoked foods, generally, must be eaten sooner than their hot smoked counterparts, which have a much larger window for safekeeping. The finnan haddie traveling with us in our canoes was picked up on the Canadian border the night before, in order to be served at lunch.

The rest of the story, to chronicle it correctly, must give equal space and spotlight to a recipe just as renowned, with the inglorious name "cullen skink." At least the origins of cullen skink are not smoking with controversy. The village of Cullen is in Moray on the northeast coast of Scotland, overlooking the North Sea. Having traveled to this region, I can easily see how a dish this hearty achieved the wide acceptance it enjoys on that craggy coast.

"Skink" is a colloquialism for the shin, or "hock," of an animal, even though no land animal ingredients are needed for cullen skink.

Known as soup where it hails from, it seems more a chowder when it ends up on a picnic table at the mouth of Tomah Stream at Grand Falls Flowage. Ray Sockabasin calibrates the right heat and height from the flame of his hardwood cook fire for the finnan haddie pot. He adds only enough water to cover the potatoes and onions I'm peeling and leaving whole, though sometimes we change up by boiling the potatoes still in their skins.

By the time both of these vegetables are softening, most of the water is gone. That's when Ray removes the vegetables, moves the finnan haddie pot to mild heat, and lays in the smoked haddock filets. He then covers them with milk. Slowly, the smoked haddock steeps. To this, on occasion, we might add half a cup of cream, or a quarter stick of butter. It's the combination of the milk and the cold smoked haddock that marries the two Gaelic recipes. Instead of placing the potatoes and onions back into the mixture, Ray and I serve them separately, leaving Bretagne to rule the waves, finnan haddie to rule the soup, and Forrest to gloriously feast his family.

The flavor and texture of finnan haddie cooked cullen skink style are memorable, hearty, and invigorating, especially when served on days that call northeastern Scotland to mind.

At least once a trip, we ask Forrest to tell the story of Charlie's trips home to Texas from New York. The two brothers shared a love for finnan haddie, a treat more foreign in east Texas than loons and lobsters. Therefore, Charlie regarded each trip home as a propitious opportunity to share a beloved meal with family. Somewhere on his person, or in a bag, exuding an aroma fishy enough to pique the olfactory curiosity of passengers and crew, there was a finnan haddie, destined for Dallas, fresh from a wharf in New York.

ONE HUNDRED YEARS
OF FISHING

U pper Oxbrook Lake, all 422 acres of it, lies within the plantation of Talmadge, Maine, about five miles due east of Democrat Ridge and eight miles north of the village of Grand Lake Stream, if you could reach it as the crow flies. It has been designated, ever since fishery records have been kept, as a trout lake. How good a trout lake is it? That's a study all its own. Abundance in the early 1900s and abundance now are different concepts. In fishery biology, this is known as the principle of "shifting baselines," a term coined by marine biologist Daniel Pauly.

In his book *Four Fish*, author Paul Greenberg describes the principle this way: "Every generation has its own, specific expectations of what 'normal' is—a baseline. One generation has one baseline for abundance while the next has a reduced version and the next even more, and so on and so on until expectations of abundance are pathetically low. Pauly expressed this as a generational memory loss . . . he has tabulated that the good old days were in fact often much better." The shifting baseline principle applies to Upper Oxbrook Lake.

The situation there may have been uniquely suited to an enviable gene pool of trout reproducing itself. While smallmouth bass migrated into most waters of the region by the 1970s, often out-competing the native fish for feed, a waterfall along Oxbrook between Lower Oxbrook Lake and West Grand Lake was thought to have kept bass out. Salmon have been taken in the upper lake but have never achieved significant numbers. The deepest hole is just eighteen feet deep. There are white and yellow perch enough to entertain children endlessly, but in Upper Oxbrook Lake's heyday, trout were its best-kept secret. Spring-fed, and well-endowed with forage fish such as smelt, common shiners, and red belly dace, the nourishment was there to endow an outstanding fishery. People made sacrifices, and went to great extremes to access trout water like this one, and then kept quiet about what they knew.

In the summer of 1913, Francis Moulton, a senior at Harvard College, stepped into a sleeper car on the overnight train from Boston to Princeton, Maine. There is no such train today. There are barely any ruins at Kelleyland Depot, the last stop before the tracks crossed Grand Falls Flowage heading to the Princeton station where Francis stepped off the train.

Francis was born in Great Neck, Long Island, in 1881; lived in Wakefield, Rhode Island, as a teen; and then went to Milton Academy south of Boston to prepare for Harvard. He took the train trip his senior year to visit a college classmate who was spending time in Grand Lake Stream. He could not have known how fateful, how significant that act would be to the future of his family, a family that did not then exist. From then on, making this journey back to Princeton and on to Grand Lake Stream became a fixed part of Francis's life.

In the 1930s, after he was well on his way professionally, having joined the Massachusetts Bar, and domestically, having started a family, the wilds of Maine were a constant companion in Francis's thoughts. He convinced three friends to go in with him on a project. They would hire local Grand Lake Stream guide Harley Fitch to build a cabin on the northeast shore of Upper Oxbrook Lake, which would then become a destination for future fishing and hunting trips.

By the time the camp was ready, so was Francis's young family. It would be the first trip for his wife, Ruth, and their three boys, Francis Jr., Henry, and Stephen. Harley had by then built a guide's cabin next to the main camp, a common practice in those days when guides and sports lived together at camp for weeks at a time. Harley brought in Jimmy Gould to help him guide the Moulton party.

Harley's wife, Helena, was camp cook. In addition to serving as camp hostess and chef, Helena prepared the shore lunches. It must have been a welcome reprieve for Helena, who inhabited a man's world, when one of Harley's sports brought his wife along.

Going to Grand Lake Stream was a tough sell to the wives of fishermen in the early days of guided fishing there. After the arduous journey to Princeton came the steamboat trip; then the buckboard ride across Indian Carry, a rocky "road" running parallel to Grand Lake Stream; and finally, the long, slow crossing from the town landing at West Grand Lake dam to the mouth of Oxbrook, about six miles up the lake. The source of Oxbrook is Upper Oxbrook Lake, which then drains into Lower Oxbrook Lake, which in turn drains via Oxbrook into West Grand Lake.

Arriving at another camp that Harley Fitch had built at the mouth of Oxbrook on West Grand Lake, the poor woman might think it her reward and resting place for having traveled so far. It was only a way station. She'd soon learn that the next leg of the trip depended on her own two legs. Everything had to be portaged the length of Oxbrook, about a mile, and then transferred to canoes for the trip across Lower Oxbrook Lake. It was then unloaded again for another portage of one hundred and fifty yards to Upper Oxbrook Lake.

Finally, a half-mile canoe paddle across that lake brought the party to the camp that Francis and his friends had commissioned Harley to build. She surely would have been forewarned not to expect the Mt. Washington Hotel. For the children, likely well-schooled in the rough and tumble prose of Jack London and Robert Service so popular at the time, it must have seemed like the edge of the boreal forest. They might have expected Buck from *The Call of the Wild* to jump out ahead of them in the trail at any time. Upper Oxbrook Lake thus entered the bloodstream of the Moulton boys.

Francis' sons, all at impressionable ages, would, for the rest of their lives remember images from this period of their father; Harley Fitch, a larger-than-life Maine guide and woodsman; and the place itself— Upper Oxbrook Lake.

Take Henry, Francis's middle son. By the time Henry was a teenager, the woods and waters of the region were aspects of his life that he only wanted to explore more and more. And yet, ominous clouds were gathering. Like his dad, Henry attended Milton Academy. He was a junior there when Germany invaded Russia in Operation Barbarossa, the largest military attack in World War II. He was a senior when war was declared by the United States, following Japan's attack on Pearl Harbor.

Before an all-too-harsh reality struck that spring, Henry and five other members of the Milton varsity football team made the trip to the Upper Oxbrook camp. Arriving there was a temporary escape from a nightmarish world of dread. For their part, Harley and Helena Fitch were pleased to entertain half the starting lineup of a distinguished Massachusetts prep school, a group of brash young men who brought new life to their wilderness hideaway.

Francis Sr., having served on the battleship *Mississippi* during World War I, surely feared for all of his sons when war broke out. Four years later, just as surely, he must have been counting his blessings when armistice came and they had all survived, healthy and safe.

During the next year, 1946, things gradually returned to normal, or better than normal since by then, both Francis Jr. (nicknamed "Pat") and Henry had found their brides.

The things the boys had thought of so often during the war—the camp at Upper Oxbrook, and Harley and Helena—now exerted their old magnetic force. That spring, Francis and Ruth ("Pa" and "Ma" Moulton) planned a trip. It would be the first chance for the wives of the young men to finally see that distant, backwoods destination their husbands went on about incessantly.

The life and times of the Moulton family have been spilling out piecemeal in my canoe during the years I've guided Henry Moulton, now 89. It is June 2011, and Henry sits in front of me in the midship seat of my Grand Laker. I know by now that his eyes, looking forward so intently, look backward, too. His reminiscences transport us both to his childhood at Upper Oxbrook Lake. He dexterously casts a surface lure as we drift over shoal water. The action of the lure reminds him of the gentle splashing sound made by deer as they walked along the water's edge of Upper Oxbrook. He can still see the porcupines around camp with their comical, wobbly walk, and the beavers working the stream along the Oxbrook portage.

He reminds me that those were the days before fiberglass, aluminum, ABS, and all the other lightweight, durable materials canoes are now made of. In the 1940s, double-end, cedar canoes wrapped in a canvas shell hardened with mineral compound were the crafts used at camp for water travel. They had only lately replaced bark canoes, which had been used by Native guides since the very first sporting business had come to the region. Motors were heavy, and much too cumbersome for mile-long portages.

From his sharp memory, Henry can take me inside the camp that Harley built. An evening fire was usually needed there to cut the chill. In any case, most of the cooking was done with wood fires—fires that Henry can still hear crackling. Before Humphrey gas lights, still used today in remote lodges, the Aladdin lamp was a mainstay. It was a tall, narrow-globed, round-mantled lantern outfitted with a sturdy shade. It had a brass or nickel-plated base, sometimes designed with wildflowers in relief.* Two or three of these handsome lamps could illuminate a modest-sized camp with an agreeable radiance in the evening, more than enough light for two tables of four-handed cribbage. Always close by was a tin of strike-anywhere matches; and always in the air, suspended like a second ceiling, floated the silky billows of Harley's pipe smoke.

Sometimes in these early guide camps, just before a particularly fine, fresh-caught fish was cleaned and prepared for cooking, it would be outlined on brown paper. Then one of the more artistically inclined members of the party might fill in the detail: the dark back,

---

* Andrew Wyeth used one just like this for his 1945 painting, *Oil Lamp*, displayed at the Farnsworth Museum in Rockland, Maine.

the spots, the square tail, and the unique jaw that distinguish a brook trout. For many fishing camps such as Harley's, these drawings became a diary. A story might accompany the catch: trolling speed, fly pattern, number of jumps, netted by so-and-so, the weather that day. Over the years, these accumulated into a camp history that could be relived with each return trip.

Coming in from a day's guided fishing, the camp would smell of whatever king's repast Helena had been busy preparing. Had they returned mid-morning, her baking time, they would have smelled the pies, the biscuits, or the bread baking in the wood cookstove oven. Listening to Henry, I can almost smell them, too. An evening treat might've been venison stew. Harley, whose hunting skills were celebrated around campfires in Grand Lake Stream, always had game meats in the larder. In a time well before deep freezes, canning was the order of the day. The homes and camps of successful hunters were stocked with mason jars full of moose meat, deer meat, partridge, rabbit, and anything else that might have strayed in front of a 12-gauge or .32 Special.

Helena was as adept at Dutch oven cooking as most New England homemakers had been since colonial times. She knew by heart the ratio of coals on top to coals on the bottom, and knew how to time her entrees to the pleasure of her fishing parties. Her venison stew was a regional standard: chunked venison, carrots peeled and diced, Maine potatoes peeled and cut into one-inch pieces, chopped onion, and broth she'd made earlier from either deer or moose meat. If one of her sports had lugged in some red wine, so much the better. A half-cup would only enhance the hearty stew.

Henry remembered never sleeping any better than he did in camp at Upper Oxbrook. The bunks were usually homemade with horsehair mattresses, though on occasion, Harley found a deal at an Army surplus store in Bangor. Quilts and comforters were the winter work of Helena and Wilhelmina Eaton White, Helena's sister. They had to be mothballed during the winter or else they became construction materials for interloping rodents. There was, therefore, always that slight whiff about them, but that was better than an empty comforter shell on a cold night.

Thanks to Francis's long history with the Fitches, the now-enlarged Moulton clan had a special place in the hearts of Harley and Helena. On one morning in particular on that June 1946 trip, Pa, Ma, Pat and his wife Alice, and Henry and his wife Betsy all gathered around the breakfast table. Harley had been churning out pancakes for the Moulton party from the galley-like kitchen in the camp. When the last of them had been devoured, he came out to ask Ma if she wouldn't like just one more. She politely declined, but Harley pressed and finally, she relented. "OK," she agreed. "Just one more." When the order was up, Harley delivered it himself: just one pancake—the size of a manhole cover. Pa laughed until he cried.

And so did Henry and I, sitting in my canoe sixty-five years later. Henry hooked and landed a seventeen-inch smallmouth bass off the rock pile we were fishing, and then held it high for a photograph. I wondered how many such photos there must be in Moulton attics or basements. We headed across West Grand Lake at a slow troll so that I could hear him over the outboard.

Beginning in 1948, different combinations of Pa and his sons returned for fall hunting trips. On one such trip in 1958, Harley had hired local guide Earl Bonness to help him with the party. Little did Henry know that thirty-five years later, he and Earl would still be fast friends. There was nothing new I could tell Henry about Earl, even though I'd known "The Old Trapper" for thirty years myself. His signature Montana herder hat dated from the years he worked horse and cattle ranches there. He was one of the last living "cookes," as those assisting the cooks from the old timbering camps along the Machias River in the 1920s and '30s were called.

Earl's house from tannery times would've been there for Francis Moulton to see when Francis first arrived from Boston in 1913. Earl's old paddle shop is gone now. When he wasn't guiding or trapping, he was at work in this shop. Few could make as trim a paddle or put as sharp an edge on a canoe axe as Earl Bonness.

I guessed out loud that when Henry first met him in 1958, he probably heard one of the sayings Earl had coined about the good old days, "when there was a pickerel under every pad and the fishin' was so good you had to go behind a tree to bait your hook." Henry sputtered into laughter and said I had guessed right. He had also seen Northeast Historic Film's production of *Woodsmen and River Drivers, Another Day, Another Era*, featuring Earl Bonness among other veterans of the river lumbering days. Henry thought for a moment, then picked up his story again . . .

In 1963, Henry and his wife, Betsy, reenacted the trip his parents had made with their children in the 1930s—they brought their own children, Anne, Sara, and Peter to Grand Lake Stream. Today, forty-seven years later, Peter and his son Julian are on a different part of the same lake that Henry and I are fishing.

On Peter's first trip, when he was just four years old, the family stayed in a cabin near the town dock, a part of Harley and Helena's business complex, which then included both Upper and Lower Oxbrook Lake camps, the camp on West Grand Lake at the mouth of Oxbrook, and cabins in town. The enterprise was known simply as Harley and Helena's Housekeeping Cottages. The kids, the third generation of Moultons to know Harley and Helena, had their first guided fishing experience with Helena's brother-in-law, Horace White. Sara Moulton landed her first salmon while fishing from Horace's Grand Laker. During their stay, The Old Trapper himself—Earl Bonness—dropped by to say hello, and young Peter saw the man who was to become a fishing icon to him for the rest of his life. In the meantime, Peter always wore his railroad engineer's cap, mimicking the one that Harley was rarely seen without.

We were now within sight of my choice for a lunchground—my own camp. I had my own reasons for deciding on it. Earl Bonness and Pop Moore built the main camp and guide's cabin (now guest cabin) in 1929, when the young men were nineteen years old.

On the way in, trolling his orange Rapala lure only fifteen feet behind the canoe, Henry suddenly sat up in his seat and stared over my left shoulder. He had just seen a swirl behind his lure. It was a short strike or, in layman's parlance, a miss. Henry instinctively let out some line, which had the effect of stopping the lure dead in the water. When the slack thus created was taken up by the boat speed and the Rapala took off again, the strike that followed was anything but short. The fish was also anything but lunch. It was much larger than the slot limit for bass on West Grand Lake. Henry's brief interaction with the hefty smallmouth left a gleeful expression on his face. It was still there when he posed for a picture.

Peter, his son Julian, and their guide met us at the dock in front of my camp. Once the lunch fire was going, the coffee water on, the fish filleted, and the potatoes and onions sizzling, Henry, with family gathered round, told of his first winter trip in 1967. It was to Lower Oxbrook Lake, where Harley had built a camp. A blizzard rolled in on top of already-deep snow, so that ice fishing could only be done on snowshoes. They had planned to use a snowmobile, that troublesome twentieth-century invention that came with its own curse: it required constant attention to run at all, and despite that, it usually didn't. As if to raise a red flag on what this new mode of snow travel portended, Harley's snowmobile was broken down the whole trip.

By 1970, Peter had turned 11, an age of awakening in the souls of fishermen. We could all glance at Julian now and see the same awakening in progress. Remembering well his own youth and what Harley had meant to him, Henry came to the most poignant chapter of his story. It was the decline and passing of Harley Fitch, followed by Helena.

In the late 1960s, Harley's heart began to fail, forcing Harley and Helena to scale down their business of running the camps and The Trading Post near the town dock. One heart attack in 1969 slowed Harley down, but a far more severe one in 1973 put things on a downward spiral. The Oxbrook era was over for good.

Before the end came for Harley, the Moultons were forced to switch accommodations from Harley and Helena's to Grand Lake

Lodge, owned at the time by Harry and "Pinky" Lewis. They were joined there by Henry's younger brother, Stephen, and his young son, Joshua Moulton. Jack McKelvy came on as a second guide.

After that, the annual fishing trips continued unbroken through 1975. The patriarch of the tradition, Francis, had passed away three years earlier. Peter was then old enough to start working summers. College loomed in the near future. In the spring of 1976, by which time the Moultons had been coming to Grand Lake Stream for sixty-two years, Henry wrote a sad letter to Earl Bonness. In it, he apologized that the Moultons wouldn't be making the trip.

We lingered after lunch, sitting around the picnic table with coffee and brownies. I asked Henry if he ever saw Earl again before his passing in the mid-1990s.

"Yes!" he exclaimed. "In 1993, I came into town on a side trip from Bar Harbor. I went down to the town dock where Harley's store and cabin had been, and of course they were gone. When a couple in a truck stopped where I was standing, I couldn't resist asking them if they knew of an Earl Bonness. They told me they had just seen him at the store. I went there but he'd left for home, which is where I found him. We had a wonderful visit."

As we took in the sights and sounds of Dyer Cove that day, I realized we were just shy of one hundred years from Francis's first trip. I felt sure that he would be gratified to know that in 2008, after a thirty-three-year hiatus, his family resumed what he had started in 1913.

I decided to choose this moment for my planned surprise, the reason I'd brought Henry to my own camp for lunch. I hadn't yet told him that Harley's stepson, Warren Arthur Whiting,* was my friend

---

* Of the many cherished items left to me by Warren, among the dearest to me is the small, leather-bound diary of Helena Fitch. Beginning in 1940, the diary details everyday occurrences, including Moulton visits to Upper Oxbrook Lake. She and Harley spent whole winters in camp at the mouth of Oxbrook, then moved to Upper Oxbrook in March for the sugaring season. They sold maple syrup to complement their livelihood.

for over twenty years until he passed away. Among many old things he left me—things passed down to him from his mother Helena and his stepfather Harley—one of them was here at my camp. I had it hanging over the doorway to the porch of the guest cabin.

I walked Henry around and positioned him so that he could see it. When he realized it was a sign, he adjusted his glasses and read aloud, "Harley and Helena's Housekeeping Camps." It was the very sign that they had used when they were hosting the Moultons all those years ago. Whatever welled up in Henry's eyes at that moment did not spill from his lips.

In fact, I've forgotten who spoke first; I only remember that it was a long time until someone did. Then Julian gave a shout from the dock where he was casting a surface lure: "Fish on!"

Josh Moulton

The fishing pedigree of the Moulton family is being fully lived and further explored today. In correspondence with Joshua Moulton, Henry's nephew, I keep up with his striped bass adventures on New York City's East River. That's when he's able to steal a few moments away from the demands of his calling and passion as a renowned chef.

Long before learning the particulars of Josh's career arc in the culinary arts, I was already self-conscious preparing a shore lunch in front of him. Surely my ham-fisted attempts were in need of refinements that might easily be elucidated if he deemed it worth the effort. When I offered myself up for overhauling and improvements, he only said, "This is good food, honestly prepared. You'll never hear a complaint from me." For me, it was a view into Josh's style and success.

Before studying at the Culinary Institute of America, before attending Yale University, and while growing up outside of Boston, Josh was receiving those same immutable messages that Francis had conveyed to his father and uncles. One of them, Uncle Pat (Francis Jr.) had a vacation home in Kittery, Maine, where Josh loved to spend time in the summer fishing, romping, and exploring.

Small wonder that after becoming a sommelier at New York's acclaimed Arcadia restaurant at age 24, after winning the *Wine Spectator* Award of Excellence, after earning his stripes as an executive sous-chef at Union Square Café, after tours at famous New York haunts such as Gramercy Tavern, Tavern on the Green, Café Luxembourg, and Gabriel's, Josh would bring that wealth of learning and experience to bear on a new enterprise. It opened in Brooklyn in 2012 with a name only those of us who know him can fully appreciate. It is called Kittery, and features coastal cooking from Maine to the Gulf.

Our language as friends around campfires is sometimes as rough-hewn as the walls of Upper Oxbrook camp were. His approach to his business, Josh says, is "to take great product and not screw it up. If I listen to the food, it will tell me what to do. That's when I know that less is always more."

More is what Josh contributed to my own shore lunch repertoire. This recipe has already proven itself to diverse parties at lunchgrounds surrounding Grand Lake Stream. I can endorse Josh's assessment that it is "foolproof."

Grilled Pork Chops, Cranberry-Apple Sauce, & Yukon Gold Hash*
Yield: 6 portions

For the Pork Chops:

12 loin pork chops, each ½-inch thick (if you can get Berkshire or
  another heritage breed, great—but not mandatory)
¼ cup olive oil
8 cloves garlic, smashed & rough chopped
1 teaspoon freshly ground black pepper
12 fresh sage leaves, roughly chopped (or 1 Tablespoon dry sage)

Trim pork chops of any excess fat (though more is better to me).
Combine all ingredients to evenly coat chops. Pack in a container
tightly and marinate overnight.

For the Cranberry-Apple Sauce:

6–7 tart apples, cored and roughly chopped (as long as you have a
  food mill, there is no need to peel apples; if not, peel and cut into
  ½-inch chunks before cooking)
1 cup sugar
1 Tablespoon ground cinnamon
⅓ stick butter (salted is fine, though I prefer unsalted so I can
  adjust seasoning as I want)
6–8 fresh sage leaves, chopped fine
¾ cup dry cranberries (Craisins) soaked in very hot water until soft

Combine apples, ½ cup water, cinnamon, and sugar in a saucepan
and cook until very soft. Run through food mill and set aside (if you
are without a food mill, cook the chunks until they begin to fall apart
and then do the next step in a separate pan; combine after sage has

---

*Chef's note:
The nice part about this recipe is all the prep can be done ahead and packed and
transferred to the campsite easily. So what remains to be done is make the hash
and grill the chops. I would have the hash mostly done before starting the chops,
as the hash requires more attention.

cooked). In a saucepan, heat butter until bubbling and add chopped sage. Reduce heat and cook 30 seconds. Add apple puree, drain cranberries (but reserve their liquid and use to thin sauce if needed). Cook 5 minutes more over low heat. Taste and adjust seasoning— salt and pepper go well with this even though it is a sweet sauce. Cool and save refrigerated for up to two weeks.

For the Hash:

8 cups Yukon Gold potatoes, peeled and diced into ½-inch chunks
1 medium yellow onion, diced into ¼-inch chunks, sautéed in
    butter or oil until soft
4 green onions (scallions), cut into ¼-inch rounds (mostly the
    green part, but some white is good as well)
¼ stick butter
¼ cup olive oil
salt & pepper

Boil potatoes in water until soft but not falling apart. Cool on a tray and save. Heat cast iron or other large heavy-bottom pan until hot. Add butter and olive oil and heat until sizzling. Add potatoes and slightly smash onto bottom of pan. Let cook until potatoes begin to turn golden brown on one side and then turn over with a spatula to brown more. This is the finesse part, where heat and stirring are very important. You want the crispy bits, so don't move the potatoes until taking a peek underneath shows the browning you want. When the potatoes are mostly browned, add the onions, salt and pepper and cook another minute or two. Just before serving, toss in the green onions and stir one last time.

For the Meal:

Remove pork chops from container and remove garlic and sage (if fresh sage leaves) as they will burn. Season with salt and pepper and grill until cooked through but not tough. Pork will dry out, so less is more when it comes to when they are done. I prefer them slightly pink (medium well), but that is up to the cook. One way or the other, let them rest at least 5 minutes before serving with hash and apple sauce (you might want to warm sauce slightly or not depending on the day, i.e. warm or cold weather). Serve with hash and enjoy!

SARA MOULTON

Anyone who has spent even scant spare time on the Food Network, or reading *Gourmet* magazine, or surfing channels for the best cooking shows, knows the name of Henry Moulton's daughter—Sara Moulton. From the time she graduated with highest honors from the Culinary Institute of America in 1977, she has made recognized, lasting contributions to the food world as a chef, cookbook author, and television personality.

The host of public television's *Sara's Weeknight Meals*, now in its third season, Sara Moulton is also the author of three cookbooks and a weekly column for the Associated Press entitled "The Healthy Plate." She began her on-camera work at the Food Network in 1996, hosting over 1,500 episodes of *Cooking Live* and *Sara's Secrets* during the next ten years. Starting in 1984, Sara spent twenty-five years at *Gourmet*, most of it as the magazine's executive chef.

As I watched Sara guesting on Rachael Ray (which she frequently does), I decided to muster the gumption to make my request for a recipe. As a fishing guide, I naturally considered what bait I might use. Henry! If I made the right cast in her dad's direction, maybe the idea would have a nice soft landing by the time it reached Sara.

Any hesitancy I might've had was misplaced. Sara, as gracious as every other Moulton I've ever met, stepped up with an idea that has the perfect flare for outdoor cooking, and eating. She even provided the recipe's pedigree:

My first official cooking job was in the mid-70s at a bar in Ann Arbor, Michigan (where I went to college), called the Del Rio. They featured live jazz on weekends. It was a democratic place; all decisions were made by common vote and it felt like one big family. The food we cooked was not all that sophisticated—chili, hamburgers, Greek salad and soups based solidly on jars of soup base—but I got into it and prided myself on my soups in particular (the only item for which we did not have a formula).

The most popular dish on the menu was a burger called the "Det" burger, which had been developed in the early 70s by one of the cooks, Bob Detweiler, when one day he got tired of making the same old burger on a bun. He topped the basic burger with what became the "Det" mixture, drained canned mushrooms, drained canned California olives, and reconstituted dried green pepper bits, covered it with a slice of onion and cheese (his wife Julie, the manager, suggested the cheese). And here is the most important point—he steamed it in beer! It was really delicious, the sort of burger you dream about.

I have developed my own version here using fresh mushrooms, Mediterranean olives, and canned green chiles to add a little bite.

DET BURGERS

Yield: 4 servings

Hands-on time: 25 minutes
Total preparation time: 25 minutes
3 Tablespoons vegetable oil
1 medium onion, sliced (about 1 cup)
8 1½-inch cremini mushrooms (about 4 ounces), sliced
Kosher salt and freshly ground black pepper
1 4-ounce can sliced, peeled green chiles, drained
⅓ cup pitted kalamata olives, sliced
1½ pounds ground beef chuck or round
6 ounces cheddar cheese, cut into 4 slices
⅓ cup beer (your favorite)
4 hamburger buns, split and toasted

Heat 2 Tablespoons of the oil in a large skillet over high heat until hot. Reduce the heat to medium; add the onion and cook, stirring occasionally, until softened, about 5 minutes. Increase the heat to medium high; add the mushrooms and cook, stirring, until the mushrooms have browned and the liquid they release has evaporated, 4 to 5 minutes. Season the mushroom mixture with salt and pepper to taste and transfer it to a bowl; add the chiles and olives and set aside. Wipe out the skillet.

Gently shape the beef into four 4-inch burgers; season with salt and pepper. Heat the remaining tablespoon of oil in the skillet over high heat until hot. Reduce the heat to medium-high, add the burgers, and cook 3 minutes. Turn the burgers and cook 2 minutes. Top each with a quarter of the chile mixture and a slice of cheese. Add the beer to the skillet; cover and steam until the cheese has melted, about 3 minutes.

Transfer the burgers to the toasted buns and serve.

HOME WATERS

S ome guided fishing days are blueprinted in the morning, first thing. Maps are spread out, coordinates taken, quarry chosen, lunchground picked out. Other days unspool without a script.

I knew from my guiding history with Rob and Rebecca that not everything had to be known in advance. Some of our most memorable days together have played out like a novella with a surprise ending. So it was natural enough on that late July morning for us to have wandered up into one of the many feeder systems that entered the lake we were fishing. Pickerel cruised such places, and nothing delighted Rob like taking one of these marauding, chain-side gators on a bass bug.

The stream we chose cut through the sedge meadows with snake-like coils. There seemed to be no straightaway stretches of more than fifty yards. Up the middle was a channel. It was rimmed port and starboard by thick rafts of lilies. Sometimes the line of lilies to either side was interrupted by a tiny cove-let of open water. Rob would hit that spot with his fly and almost invariably receive a shock and awe response from an old sawtooth. Involuntary shrieks of glee left Rob's lips every time this happened.

The snakier streams hold the most surprises in store. Anything may lurk around the next bend. Will it be large boulders sheltering trophy smallmouths? A fallen tree, blocking passage? Not this time. It was the hulking carcass of a very dead, very bloated bull moose. Flies had already eaten away most of the summer velvet from its antlers. I was sure from the sight of it that ravens, eagles, and snapping turtles had also staked out the bonanza feed bag that would sustain them for weeks to come.

As we approached on the downwind side, the stench hit us all at once. "Aaagh!" Rebecca grunted. "Ripe!" Rob piped. There was nothing obvious that gave away the cause of death. I have found other moose carcasses, and sometimes I've been able to puzzle out the scenario that probably led to their demise. One spring, I came upon a cow moose of middling weight that had crashed through a patch of thin ice and couldn't get out. The thinnest ice would be in the middle of the stream where the current is strongest. Once the moose was down in deep water, it was most likely the thicker ice at the edges that prevented its escape.

Another young bull I found had obviously stepped into thick, oozing mud and couldn't extract its legs. It wasn't the quicksand of old Tarzan movies that kept sucking its victims down until they were out of sight. It was just plain mud. Deep mud. It creates suction. I've had to step out of my hunting boots and reach back to retrieve them in similar situations. I imagined the moose walking in until all four legs were knee-deep in the suction chamber. It bothers me when an animal so majestic is wasted in this way and when its expiration was obviously not quick. Happy to be upwind, we lingered, looking for any cause we hadn't thought of, but nothing presented itself.

The fly-fishing action was steady. Each new bend in the river begged for exploration. We were being swept upstream in a vortex of ever-expanding fishing opportunities daring us to come farther. Finally, there were no more bends. The stream narrowed, the flow increased, and up ahead, we all could make out a dark wall across the water. At that point, the stream was barely the width of two paddles end-to-end. When we got closer, we saw that the painstaking efforts of beavers had paid big dividends—for them. Above the dam was a small pond they'd created for themselves. With a little more work, they might actually turn this construction site into a home, one that would serve them all winter once sufficient depths were achieved from the effects of the dam.

On our side of the wall made of branches, the water had already deepened. It looked as if the buck-toothed furbearers had blocked all passage. That meant that any smallmouth bass wishing, as they naturally do, to migrate farther upstream would be stopped short right here. I counseled Rebecca to land a fly just inches from the beaver dam while I feather-stroked the paddle blade to hold the canoe in the current forty feet away, side-to to the dam. She executed the cast perfectly, placing her fluffy bass bug in a spot that screamed "Big Fish!" This time, Rob's involuntary shriek was vicarious glee. Rebecca's rod tip came up, the line went taut, and the bass went airborne. Seventeen inches of pure muscle and fight—the effects of living in moving water—registered at Rebecca's wrists. She prevailed. The red-eyed bronzeback stilled itself briefly in the net before finding a new lease on life.

Minutes later, I was still feathering the paddle blade, staring at the beaver dam, when I realized that both Rob and Rebecca were repeating my name. I looked at each of them and said, "Wanna try something?"

"Sure!" Rob chimed from the bow. It wouldn't be the first time the three of us had tried something. I pulled the paddle in forward strokes until the bow grazed the branches on the left side. There was a rock there, which would serve as the stepping-stone to the dam. I handed the paddle forward so that both of them could use it as a wading stick until they'd planted themselves firmly on the catwalk on top of the dam. Beavers often make the top easy for themselves to walk across.

Tying off the painter to some puckerbrush on shore, I stepped out into the warm water on the upstream side of the dam. I pulled out a few branches while my friends waited patiently. I didn't want to destroy the dam, only make a small renovation so as to pull the canoe through. The day was calm, the sun was shining, and it was too late in the season for biting bugs. Standing knee-deep in that stream, I decided I was having fun. The next thing I knew, Rob and Rebecca were repeating my name again. Then Rob said, "You all right?"

"Definitely," I smiled. "Just thinking."

With only a little work, I could see now that getting over the dam was possible. When I backed up, hit the throttle, and drove the bow over so that it slapped down on the upstream side, I felt a rush of the kind eleven-year-olds feel when they let go of the rope swing over the river. I picked up my passengers on the other side of the still-intact dam. Rebecca said, "That was interesting." Rob was already changing flies and looking upstream. And my daydream had just begun.

It was 1973. I'd just completed my summer's employment at Darrow's Wilderness Canoe Camp in Grand Lake Stream. It was a job that showed me the wilder parts of Maine, which, after my sedentary college years, I felt I needed. Oftentimes I'd find myself sleeping on the ground outside, in a tent, or in a van while waiting to meet a canoe party at some waypoint. My job was to resupply them for the balance of their trip. A favorite memory from those resupply missions was waking up at the edge of Baker Lake near the headwaters of the St. John River to see a cow moose and two calves standing in the water outside my tent flap.

In late August I walked away with $350 in my pocket, the whole summer's pay, which had also included room, board, and a shop to work in as I refurbished a 1957 Old Town river canoe. It was a good place to save money, since there was no place to spend it. My VW Beetle had been sitting all summer at the town dock parking lot, only occasionally getting started when I passed through on my way up or downlake. I paddled the twelve miles downlake that last day with nearly all of my worldly belongings in the fifteen-foot canoe. Once I reached town, I secured the inverted, double-end canoe on the roof of the bug with lots of rope and rags, tying it off twelve ways to Sunday. When I finished, the bug looked like a turnip with a Bonaparte chapeau.

That's the way I drove it to Sebago, Maine, straight through, five hours. That was plenty of time to wonder, or maybe fear, to what extent Sebago had changed. If there's one thing that youth remembers from enchanted summers, it's the details. The last two farms on the way to the camp road. The rocky, rutted way in. The dilapidated brown gate bolted to a post on one side and chained to a concrete pillar on the other. The first view of the lake from the Burnell camp.

By the time I graduated from high school, our family vacations to my Uncle Henry's camp on Peabody Pond were a thing of the past. By that time, Mom and Dad were going on golfing vacations, cruises, and cross-country car trips. All three brothers headed off on different life paths. Now I hoped Uncle Henry would be sitting there with Aunt Ethel when I arrived unannounced. They'd taken to spending summers at the camp since Henry retired from his job as a Connecticut State Bank Examiner.

To my delight, Fitch's store was still open in the town of Sebago. It was the store that had everything Walmart has now, save the plastics and electronics. I picked up a salami and cheese sandwich at the deli counter and pulled a bottled Coke out of the old coin-op cooler. Before leaving, I made mental notes of the inside of Fitch's, knowing it couldn't last. Fitch's was a prototype general store of the kind that once sustained virtually every town in Maine. It used to be said of its owner, "If Fitch hasn't got one in the store, he'll sell you his own!"

From there, I had only to motor up the mountain toward Douglas Hill, heading northwest toward Peabody Pond. Route 107 would take me through Mud City, a half-horse adjunct town to Sebago that hosted bean suppers in the Town Hall. Stub Stacey's store was the little brother to Fitch's in terms of supplies, but less of a haul from Peabody, so Dad could stop there first if he needed shellac or nails or turpentine. Which he always did. Maybe it was an excuse to pick up a paper, smoke a pipe in peace, and see what the mountains looked like before the sun got too high. He was in full vacation mode, having traded in his Argyle knee stockings, pressed slacks, and starched shirts for white sweat socks, khakis, and a T-shirt. Once in a while I'd stow along with him just to hear Stub talk. I've never before or since understood less from a man speaking the same language as me.

All this flooded my brain as I drove the top-heavy Beetle up the last steep incline, past the Hancock Pond Road on the left, the Folley Road on the right, and finally to the entrance to the Peabody Pond Road on the right, just after "the old Brown place." When I was a kid, that's the way grown-ups referred to homesteads when generations of the same family had lived in them. Of all the unlikely colors in the spectrum for a rural, barebones abode, it was pink. That stuck in my mind for good after first seeing it at the age of eleven. That was the first year that Dad, Uncle Henry, my older brother Al, and I parked across the road from the Brown place, in order to snowshoe the road into camp. Amid all that snow—windrows over my head at the road's edge—and up to my thighs everywhere else, there was that inescapable, eye-catching swatch of pink. "Why wouldn't the Browns paint their house brown? What color would they paint it if their name was Pink?" Certain thoughts help to take the mind of an eleven-year-old off the biting cold that's already penetrating two pairs of wool socks.

Nobody else I knew had a February vacation like that one. Snowshoeing almost two miles into a rustic camp on a lake. Warming by a wood fire (even though I thought of it as thawing). Chopping out a water hole in ice that was three feet thick. Getting my first smell and taste of venison from the buck deer Henry had shot the previous fall.

He told the whole story of the kill one night in camp. There is a Philip Goodwin painting that almost perfectly depicts that story. Henry had walked the Northwest River down to the Folley Road and back. He had his .32 Special draped across the inset of his left arm, right hand over the trigger guard. There was no snow on the ground yet, so good tracking was out of the question. Back on the camp road, he decided to walk up Tiger Hill before heading back for lunch. There were some old granite foundation walls still visible along the Tiger Hill Road then. All of the old farms had gone to seed, but the rock walls where fieldstones were stacked were still there, in various stages of disrepair.

Henry's buck took a wrong turn that day, something they seldom do. He'd been on the uphill side of one of the rock walls, with Henry on the downhill side. Something spooked the deer. Maybe it was the snap of a twig, the sound echoing off the rock wall. Maybe Henry's own scent swirled around the hill in an eddy and wafted toward the buck. Whatever it was, it was enough to start him on a run, but then there was the rock wall. No problem for a whitetail. The ten-pointer made a majestic leap that would've measured twenty feet on a gym floor, but Henry had his gun up before the deer ever left the ground. He'd heard a snort as the deer took off. His shot was clean, sure, quick. The deer was dead at Henry's feet when he'd steadied his own heartbeat enough to check. It was a downhill drag to the road, an easy pick up with his vehicle, and now fine fodder for wide-eyed kids on a midwinter's night. How's an eleven-year-old ever going to forget a story like that?

These days, I knew his health wasn't great, and the two to three packs a day of Chesterfields didn't help. But he was where he truly wanted to be, and how many people can say that? "Oh yeah, the Chesterfields," I mused. Another eleven-year-old's memory. Uncle Henry could reach into his khaki pants pocket, where he always kept a pack of unfiltered Chesterfields, fiddle around for a few seconds with his fingertips, and then pull just one cigarette out of his pocket. Most people wouldn't trouble themselves. They'd just take the pack out of their pocket, tap it on their knuckle and let one fall out. Why does a kid's mind permanently record every one of these family nuances as though they carry some lasting meaning?

"Well, you're a sight for sore eyes!" Henry said at the camp door.

"Have you eaten?" Ethel asked, without showing a lick of surprise. Then she pulled me into a bear hug. "Oooh, you're thin!" I mentioned my salami and cheese, which was enough to set Ethel in motion. A still-warm pot roast was in a Crock-Pot on the stove, but my hopes were focused on the fridge. Ethel's homemade tapioca pudding was the most exotic dessert of my youth, and I was wondering what the chances were that she still took the time to make it nowadays. When they'd both watched me polish off the remains of their supper, Ethel piped, "Think you've got room for some tapioca?"

I told them I'd come on a mission: to see them, and to give this restored canoe of mine a baptism on my home waters. That's what I considered Peabody Pond to be, that and much more. I then turned to Henry. I said that I'd learned of an old ritual among the men of certain tribes that some observe to this day. The belief is that by returning to the place where they became a man, they will remember the things they need in life in order to be fulfilled.

Nothing perked up Henry like the subject of Natives or American history. He was a history buff who read tirelessly of Manifest Destiny and the so-called Western conquest. He'd been the first person to tell me that there might be something amiss with the versions of that story taught in school to his generation and mine. He could quote statistics such as numbers of foot soldiers, cavalry, and Natives in key battles. He knew the names and dates of all the treaties broken.

He was better versed than anyone I knew in some of the worst chapters in American history, and, as scandalous as it was when I was a child, he loved to talk about them! Among his favorites: Andrew Jackson's Trail of Tears in 1838 when 16,000 Cherokee were forcibly marched westward out of their homeland, a brutal march that killed 4,000 of them. Also the Wounded Knee Massacre of 1890 in which as many as 300 Lakota Sioux men, women, and children were slaughtered by the US 7th Cavalry and dumped into a mass grave.

He hadn't lost his knack. He loved hearing about the tribal tradition and approved of my mission. Looking back, it's easy to see that the ritual worked, and that in some small way, the road to becoming a guide opened for me on that trip. I stayed up late listening to Henry that night. Ethel was probably glad for him to have a fresh audience. By the time we were finished, I felt like I'd smoked a pack of secondhand Chesterfields, but I thoroughly enjoyed being a student of Henry's unsanitized history once again.

When he crushed out his last cigarette, I retrieved a rollaway bed from the bunkhouse and brought it up on the camp porch. That way, I could listen to the loons at night and let the morning's first outboard motor heading out from the nearby boat launch be my alarm clock. Dreams of enchanted summers accompanied me until I heard that sound, the same sound from so many mornings of my childhood. *Put-put-put-put-cough* was the sound of an old Johnson Sea-Horse doing its best to run at an idle without stalling.

After breakfast with a special tapioca dessert, I paddled away from the dock as Henry and Ethel waved from the porch.

"See you in a couple days!" I called back. I'd never see them again.

I wondered if Rob and Rebecca noticed anything. How did a person straddling two worlds look? From my stern seat, I had two views. One was over Rob's shoulder at the stream ahead, where we actually were. But in my mind I was also looking at the mouth of Cold Rain Brook, my destination that morning on Peabody Pond, thirty-seven years earlier. There wasn't much about the entrance to Cold Rain to jump out at you if you weren't looking for it, but I was looking for it. Only a slight parting in the pickerel grass gave it away.

I'd known about Cold Rain since my brothers and I, and our friends, the Burnell brothers, had scoured every inch of every shoreline on Peabody Pond until we were sunburnt, chafed, bruised, abraded, and bug-bitten. I'd just never explored Cold Rain Brook past its entrance to Peabody Pond in Pickerel Cove. The fact that this one place had gone uninvestigated had permanently cast it in my mind as a mystery. I knew that the source of Cold Rain Brook was Cold Rain Pond—that was evident enough on maps. Now, I meant to see them both, using my vintage canoe.

Suddenly, back in the present, Rob hooked into a large, dark, river bass that gave every sign of never having been hooked before. Here it was, trapped above the beaver dam with nothing to do but grow on the plentiful forage in this hidden habitat. Of the roughly 2,000 to 2,500 smallmouth bass I typically handle each season, this one impressed me more than most, especially because of its strength. Now Rob was completely taken by this stream and its offerings. Two more paddle strokes after releasing the bass, and I was released back into my daydream.

Every cast for the first hundred yards of Cold Rain Brook produced a pickerel that morning. I'd packed a spinning rod, since I came prepared to camp out one or two nights. There'd be no going hungry today with the sandwiches Ethel packed for me, nor tonight, from the looks of the fishing. Before long, the weeds gave way to shallows and rocks. Then I saw the beaver blockade up ahead. Well, I had all day, so I pulled the canoe off to the side, stepped out in my sneakers, and surveyed the situation. It was no use. This barrier was many years old. It was rooted in the river. Heaving ice had accomplished that. The beavers had built stories onto it over time, and added mud. I walked upstream a ways to find that the stream narrowed to a brook coming toward me from a steep grade. I was hiking south while the stream was flowing north. According to map calculations I'd made earlier, the pond couldn't be more than a few hundred yards away. I looked back at my canoe to make sure it was secure, and started hiking.

The brook soon became a cascading waterfall. I had to take to the woods to get around it. Up, up, away from the falls I hiked, until suddenly, things turned very quiet. Too quiet. I knew this sensation. I squatted down, watched, and waited. Finally, there was the loud crunch of a twig, then the *whooosh* of brush glancing out of the way. I stood up slowly to see the rack of a bull moose towering over the understory where he'd been browsing. When a moose moves, everything goes still. Past him, I saw through the dark woods a large opening of light. Cold Rain Pond! The moose never picked up speed, but just ambled away until I could no longer hear his footfall.

Cold Rain Pond had haunted my youth in ways that keep kids awake at night. I've since read USGS information on it from the Department of Inland Fisheries and Wildlife. These days, it holds brook trout. It is considered a southern Maine pond with northern Maine characteristics. The official description: "Cold Rain Pond thermally stratifies each summer and contains a sufficient volume of cold, oxygenated water suitable for brook trout management. The Department began stocking brook trout in 1990." But in the summer of 1973, as I prepared to demystify Cold Rain Pond for myself, it was still thought to be a panfish pond, hard to access and therefore barely worth it. Average depths of fifteen to eighteen feet would seem to support the panfish hypothesis. But then there were pockets of thirty feet and more. Were trout there even then?

Rebecca was now on to a fish, one that had been lurking on the downstream side of a root system reaching from the base of a black spruce out into the stream. She had sidearmed a cast under the limbs so that the fly skittered across the surface several times before reaching its target. The peace of the moment suddenly erupted into war, one that Rebecca wasn't winning in the early part of the campaign. Tail walks, head thrashings—this fish unleashed a force greater than befit its size. Being well-hooked was its only failing. Rebecca, no stranger to fish fights from the much larger bass that this fish mimicked, began to make gains. Her imitation dragonfly did not. When she played the fish up to the canoe and I unfastened the bass bug, I saw that it now looked more like a tsetse fly than a dragonfly.

When I came out from the dark woods to the shore of Cold Rain Pond, the opening to Cold Rain Brook wasn't much more than a rivulet. It was late August, when most lakes and ponds are nearing their lowest levels of the year. The pond was a mirror. Out near the middle was one huge, rounded boulder. It was sloped on one side so that it might be possible to climb, depending on how deep the water was right next to it. I'd gotten used to wearing a bathing suit under my jeans all summer, and today was no different. As I slipped out of my jeans and shirt, I was posing the question that tempts the fates more than any other: What's the worst that can happen? I supposed I might see a snapping turtle. I trusted in my swimming skills. One of Maine's many graces is its scarcity of man-eating predators. I decided to swim for the rock.

Cold Rain Pond had nothing sinister to offer. The fates were asleep. It was a leisurely swim and there were shallows around the big boulder, making it easy to get a leg up. From a splendid perch atop the rock, I could see only one camp along the shoreline of this thirty-eight-acre gem. It blended perfectly with everything around it. "Lucky folks." I felt a life goal crystallizing. Someday I needed to find a place like that. While staring at it, I went from a cross-legged, sitting position on the rock—to lying on my side with one elbow propping my head up—to lying on my back—to sound asleep.

Next thing I knew, an alarm went off. A shriek. I moved to cover myself, feeling practically naked on my rock. Suddenly, I was back in my Grand Laker, realizing both Rob and Rebecca had fish on. A double hook up! It seemed as if Rob was going to be able to play his fish a little longer than Rebecca, so I could tend to hers first. Rob's bass was ranging back and forth the width of the stream, ahead of the canoe. Rebecca's was on a short line and perilously close to a thick weed bed. The days of needing blow-by-blow coaching are a distant memory between us. She raised her rod, stripped line, and quickly got the bass's head out of the water, drastically reducing its horsepower. My pole net closed the deal. When I looked to the bow, Rob was already lipping a fine smallie. We worked like a team. My misgivings about indulging in this daydream were fading.

Waking up on a rock in the middle of a lake, you only see sky. "Is this heaven?" It was several seconds before I rounded up my wits. It was the sound of water licking the rock that did it. A light breeze had kicked up a ripple. Had I slept an hour? The sun's angle was definitely different and I felt heat on my skin from a possible sunburn. The granite protrusions had made a checkerboard of my back. The swim toward the outlet was slow and soothing, and my heart sank a little when I stepped out. I had met Cold Rain Pond. Demystified it. It would no longer loom mysterious. I vowed that day to be sure and save up some mysteries—that they shouldn't all be solved.

I found my canoe as I left it. Stepping over the beaver barricade, one stick caught my eye. It was a shillelagh! Destroying a beaver dam in the state of Maine is illegal, but surely one stick could be forgiven. I pried it out of the maze and set it in the canoe. I thought it might one day be conscripted into service as a walking cane in my dotage.

Today, my Cold Rain shillelagh hangs on a peg in my canoe shed, awaiting dotage duty.

Smallmouth bass were brand new to Peabody Pond in 1973. They seemed easy to catch compared to salmon and trout, but that may have been because they weren't yet used to being fished. Camped out under the galaxies on Weeman's Beach that night with a belly full of fish, I counted up the constellations I could recognize: Leo, Scorpio, the big bear, Ursa Major. August in Maine is a good time for stargazing.

Rob, Rebecca, and I had solved the mystery of what was beyond a beaver dam, one that for me had opened a window to another. I never told my friends where I'd been that day in my imagination. If my guiding focus seemed off to them, they were kind enough not to mention it. Finally, just like Cold Rain Brook, the stream we were on also had a beaver dam that was impassable. It was layered thick and tightly with building materials from a forest partially felled by beavers. Beyond that dam lies a mystery I've decided to save up.

I missed Henry and Ethel when I paddled downlake because they'd gone to town on some errands. I'd come down in the morning in order to make a long day of it on the road. After I left, Peabody Pond would produce one more mystery for me, one that I'll never solve. "Asphyxiation from propane gas" was the Medical Examiner's official finding. Why had the pilot on Henry and Ethel's gas refrigerator gone out overnight while they were asleep? Apparently because of the night's chill, the camp windows were all closed up tight. The gas had nowhere to go. When they hadn't been seen or heard from for a few days, a neighbor and friend stopped in to check on them. It was none other than Franklin Burnell, the father of my boyhood Peabody cohorts. When he opened the door, a wall of gas nearly knocked him over. Henry and Ethel were both dead in bed.

I've always been grateful for the one last visit I had with Uncle Henry, the closet historian, and Aunt Ethel, whose tapioca recipe I wish I had today. I'm grateful to them both for supplying my youth with its home waters. My father purchased the place from Henry's estate and regularly went there himself until the year before he died at the age of eighty-eight. The place then passed to my brothers and me. I still return there, when the spirit moves, to remember important things.

MIHKU AND HIS RAVEN

I t behooves any fishing guide to find havens from weather, especially wind, to cscape to on days that would likely be a total loss if spent out in the open. Over the years I've searched out such placcs on days off, fishing them not only for fish, but also for other attributes.

The sprawling lakes of the region seldom provide good refuge from big blows. Wind can sack a fishing day much faster than rain. On those days, it's good to withdraw to narrower waterways that deny wind a running start. It's usually going to be a river or a stream. In such remote, less-fished locations, make-your-own lunchgrounds may be necessary. A fire grate can be made using the broiler basket from a guide's bow bag. A cut, peeled spruce pole can be positioned so that its end hangs over the fire, allowing a bailed chowder or coffee pot to suspend there and cook. A table is fashioned from a flat, weathered piece of washed-up dri-ki (the Native word for driftwood) positioned across two boulders. There's always a deadfall around to summon into service as a bench seat. For some reason, the fish cooked over that fire; the chowder made there while the wind howls in that other, unkind world; and the coffee made in that suspended way all taste better, as if the senses are enlivened to a new pitch owed to the sweetness of having gotten away with something, of having rescued a day.

One of my havens is a stream miles back into tribal land, but I access it by first crossing a lake that is not boundaried by the reservation. My intentional geographic vagueness will be noted here, for reasons that will quickly become obvious. I had discovered this stream on a calm day in May, while fishing the lake with two sports from Houston. Why I hadn't noticed it before baffled me. I supposed it could have been the stump statues arrayed like sculptures in a Roman garden that camouflaged the opening to the stream. Somehow, that day I noticed it. Rather than indulge my two clients on a possible wild goose chase, I made a mental note to return and explore it on my next day off.

When that day came in early July, it took me half an hour to find the opening again. I considered the possibility that some of the stumps were not attached to bottom—that they were moving— and this helped keep the mouth of the stream hidden. After picking my way in through the deadwood, I had a wonderful surprise. The stream turned navigable with the outboard for at least four-and-a-half miles! Even so, I paddled and fished a good part of the way. It had a distinctly wild feel. Only game trails came up to the water's edge on either side. It was easy enough to see where moose or deer crossed. It took a closer look to notice where beaver, otter, and other critters had slithered into the stream.

When the stream finally turned shallow and bony, I was able to tilt up the motor and still paddle on. Right about then a raven's call jolted me out of pleasant reveries. I paused, looked around, and heard, up ahead, the sound of whitewater. That would be the end of the line as far as canoe travel was concerned. By late that afternoon, I'd had more than one person's share of fun catching smallmouth bass in the slower water and then, where the water was faster, catching brook trout on a fly rod. At that point, I was deeper into Indian land than I'd ever traveled by water in my guiding career.

Since that discovery, I have returned several times to that sheltered haunt when I needed to salvage a guided fishing day. On one of those days, with sports in my canoe, I made another discovery, though I never mentioned it to my two clients. When we were heading upstream from our makeshift lunchground and I'd reached the first boulders close to the fast water signaling me to tilt up the motor and start paddling, a raven let out a sudden "QUARK!" up over my left shoulder. It dawned on me that every time I got precisely this far in the stream, a raven sounded. From the shore on the left side, a bluff the height of a two-story building towered over the stream. The embankment was completely canopied by old-growth hemlock. Hunters will often refer to such softwood growth as "darkwood," for two reasons. On the brightest of days, only an occasional sliver of sunlight makes it all the way to the forest floor. The second reason is spookiness. On one of those hemlock limbs sat the raven with the great set of lungs.

If it weren't for the raven, I wouldn't have made my discovery: At the top of that bluff, situated back amongst those huge hemlocks, I could make out a structure. It didn't look so much like it was built there as grew there. A part of the landscape.

From what I could see, it wasn't dilapidated. Untended, deep-woods structures go downhill fast. The weight of unshoveled, wet snow can belly the ridgepole and sag the roofline. Frost heaves, after melting, can settle the sills into the ground and rot them. All of this movement reshapes doorjambs and window openings. If there is a body of water or stream close by, the structure will tend to lean in the direction of the water. No one seems to know why. Sometimes, if there's a porch on the neglected cabin, it will look as if the porch and the main structure are working at cross-purposes, so that the whole spectacle, if painted, would be labeled a sure Picasso.

Not the case here. A shiny, galvanized stovepipe poked through a newish-looking roof jack. The green, rolled roofing, which only helped the building blend into the hemlocks, appeared to be in good shape, too. With one more paddle stroke I could see a waterline that came off the side of the bluff, traveling a route through roots and rocks down to the stream. It most likely meant the cabin had a pitcher pump in use. The pipe would be hauled out before each winter. Just beyond that, an inlet perhaps five feet wide came into the main stream. Something about that inlet gave me the impression it was man-made. Neither of my sports noticed any of this as they were busy casting. It all went by in just a few paddle strokes until the bow sport hooked a fish and let out a shriek.

While tending to the action in the bow, I for some reason glanced back up to the bluff to see the outline of a man standing half out of sight around the corner of the cabin. My attention was then commanded by fish and fisherman all the way to a successful netting of a fifteen-inch brook trout. It made a fine photograph right before being released. We continued upstream to the fast water, and by then it was time to begin our long journey back to the boat launch many, many miles away. Just before the stream began to deepen, where I'd be able to let down the outboard motor, I scanned the shore to my right. Wasn't this where the raven sounded? Busy with my clients, I'd forgotten to make mental coordinates. With both sports now facing forward in the canoe, I squinted, craned my neck, and peered as deeply through the dark conifer maze as I could, and still saw neither cabin nor waterline. I thought, "That'll teach me to mark a spot."

All the way back to the landing I thought about that cabin, the only sign of life for many square miles in that entire region. It certainly was not new. The blanched logs dispelled that notion. If the builder or builders meant it to blend in, they'd succeeded. That it was inhabited, or at least being visited, succeeded in stirring my curiosity.

There were no days off for the foreseeable future. I might have to wait until fall to come back on my own. That was a long time to nurse a bad case of unsated nosiness. Then, the last week of July, when I had a booking with another guide on a party of five, there was a last-minute cancellation.* At the last minute, the party was reduced by two when the couple I was going to take decided to drive to Bar Harbor to go on a whale watch. They would pay their guide anyway in view of the short notice, and hoped there wouldn't be any hard feelings.

---

* The reason for the odd number was the other guide's Quebec-style canoe. It is both broader of beam and two feet longer than the standard Grand Laker design. He can guide three sports instead of two if necessary, especially if the third is a child, which was true in this case.

A paid holiday! Hard feelings? I wasn't long deciding what to do with that gift. One day off is almost a problem for a guide since, in the well-worn words of The Old Trapper, Earl Bonness, "One day ain't enough time to have a nervous breakdown." Might as well get back on the water. I put together my own shore lunch, which was easy since I planned to have fish, fried potatoes and onions, guide's coffee, and a fudge brownie that measured three inches square and one inch thick. Just before hitching up the canoe trailer and heading out, I had a late thought that led me back into the house. I doubled the dunnage and now carried lunch for two.

I stopped at The Pine Tree Store and had a leisurely visit with Kathy Cressey on the Liar's Bench: she with her peanut butter toast with honey on top, I with my breakfast sandwich. We each shared all the news the other might not have heard, which in Grand Lake Stream can take a while because of a large margin for gossip. To tempt her, I told her I had an empty canoe for the day, and not only that, I had stocked lunch for two. I saw from her reaction that she would've loved nothing more than to go fishing but had no one to cover the store.

The day was friendly. Up till now, I had reserved my little no-name tributary for wild weather. I'd added it to my private deck of guiding cards to be played in times of need. This was not one of those times. Reaching the launch where I would put in, I sized up the perfect weather conditions and decided it would rain for sure the next day. It was just too nice. I thought of Tom Hennessey—artist, columnist, author, and Maine state treasure—who put the same feeling this way: "If it had been any more beautiful, it would've been unbearable." It was that kind of day—the kind that removes any doubt that the opposite kind of weather is on its way. And it almost always is. Maine guides see so much weather adversity on the job, it leads to a certain suspicion of perfect weather. I could now more easily recognize the Roman garden of stumps that gave away my turning point into Unknown Stream, as I jokingly decided to call it. It comes from a tradition of friendly deception among guides. When one has had spectacular luck at a certain spot but doesn't want to

give it away, he or she will reply to a snooping colleague, "It's just off
the mouth of Unknown Stream." That's the sure sign that someone
has something to conceal.

"Well," I thought, "I'm here, the day is perfect, so why not fish?"
Within minutes, I noticed something I'd seen twice before while
fishing with Rob and Rebecca Lekowski. It was a hatch of mayflies
that had been discovered by the bass in the slower, deadwater
stretches of the stream. Fish rising to mayflies is usually discussed in
the context of trout or salmon, not smallmouth bass. The surface was
dimpling everywhere. I scooped one up for a look. It was *Hexagenia*
all right. I threaded my Double L, nine-foot, five-weight fly rod, and
then copied the pattern from my fly box, tying it onto a 5x tippet.
I got the fly overhead, false casting while scanning for a dimple.
When one showed, I set my match to the morning's hatch down
within inches of where a bass had just taken a mayfly, only to see him
come back for seconds. The tip of the Double L sent the message
back to me that this was a fish not used to being caught. Stream fish
are always stronger—that's one thing. But wilder fish, a safe distance
from well-known fishing haunts, haven't yet been duped so often by
hooks dressed with feathers. The proof is in the fish fight.

On a jump, the twelve-inch smallie loomed like lunch the minute
it broke the surface. Even more so in the bottom of my rubber mesh
net. I said quiet thanks to the Bar Harbor couple who had paid me
for the privilege of this outing, and hoped that even now they were
spotting whales. The hatch lasted most of the morning and so did
the action on the fly rod. The morning record was an eighteen-inch
smallmouth that rocked my canoe with water it displaced every time
it jumped. None of the fish I'd played had the feel of fished-for fish.
This was truly a garden, one that I'd henceforth describe to anyone
asking as being "just off the mouth of Unknown Stream."

When small riffles up ahead signified an increase in stream flow,
I looked over the side, and sure enough, underwater boulders were
visible. Just as I shifted in my seat to tilt up the outboard, a "QUARK!"
sounded from close quarters. Though startled, I smiled, realizing
the raven had just reminded me of my whole purpose for coming.

Squinting once again into that tangled webwork of darkwood, I saw what I was looking for.

As I moved forward with short paddle strokes, the cabin made of vertical cedar logs played hide and seek behind the trees. Now the waterline came into view, and I remembered the little canal just upstream from it. I executed several J strokes on the right side, bringing the bow of the canoe perpendicular to the opening of the inlet. A few forward strokes had me into the canal, bordered on both sides by black alders, the limbs of which had been pruned so as not to block passage. It was proof of my theory that the waterway was either man-made, or man-improved. It wound around to the left, presumably toward the back of the cabin. Grasses gently brushed the canoe sides as I poled along with my paddle.

Then, the oddest thing came into view. It was a kind of roller assembly reaching all the way from the top of the bluff down to the canal. Its side rails were about three feet apart, with rolling-pin-like members notched into these rails every couple of feet. "A launch!" I thought. It was a micro-version of the type seen in old footage when a liberty ship was christened and then rolled down into the water. It was made entirely of peeled, hewn spruce logs. I saw no nail nor any hardware until, with one more poling, I could see, at the top, a block-and-tackle pulley system attached to a tree.

I set the paddle down across the gunwales and cupped my hands to shout "Hello!" when, "Tahn Gok!" The voice that took my breath away didn't come from the general vicinity of the cabin where I was about to yell a greeting. It came from behind me! I spun around so fast, the canoe would've upset had it not been in a canal barely wider than its beam. There, almost touching the propeller of my upturned Johnson outboard, was the bow of a bark canoe. In it was a Native man smiling a wide, toothy grin.

"Assokitahasi," he laughed. I sat agape, unable to speak. Only once had I even heard of someone being that quiet in a canoe—and when that thought struck me, I looked at the man again. He must have come into the canal almost immediately after I did. He must have timed his paddle strokes or polings to coincide with mine to mask their sound. His canoe would be far lighter than mine with no motor or guide gear; it would therefore draw less, sitting higher in the water. And he spoke Passamaquoddy to me! No Passamaquoddy speaks in his Native tongue to a white man unless they are friends or he has some reason to believe the white man will understand him. He was dressed traditionally. Long black hair parted in the middle and braided. Beaded breastwork. Various amulets and talismans around his neck and wrists. A smile that began in the pit of my stomach made its way to my face. The image before me coincided perfectly with Drummond's description of the Native man who suddenly appeared near his eel sluice on that eerie night six years earlier in Township Unknown.

"Mihku?"

"Aha!"

"Mihku Wihwahsin?"

"Aha!"

The word he had startled me with, *assokitahasi* is the Passamaquoddy rough equivalent of "surprise!" An understatement in this case, but then the Passamaquoddy language is understated. Often, one word adequately expresses concepts that in English require whole phrases or sentences. It's as though, long ago, there was an agreement that language shouldn't be unnecessarily time-consuming. For example, the word *ehetuwonekosuwok* means that there are two beds in a room, all made up, facing in opposite directions. One word!

It's an oft-repeated anecdote in guided fishing that when white people end up in a boat with a Native guide, it's too quiet. They wonder if something is wrong. Nothing's wrong. The Native inclination to let silence speak for them is always disconcerting for those made uneasy by a lack of conversation. My guiding colleagues who are Native live under no such burden. They might not say much, but they don't miss much either.

Mihku stepped out of his canoe first and approached me with an outstretched hand. When I moved to shake, he pulled me up onto my feet in my canoe and then helped me step out. He called me by name, then glanced at my stringer. "Nemass!" he exclaimed. Fish! He then went back to his canoe and picked up a forked stick with two trout on it. "Nemass," I said. "Aha!"

Aha is a kind of all-purpose "yes" or "okay." I knew that Mihku spoke English. It is the first language of the tribe, although, unlike many other American tribes and aboriginal bands of Canada, the Passamaquoddy language has been carefully and painstakingly preserved. That effort has been a concerted one, supported by tribal leaders, elders, teachers, and council governments. It has resulted in a modern ten-thousand-word dictionary. The consequences of losing a language were considered to be so profound—taking with it culture, traditions, rites and rituals, medicine, and many other integral parts of Passamaquoddy history—that it was to be avoided at all costs.

Sadly, what the Native is used to from non-Natives is a lack of interest in their language. It is felt as a compliment when an effort is made to learn to communicate, however unskilled, in their tongue. Because of my limited abilities, not his, Mihku and I used a hash of expressions, mixing both English and Passamaquoddy. When I offered to cook lunch I used the word *pasquhihpu* for "lunch" and he approved with "Aha!" I returned the compliment by saying, "Kchi woli-won," which means "thank you very much." I would cook *nemass* (fish) and also *pocetesol* (potatoes). "Sounds scrumptious," said Mihku, switching back to English, and we both had a big laugh.

I unloaded my cook gear, lunch basket, and stringer. Mihku pulled both canoes up onto the canal bank, and I took a moment to admire his. The late and legendary Passamaquoddy guide Lola Sockabasin had explained to me fifteen years earlier how they were made.

The bark shell of a birchbark canoe is wrapped in reverse to the way it wrapped the tree. On the canoe, the smooth or underside of the bark faces out. One piece stretches across the entire bottom of the canoe and about halfway up the sides. The side panels, which come up to the inner wales and outer wales, are sewn to the bottom piece, forming a seam all the way around the canoe. That seam is sewn with black spruce roots. The roots are pulled right out of the ground near the base of a mature spruce. They are then cleaned and skinned and finally split into various sinews so that each root makes more than one sewing thread. The roots are also used to lash inner and outer wales together. Cedar logs are split down to the thickness needed for both ribs and planking. These are then boiled for bending. When everything is in place, the seams are gummed with tar or pine pitch that has been boiled.

Though it is uncommon to find true bark canoes made like Mihku's in the traditional way, those you do see will likely be decorated at the bow or stern, or both, and possibly along the sides just under the gunwales. These designs, some of them finely detailed, are literally scraped into the bark with a sharp tool, making this rare art form a first cousin to wood etching. I pointed to the design on the bow of Mihku's canoe and took a clumsy stab at the word *kchee-ga-gog*. "Raven!" Mihku affirmed. He also asked me if I'd seen his raven. When I said I had, he told me it is his sentinel, or gatekeeper, alerting him to visitors. He said he had seen me once before, earlier in the summer after the raven had alerted him. Today he was fishing the whitewater just above the cabin when the raven sounded, and he headed back in time to see my upturned propeller disappear into the canal.

When I asked about the canal and pulley, he motioned to follow him. We carried fish and cook gear up the bluff. On the way I could tell that he was fit and agile for his years, which my best guess figured to be around fifty-eight. I also knew that he could easily be ten years older than that and still look fifty-eight. Off to the side was a sight that jumped out of the pages of my own imagination, something that only existed there thanks to Drummond Humchuck. It was a rowing pen up on sawhorses, probably the very rowing pen (or paddle pen) Mihku used to transfer eels from Drummond's catch box to the truck that took them to market. Instead of thwarts, the pen had wells for holding eels. I could tell the boat was very old.

I felt boyishly overwhelmed to be there. It was a place I'd felt drawn to by one intuition after another, beginning in the spring, without ever knowing why. Now, I knew why. As I climbed the rest of the way up the bluff, the cabin on the flat ground at the top—roof, eaves, windows, sills—came into full view. I had to stop. It was as though someone had lifted Drummond Humchuck's cabin out of Township Unknown and deposited it right here in these woods, deep into reservation territory.

I looked at Mihku. "Assokitahasi," he said. Yes, it was a surprise, but it probably shouldn't have been. His father, Moses, the man who'd helped Drummond build his cabin, clearly had applied the same skills here. "Mihtaqsol," I said, nodding toward the structure. It means "father" and Mihku answered that yes, it was the work of his father—and Drummond! They had helped each other build their cabins. The cedar logs had faded on the same timetable as Drummond's, and so I calculated their ages to be about the same. Mihku asked if I'd like to see the inside.

Between where we stood and the cabin, in a small clearing just steps from the camp door, there was an outdoor cooking area. There was a fire pit surrounded by fitted stones, with a cooking grate across the top. Spanning its length above the grate was a steel bar. Hooks hung from it with various-sized skillets, a broiler basket, Crock-Pot, colander, chowder, and coffee pots. I set my bow bag down, we hung our fish stringers over the bar, and then I stepped past the sturdiest looking picnic table I've ever seen. It was hand-hewn from hemlock logs. Before we got to the door, I was able to look out toward the water from the place Mihku was standing when he saw me on the stream earlier in the season. As is always the case with camps behind a good tree-line screen but near the water, the view out is much clearer than the view in. Doubtless, that had been Moses' intention in selecting this perch.

Had Drummond Humchuck been seated in the doorway of Mihku's cabin, teetering on his twig rocker and puffing on a pipe full of red willow, I couldn't have been too surprised. One structure was the twin of the other. Likewise the interior layout, though Drummond's has more clutter due to the various enterprises that keep him busy indoors when he's not busy outdoors.

I saw no evidence at Mihku's of soap making, for instance. Or raspberry-vine pounding for lamp wicks. I did, however, see a bottle of bogwani on the counter. Then I realized that the whole flow of the interior led the eye to a display shelf. It was clearly meant as a place of honor in this camp. On it was a Popsicle stick model of the Brooklyn Bridge. Before I could speak, Mihku said, "Kehcikotonet," which means "the old one," or "the elder." Yes, it was Drummond's work all right. Who else would care to carve the individual strands of a cable, whittle turnbuckles and spires so true as to give the work a magisterial prominence even here in Mihku's cabin? The work would command the same authority hanging in the Capitol Rotunda in Washington, D.C. Mihku was obviously proud of the piece, which I praised the most lavish way possible—by staring at it, taking a step forward, then a step back, and shaking my head back and forth for the longest time. He was clearly pleased.

He then led me to one corner to see a kind of open-faced pantry full of shelves, many of which were stocked with various staples. Mihku said, "Kehcikotonet" again, and then I realized—this was Drummond's cache, the things Mihku stockpiled to bring to him from the proceeds of their eel barter. He said that by the time of the hunter's moon, all the shelves would be full, and it would be time to make his journey. He apparently saved things up throughout the year, adding the comestibles just before heading out to Drummond's.

Outside, Mihku and I went about the chores of preparing a lunch as though we had been guiding together for years. No guide loves anything more than to see the way another guide cleans fish, as each will have some peculiarity or trick of his own. Mihku, though not a guide as far as I knew, had more than enough skills to be one. He cleaned his two trout so fast that when he was done, I couldn't say exactly how he'd done it. I was still working on the first of my two smallmouths. As I started on the second, Mihku got a good fire going. He had both an outdoor and indoor pitcher pump, the outdoor one close by the cooking area. With a few primes on the pump handle, he brought water up the pipe and filled the coffee pot. I peeled potatoes, chopped onions, and then mixed up the coffee with a whole egg. Mihku nodded his approval. Soon enough the coffee pot was at a full boil, and I handed him the mixture. He poured it in, watching it fizzle and froth until he set the pot down in front of, but close to, the fire. This kept it at a front-to-back rolling boil without boiling over.

Oddly, for two people who had never met, we worked as a team. The fish were all fried in a skillet Mihku chose from his rack. I used one from my bow bag for the potatoes and onions. One hand seemed to know what the other was doing, with the effect that everything was ready at the same time. "Kisaqosu!" he said, scooping up the fish. "They're done." I opened my basket and took out my blue enamelware. It was a fine lunch. The taste of trout so late in summer was truly a treat. Mihku showed his approval of the bass by bringing his hands together over his plate in a prayer gesture.

Once we'd overpowered our plates, Mihku poured coffee into tin cups and I unwrapped two brownies. We then turned around to sit facing the fire on the bench seat of his hemlock picnic table. At that moment, William Underwood popped into my mind. I'd written about him being guided, over one hundred years ago, by Joe Mell, a Passamaquoddy guide, woodsman, and canoe maker. Their friendship lasted decades. Underwood wrote two books in which he recounted many of their adventures. Reading them, it is impossible to miss the affection Underwood felt for Joe. Though a man of few words, Joe Mell's company was very agreeable to Underwood, the noted photographer and author. Thoreau, in *The Maine Woods*, wrote similarly of Joe Polis, the Penobscot Indian who guided him to Katahdin. The interplay of honest, direct conversation and quiet must have been refreshing to Thoreau, who by all accounts loathed tedious prattle.

I recognized that it was the same with Mihku. What may have removed the awkwardness from our long silences was the strangely comfortable sense that we were pondering the same things. Our thoughts were conversing, if that's possible. It had seemed that way since we shook hands. The first word he spoke after we finished our dessert proved my theory to me. It was *nsiwehs* or "brothers." Then, as though filling in some gap in the silent conversation of our thoughts, he explained a lot to me in a very few words . . .

His father, as I knew, had died when Mihku was very young, but not so young that he didn't remember him. He insisted he did, anyway, even if his mother had always assured him he was too young. The man who stood in for his father, teaching him everything that Moses would have taught him, was Drummond. He came to this cabin often as a younger man, and also brought Mihku out to his own. They fished, hunted, and trapped together in the territory I call Township Unknown but that they called "Kiskesasik" or (roughly) "garden plot." Then, after Mihku was grown and had his own family, they lost touch for many years. Only in more recent years had Mihku gained a greater appreciation for what Drummond had given him. That's when he returned to Kiskesasik and surprised his surrogate father at the eel sluice. Thanks to this account, I now knew that Drummond, once he got close enough that morning on the stream, would surely have recognized Mihku.

In the years since then, he had been happy to learn that the aging Drummond had a friend—me—who came to see him regularly. He got the impression Drummond was a teacher to me, which he said for Native peoples is almost the same as a father. By that reasoning—the two of us sharing Drummond as *kehcikotonet* (the elder who teaches) he decided on the word *nsiwehs* (brothers) when referring to himself and me. I nodded enthusiastic approval.

I felt comfortable enough to ask Mihku about family. He told me his children were grown and gone now, leaving only his wife and him at home in Indian Township. His mother had passed on three years previously. He comes out here to fish, hunt, or work on various projects like the paddle pen.

I was glad to have that opening into the question I wanted most to ask. The fact that the eel pen was here at this landlocked camp meant that he must somehow be able go to Drummond's eeling stream from here. I couldn't fathom it. I traveled such a different route from Grand Lake Stream to Drummond's cabin that I couldn't navigate in my mind what water route there might possibly be from here.

And yet, there was the paddle pen and no means of trailering it out of here.

Mihku said the trip was indeed possible, but only in high water. That meant early spring or late fall. Drummond showed him the way when he was very young, long before the Maine Indian Claims Settlement Act of 1980, which conferred reservation lands. Some of the waterways are barely passable, "About like the canal," he said, pointing down toward his. He always brings a chainsaw and usually needs it. Dead trees and limbs that have fallen would block him otherwise. He said that when he makes the trip, it requires him to sleep out one night. He does cross under one paved road, towing the pen through a wide-diameter culvert. It's the same road where he meets the eel vendor that takes the catch to New York City in the refrigerated truck. On the way out to Drummond's, his wife meets him at that road just in case he needs anything. It is always in the middle of the night, as he is not interested in having his destination known. She insists these days that he carry a cell phone, but he confessed that he keeps it off most of the time, and barely knows how to use it anyway. He pulled it out of his pocket and showed it to me. We both had another big laugh.

"Kiskesasik." I tested the word out loud, subduing the middle syllable to accentuate the music. Mihku said it after me. I told him I had only learned of the friendship between his father and Drummond earlier this summer. I had gone to my friend in grief after being unable to save a life. He had told me the story of Moses and of his tragic, untimely death. It was Drummond's way of lightening the load I was carrying. I told Mihku that when Drummond was speaking about Moses, I could tell it must have been quite a friendship.

Mihku said it was a friendship of an older kind, based on helping each other in almost every way. "Esunomawotuwok," he said. It sounded like the opening notes of a song. It means "they traded." It was with Drummond's help, for example, that Moses provided so well for his young family, harvesting fish, game, and furs. Money was almost never exchanged between them. Of all the things one person might give to another, money, for them, ranked close to an insult. For them, it was too expendable, leaving no imprint of the payer on the payee. Mihku used an allegory: "If one man helps another split his wood for winter and is paid money for it, it's a lopsided deal. One keeps warm for months, and the other's payment is gone before the week is out."

Mihku's understanding of Drummond certainly coincided with mine, but I was grateful for this much larger window into Drummond's life that reached back long before I knew him. Now it was clear why Mihku chose the eel barter as the best means of reconnecting with his *kehcikotonet* or father figure, resuming the kind of relationship his own father had with Drummond Humchuck. Drummond wouldn't have known what to do if Mihku had offered him his cut from the eel trade in money. Few things are more useless to Drummond Humchuck than money.

As I was cleaning up and making to leave, Mihku saw that I was fascinated with his pulleyed launch assembly and offered a demonstration. It was easy and graceful, requiring so little effort on Mihku's part that I was even more fascinated afterward. He let the vessel down on the rollers, set his tension in the lines, and simply let it down so gradually that it barely splashed the water in the canal. Then, with block and tackle, he just as deftly pulled it right back up.

There was just one more thing I had to address with Mihku before leaving—the raven. *Kchee-ga-gog*. It had faithfully given a signal every time I'd come close to Mihku's cabin, even on those occasions earlier in the summer when I didn't know the cabin was there. A trained raven? A predator domesticated as a sentinel?

I'd had an abiding interest in this particular raptor ever since reading a book called *Ravens in Winter* by Bernd Heinrich. A professor at the University of Vermont, Heinrich decided to study ravens in western Maine in the mid-1980s. He trucked in eight tons of bovine carcasses, staking them out hundreds of pounds at a time over four winters, within studying distance of his tarpaper-shack headquarters. He went to great personal sacrifice to either explode or corroborate the myths that surrounded this mysterious bird since ancient times. The raven was already listed in the *Audubon Society*

Encyclopedia as having "the highest degree of intelligence to be found in any birds." It was already known for having social skills enough to cooperate with wolves on hunting expeditions. The wolves, in turn, would help drive off the raven's two chief predators: the great-horned owl, and the red-tailed hawk.

Raven symbolism has flourished since the Norse god Odin carried one on each shoulder—representing thought on the right shoulder, intuition on the left. Bran, a mythological Welsh hero whose name means "raven," was the "holder of ancestral memories." Among various Native peoples, ravens have been thought to be the carriers of certain knowledge—life-and-death knowledge as well as the ability to tell friend from foe. They are the largest in the whole *Corvidae* family, which includes crows and magpies, and their life span can exceed thirty years.

And so, Bernd Heinrich set about his long, cold, lonely study of *Corvus corax*, the raven. Of his many fascinating findings, some of which support the beliefs and traditions of the tribes, the most startling centered on the raven's social development. Ravens, he found, especially juvenile ravens, enact an etiquette of sharing when carrion is found. Time and again, after Heinrich had staked out a bait site, he observed the moment of discovery by a single raven. This bird then found a perch overlooking the meat and began recruiting its own kind to share the bounty.

Other experiments were chronicled in yet another book by the professor of Zoology, *Mind of the Raven*. Ravens can use tools to access food, and in some cases they have been known to make tools. Their abilities in terms of elocution probably exceed those of any birds except parrots. They have been taught to utter words and phrases that sound nothing at all like their native "QUARK" call. Day in and day out on the water, watching what the ravens are up to is every bit as interesting to me as watching the eagles. They seem to know things, if it's possible to put it that way, but then I tend to side with the raven on Odin's left shoulder—intuition.

Mihku said that a raven had been here all of his life, doing the same thing. That meant that the assignment of watching over his cabin was passed down over two or three generations of ravens. He believed that his father had trained the first one, an idea that is not so outlandish. Ravens and other birds are now known to be trainable in many areas. They are also capable of learning behavior from a parent. Local guides know of loons that will swim up to a canoe and eat a bait fish out of a person's hand because they are the offspring of a loon that learned the same thing from a parent, and so on. Why not expect something similar from a raven? If any bird could rise to the station of reliable sentinel, it would be the raven.

I expressed my hope that Mihku and I could get together again. Since my warm-weather months were spoken for, maybe we could have a visit in winter. He liked that idea. He helped me load up, we shook hands, and he gave the bow of my canoe a gentle shove as I poled backward out of the canal. "Kchi woliwon!" I called back.

Out in the stream, for the first time that season, I saw that the shadows had lengthened by late afternoon. It always comes with a hint of melancholy—this realization that the summer has aged and won't last forever. I glanced up to the hemlock bluff to see Mihku waving from the spot where, a few hours earlier, I had looked out at the stream. I raised and flashed my paddle blade to him. It caused something to flutter in the trees, catching my eye. It was the iridescent, inky silhouette of Mihku's sentinel, perched solemnly on the high hemlock bough, at its post and on duty.

THE MANDOLIN MAN

I was refreshed from my unscheduled day off spent with Mihku. I didn't, however, want to return to the mouth of Unknown Stream too soon. I would continue to covet that treasure, naturally camouflaged and thus protected from too much human visitation. I had overlooked its entrance scores of times myself. Now, having discovered his whereabouts, I wanted to avoid even the slightest chance of crowding Mihku. He seemed happy in the same peace and solitude his father had known before him in that special place. Mihku's cabin had seemed to become a feature of the woods around it as if, with age, it had gained title to the natural order of things. I had only felt this kind of solemnity associated with a place a few times before.

Summer's candle had burned low, and some long-standing clients were already arriving for their favorite time of year. Those September days, though shorter, somehow turn more contemplative. There's something about the light, too, that can't be discounted. Landscapes and lakescapes alike present themselves more intensely, as if their colors shout with vividness as the sun scribes a lower arc across the sky. For these sports, the imminence of fall affects mood positively. They also agree that when it comes to taking it all in to the fullest, canoe travel is hard to beat.

I often suggest to my sports that one year, if at all possible, they should fly into camp on a floatplane. When they do, they see that the land, lakes, rivers, and streams below present themselves as one big circulatory system. And that's what it is. With all those watery routes, most of them connected, leading off farther than the eye can see to all points of the compass, one wonders how they could all be navigated. And yet, for thousands of years, Natives thrived and traded on those life-giving arteries and capillaries connecting them to far-flung communities.

What the guide's canoe offers, in contrast to sparkle boats and other pleasure craft, is the *process* of travel. It's a meditation more than a mere crossing. If careful observation and quiet contemplation are valued by the wilderness traveler, the guide canoe is hard to beat.

People think in canoes. And yet, even as their thoughts turn inward, they're apt to speak more outwardly than usual. All guides hold much in trust. When someone has fished with you for many years in that setting, you're carrying a great responsibility. But what happens to those illuminating life stories after the people who lived them have passed on? Sometimes I look back on those installments, those annual visits of someone dear to me, and they seem like the verses of a song.

Arthur was not his real name. In observance of the unspoken oath, that's the name I'll use. He's gone now, but his words still hover over certain pools on quiet days when I guide fly fishermen on the stream. They wait for me on the lakes too, in coves where we kept counsel for so many years. Arthur had favorite places, especially in his eighth decade, because something about them created the mood he was looking for.

Arthur told me that after living beyond his allotted "three score and ten," he wondered every day at his longevity. That was over ten years ago. To be able to draw breath, he said; to get around; to find small, unexpected comforts seemed undeserved now, especially when he thought of so many of his friends who'd passed on much earlier. "A lot of them lived healthier lives than me," he'd say. Arthur's life spilled out not in any linear, consecutive way. Just a verse, here and there.

When he was impressed by the truth of something, his favorite expression was "You can take that to the bank!" We had a big laugh on that last trip when Arthur started to use his pet phrase, but stopped short. "Well, I guess I'd better not say that anymore." It was the year the five biggest banks in America had collapsed, and with them, faith in big banks in general.

That same day, Arthur told me that the very elderly are far more liberated than most of us think. "What do you mean?" I prodded. He said that most of what he would now recommend to younger people were ideas that he himself didn't live. It's the things he almost did that he would urge them to do.

"The things you almost did are the things you think about late in life," Arthur told me. "You wish you'd given yourself permission to do them." Arthur bestowed that little nugget while casting a #18 Adams dry fly to a rising salmon in the Dam Pool.

On another day, lake fishing a few years back, Arthur became autobiographical for a whole morning. I didn't know what it was that had opened those floodgates, but it was one of those late-summer reflective days that cause some people to take a long view backward.

"By the time I graduated from high school, the war [World War II] was on. Four years later, after my discharge, there was a moment when I almost made the decision to go back to school, to put myself through college even if it meant working part-time. I decided against it and just went to work. Engagement, marriage, and family took over and another moment like that one never came again. That decision followed me all my life. Dogged me—that's a better way to put it. I usually got passed over for job promotions because somebody else, someone who was actually less qualified, had the sheepskin and got it instead. After this happened several times, I was bitter. How could a piece of paper entitle you to something unearned?

"I never really outgrew that bitterness while I was working. It would come out when I was around sheepskin types. I could scent them. They always seemed more confident than me and that infuriated me. What was it that they knew and I didn't? I couldn't put my finger on it, but it formed a raw spot in my craw that was easily inflamed."

I had a hard time imagining that this was the same Arthur I'd known as my fishing client for thirteen years. Still, he was in his eighties now, and I'd only met him after he'd retired from his job in South Portland and settled in mid-coast Maine. The whole time he was telling this story, he was casting a chartreuse popper fly, and smiling.

"If I got a few drinks into me, I'd get very vocal about this thing in my craw. I was at a dinner party with my wife one time and I wrecked the whole evening. I got tipsy and then a sheepskin-type said something that lit my fuse. Right there at the dinner table I stood up and said, 'Let me tell you exactly what your college education is worth in Maine. Maine is made up of high school grads who know how to do things—millwrights, loggers, mechanics, welders, fishermen, and farmers—and run by college graduates who don't know how to do anything.' I actually said that! I wasn't looking for a big laugh, but it got one anyway. Then, later, everyone ignored Esther and me until we left. She was furious with me for days after.

"As far as I was concerned, the educated were guilty until proven innocent, and the fact that they read books or seemed to 'know' things amounted to exactly nothing in the hands-on world I lived in, where things were made or actually got done. I told myself I'd have my revenge on them by passing my ideals on to my own children, making sure they had a trade, something useful. And do you know what? As if to spite me, both my kids went to college! One was a philosophy major and the other became an artist! At the time, I didn't think they could've come up with more useless occupations. And soon enough, I started feeling that old insecure feeling around them! Now, they, too, knew the secret. And they wouldn't tell me what it was! No one would. My bitterness festered, and eventually it showed up in ulcers—and hypertension."

That morning, Arthur took several nice smallies off a sunken island when he switched to a dragonfly imitation with red rubber legs. It was his favorite popper fly. It had a good, hollow face, which caused a tall bubble and Bloop! sound when he flicked the fly rod tip or stripped line quickly. Two of the fish were within the slot limit on that lake, so they went on the stringer for lunch. The picnic spot was on an island, but first we cast its shoreline all the way around. I had the impression that Arthur was listening to himself right along with me.

"How did a piece of paper give these people the confidence that I could always smell on them? It gave them the courage I lacked. I'll give you an example. I had a lifelong dream to have a little business. As time passed and I kept shying away from doing it, I always told myself I couldn't risk my family's future and security. You see? I was acting responsibly. I was resisting the temptation to do something frivolous. That sounded heroic, much better than admitting I didn't have the guts. But I knew the truth.

"My dream was a sporting shop. I would carry fishing tackle, materials to tie flies, bait, knives, and a few other things like good boots and woolens for the cold-weather sports. I'd conduct classes on fly tying in winter around a ram-down stove in the middle of the store. On lunch hours or when I was bored at my real job, I'd conjure up the image of the shop and inhabit it. I'd see myself behind the counter chatting up customers about fishing and hunting. I'd run it primarily alone, but in busy times I might hire some kids to stock shelves, count out bait, stay ahead of inventory. Esther, whom I was sure would laugh at the idea if I ever shared it with her, was strangely absent from my daydreams of the shop. How I loved to visit similar businesses whenever I had the chance. I felt like a private investigator walking up and down the aisles incognito, deciding how I could improve on all sorts of things. I collected and stored ideas in the back of my mind and never felt more alive than when I was doing this. I never felt more desolate than when I realized later that I wasn't going to act on my dream."

I broke in to ask Arthur if he was sure Esther, whom I'd met many times, would have opposed his dream. "No," he said. "I'm not sure. I never gave her the chance, one way or the other. That way, I could make her part of the reason I never did it."

That confession took place on the second-to-last time we fished together. There was no trace in his narrative of any of the bitterness he was acknowledging from his earlier life. There was no disdain for his children, of whom he was fiercely proud. The whole time I knew him, Arthur saw humor and irony in almost everything. He seemed a very wise man to me, sheepskin or not. His wisdom was the kind reaped from a long life of sifting through what was valuable and what wasn't.

"Did you ever figure out what the secret was?" I asked him.

"Yeah," he laughed. "I figured out that there is no secret. You know how? I went to college myself! It wasn't until after I retired, and it wasn't a real college. It was a library. My tuition was free—a library card! Ha! There wasn't anything I wouldn't read, and every time a word tripped me up, I'd get out my pocket dictionary. I started out with American history. That led me into American authors like Melville, Faulkner, Emerson, and Thoreau. One thing leads to another in a library. Those authors led me to European ones and to European history, and that led to the classics. Reading is the secret, and if there was one thing everybody but me seemed to know, that was it. Soon, I wanted to keep all the books I'd read, so I started buying them from bookstores instead of checking them out of the library. There were stacks of them all over the house, driving Esther crazy. When I was seventy-two, I built six bookcases and immediately filled them all. For me, browsing my bookcases is like looking at my diploma."

Arthur's last trip with me preceded his death by only four months. He died in December, but he was in fine form that early September. He loved September for his kind of fishing. On that last day, we drifted down a slow-moving river within a fly cast of shore. Once again, it was the dragonfly with the red legs. He was up on the casting seat, a smile on his face, as always, presenting a textbook cast as effortlessly and accurately as I've seen.

"You know, I always loved music. In high school and during the war years it was all big-band music. That's what you danced to. That's how you met girls. Everyone in those days had the same heroes," he said. "Tommy Dorsey, Count Basie, Duke Ellington. Then, when I came back home, I loved tuning in to the WWVA Jamboree out of Wheeling, West Virginia, and the National Barn Dance from WLS in Chicago. That's where I first heard Hank Williams, Hank Snow, the Sons of the Pioneers, the Carter Family, and so many others."

"What I wanted more than anything was to be able to play along. Not to be a star, or even a performer, just someone with the ear and the dexterity to play some instrument like a mandolin or banjo and keep up. I still felt that way after retiring but couldn't use my old standby excuse—not having the time. So you know what I did? I went out and bought a mandolin and signed up for lessons. I learned the basic chords and learned how to find the key of the song I was listening to. I'm no good, but it has made me as happy as anything to sit and play to the records I love."

It was so easy to picture Arthur sitting next to his stereo turntable strumming along to Hank Williams or Hank Snow. I asked if he'd play for me sometime and he laughed it off. "I play for these ears only."

As usual, Arthur caught his own fish lunch on the river that day. I had no doubts he'd be back the next season to do it again. The letter from Esther arrived on December 23. He had died on the nineteenth of a cerebral aneurysm. "He had not been ill and it was very fast," she wrote.

I called her the day the card came. She said he had played his mandolin the morning he died, to "Wildwood Flower" by the Carter Family. She confessed to having eavesdropped from the top of the cellar stairs. I told her not to feel bad—I was a professional eavesdropper, which brought a chuckle from Esther. After I hung up, I used my computer to search for and download a copy of "Wildwood Flower." As it played, I listened carefully for the mandolin part.

Here I am with a young sport in my Eastporter boat.

Salmon jumping in Grand Lake Stream. Photo courtesy of
Carl Mahoney.

Joe Verlicco, left, and Mike "Tyke" Aniolowski, right, with friend, guide, and lodge owner Chris Wheaton, center. Photo courtesy of Joe Verlicco.

A GOOD CATCH — Lola Sockabasin proudly looks at the 15 muskrat stretches at Peter Dana Point. (NEWS Photo by Clayton Beal)

Lola Sockabasin with muskrat hide stretchers. Photo courtesy of Donald Soctomah.

Passamaquoddy in a bark canoe.

Forrest Lipscomb can still land the big ones.

Portaging a canoe, circa 1940s. Photo courtesy of Donald Soctomah.

Henry Moulton still has his fishing chops.

Rob and Rebecca Lekowski fishing the stream with (now deceased) guide Richard Turmenne.

Craig Fowler hoists a beauty.

Guide Ray Sockabasin and David Kotok at a lunchground.

John Jewett and his Vietnam-era crew chief, Dean Cameron.
Photo courtesy of John Jewett.

Sandra Lloyd playing a landlocked salmon on Grand Lake Stream.

Here I am releasing Sandra's catch.

Skip Burnell, right, poses with Scott Cressey and an Atlantic Salmon in 1981.

Ray Plewacki and friend Jim Budny on Chance Pool, Margaree River, in Cape Breton, Nova Scotia. Photo courtesy of Ray Plewacki Jr.

Here's Shelley guiding me.

Newly painted canoe, turned over.

A victim of the Rolling Tier slaughter.

Common Loon, mother and offspring. Photo courtesy of Jessie Tompkins-Howard.

Twin chicks at Mud Lake. Photo courtesy of Jessie Tompkins-Howard.

My guiding outpost in 1939. Photo courtesy of Barbara Wheaton.

My Grand Laker docked while at a lunchground.

Camp at Christmas.

My camp after the storm.

Moose at the beginning of Machias River below Third Lake Outlet.

Opening day on Grand Lake Stream.

GRAND LAKE STREAM'S MOST FAMOUS FISH

Too nice a day can be a guide's nemesis. Too many nice days in a row, a nightmare. It was late August, and we were locked into a high-pressure system that had guides griping. If things didn't change, and fast, all this good weather was going to put us out of business. A succession of bluebird days had voided any chance of good catching, no matter how much good fishing our sports put forth. Most guides had cashed in their whole repertoire of tales, tall or otherwise, and were getting desperate for ways to while away the hours, knowing there'd be no welcome interruptions from fish. It's a portrait of powerlessness that's bound to happen at least once a season.

I still had one ace left up my sleeve, but I was saving it for the right client. Finally, he arrived from Seattle on the final day of the front. The fish still weren't budging. By 9:30 a.m. we had nothing but a ten-inch bass to show for all of Craig Fowler's best efforts. Craig was fast and accurate. He had fly-fishing, spin, and bait-casting skills, but even this triple threat couldn't crack the code. For Craig not to raise fish was a compelling litmus test of just how flat things really were.

Well, I reasoned, I'd spent the lion's share of the season listening, anyway, and if ever there were a day to run my mouth, this might be it. It would be the ten-year anniversary telling of Grand Lake Stream's most unbelievable, yet true, fish story.

No fish had ever put the fishing-famous town of Grand Lake Stream, Maine, on the national map like this one had. What's more, as if to stretch the limits of irony, there was no picture, no taxidermy, not even a tracing on a brown paper bag to prove that the fish had actually existed. And yet, it had.

As I told Craig, it was a story read thousands of miles away in Grand Rapids, Michigan, and in Grand Forks, North Dakota; in Naples, Florida, and in Nome, Alaska. And yes, even in his Emerald City of Seattle. Thanks to the Associated Press, it landed on lunch counters across the country, confirming the AP's hunch that there was nothing the American public would love reading more than a good fish tale, full of intrigue. When it appeared above the fold on the front page of the Wall Street Journal, the paper's online counter showed it to be one of the most-read stories of the day.

"All right, already!" Craig called from the bow. "So tell it!"

I told him I was starting at the end for reasons that would be revealed.

I asked Craig to visualize a small courtroom in Calais, Maine, on the US-Canadian border, packed to the rafters with spectators. A man sat on the witness stand, rumpled and out of sorts. His eye contact with both the judge and attorneys was conspicuously poor. The sixty-ish man, with his shock of gray hair, looked uncomfortable in his clothes, squirming in his seat just a few feet away from the judge as questions directed to him began.

". . . And sir, isn't it standard to take pictures during an undercover operation?"

"Yes."

"And yet you didn't in this case?"

"That's correct."

"And isn't it also standard to make videotapes and/or sound recordings?"

"Yes."

"And yet you didn't in this case?"

"No."

"And you took no notes?"

"That's correct."

"And the so-called third fish that you allege your guide allowed you to take over the limit of two—what happened to it?"

"I ate it."

The laughter in the courtroom was immediately gaveled quiet by the judge. The witness's face contorted. He was a veteran warden, about to retire, when he'd been sent out for two days on a sting operation, undercover, to fish with a registered Maine guide. And yet for all his experience, he'd somehow forgotten his camera, had made no tapes, took no notes, or had any evidence. At the moment, however, in this courtroom, he was under enormous pressure to turn the tide of what seemed a colossal, Keystone-Cops farce set in motion by his warden superiors.

The legal limit on bass of legal size for a licensed fisherman was two, which meant that between he and his targeted guide, they could bring four into lunch. Every guide knows this rule—it's one of the first things you learn on the job. During this particular day of fishing, three fish were brought in. The question the case hinged on, the one the warden's higher chain of command decided was enough to bring a case against the guide, was: Did the guide let the undercover agent catch one more than the legal limit?

But the *real* question, the part that had never been satisfactorily answered by anyone, despite withering inquiries from the press, was why? With no leaf unturned, all the investigative reporting reached the same conclusion—the targeted guide had no record as a fish and game offender. There were no summonses, no violations, not even a ticket for a blown trailer light. And yet, with the full reach and power of the state of Maine's fish and game law enforcement arm, a case based on one eleven-inch bass was launched and pursued through eighteen months and two trials. The intent seemed to be to take down this particular guide at any cost. News outlets seized the story as a David versus Goliath parable.

In earlier questioning, the undercover warden had admitted that he'd caught and released approximately one hundred fish during his two days fishing with the guide. "So the fishing wasn't like it is today," Craig chimed in, throwing a monkey wrench into my rhythm. I paused, but then he laughed and gave me the rolling wrist gesture like pitchers give catchers.

On the stand, the poor warden looked more and more round-shouldered as the proceeding continued. Then, the judge began to theorize. He especially wanted to know about the partnership between guide and sport, which seemed to him to be unique—one hired to help the other, both handling the same equipment and fish all day. Say that between them, they caught several fish, the judge postulated. Since one was guiding the other and hired to help, what was the exact language of the law in determining who caught which fish?

The judge, of course, knew the law, but his question suggested an interesting angle, one which, apparently, no one had considered. It seemed to suggest that since the guide was there in the first place to assist the sport, that no matter who caught the third fish, they were still within the law. It seemed to infer a boat limit in the guide-client relationship instead of a per-person limit.

The judge should've been in the perfect place to have his question answered. Seated in the back of the courtroom were the chief of the Maine Warden Service; the young, ambitious district game warden responsible for bringing the case; and a game warden sergeant who was his immediate superior. The entire chain of command was present and accounted for. But suddenly, all of their faces went blank, in unison.

From the stand, the undercover warden was powerless to help them. After articulating his question, the judge waited patiently. The game wardens, top brass and all, scrambled into a huddle along with their assistant district attorney. All eyes in the courtroom watched them as they quickly flipped through the pages of their own regulations manual, unable to find the wording requested by the judge. Did it not exist?

After several minutes and an objection by the defense attorney over the delay, the assistant district attorney asked the judge if they could request a dictionary. The gavel once again silenced guffaws in the courtroom. Then, from an adjoining office came a secretary, lumbering across the courtroom carrying what looked like the Gutenberg Bible. Its alphabetic letters were leafed out for easy referencing, which is how the whole courtroom knew that the game wardens and their lawyer were looking under the "F" section.

"You making this up just because the fishing's lousy?" Craig asked between fruitless casts.

"Nope," I quipped back. Satisfied, Craig rolled his wrist again.

When the prosecutor came out of the huddle to read from the massive tome, the courtroom went silent. From his air of solemnity, he looked as if he might have been steeling himself to read a new commandment fresh from Mt. Sinai. He began tentatively at first, then read to the court the definition of "to fish."

Mouths fell open, though the judge, amazingly, managed to remain composed. Sensing that an answer to his original question was not forthcoming, the judge raised his hand, interrupting the prosecutor—who promptly took his seat with the cumbersome volume still open on his lap.

Measuring his words carefully, the judge said that the most compelling testimony he'd heard all day was from the undercover warden himself, who had testified earlier that during the sting operation, he asked his guide whether he sometimes let his sports keep extra fish. It was an opening, an invitation to incriminate himself. "This guide's answer was 'No,'" the judge noted. "Here is when the dishonest guide says, 'Oh, we can talk about that . . .' The honest guide says, 'No, I won't.' That's what this guide said, and I believe him."

His final gavel stroke came down, ruling in favor of the guide that no violation had occurred.

The press section of the courtroom, which had been full, emptied. As soon as the final gavel came down, the primly uniformed, forty-five-year-old warden chief rose abruptly from his seat and beat a hasty retreat from the courtroom. Reporters ran down the hall after him. One's voice rang out above the rest: "I guess this means you're not going to talk to us!" The warden chief spun on his heel, revealing his neck, face, and ears flushed crimson. He yelled back to the oncoming journalists, "I'd do it all again!" which, of course, got printed.

"Yeah! Now I remember this," Craig piped, as he bulleted a Rat-l-Trap lure up under a spruce limb hanging out over the water from shore. "There was a backstory to this, right?"

"You could say that," I teased. "But so much for the end of the story. I'll save the beginning for after lunch." I could already tell I'd better milk it into two installments. The weather so far showed no sign of the change that had been forecast to begin that afternoon. The scorecard was still just the one ten-inch bass, not a tally that Craig Fowler was used to. The best I could hope for was to keep him entertained and hope he was happy just to be there. It crossed my mind too that if tomorrow's fishing was equally slow, I'd be in trouble for material.

On the westward shore of Bear Island in Junior Bay at the head of West Grand Lake, there are some camps. One is so well camouflaged that it takes squinting to make it out—another example of a Teddy Roosevelt cabin, rustic in every detail right down to its deer antler door handles. It's owned by a friend who's given me permission to host sports there for lunch. I'd brought Craig here before; I knew it to be one of his favorite spots. Moose occasionally graze in Morrison Bog on the mainland, directly across from the camp. There are large boulders on shore, with a steep drop-off where Craig sometimes casts to his heart's content during my prep work for lunch.

"Yup, it's coming back to me," Craig said as we got the last of the cookware and firewood up to the picnic area. "How many years ago was that? Didn't some deep-pocketed bankers or somebody like that take the guide's side?"

"Something like that." I could see when Craig sat down that he wouldn't be fishing off the rocks today, and I couldn't blame him. On a more typical day with Craig, I'd be preparing a fish chowder right now. Instead, I laid out the standard dill pickles and sharp cheddar cheese hors d'oeuvres, then talked as I got a good cook fire going, peeled potatoes, chopped onions, and took the two, inch-thick pork chops out of the marinade to rack them into the broiler. Talking while working is an essential credential for guides.

I coaxed Craig's memory by telling him that a big name in the financial world had become involved in the case. This in turn captured the attention of the financial networks, as well as the *Wall Street Journal*, all of whom suddenly focused on a tiny fishing village in Maine that most of their readers had never heard of.

This man, I told Craig, was very high-profile. That's why they paid attention to what he did. When he wasn't traveling the world as a lecturer, author, or advisor, when he wasn't promoting charitable, philanthropic projects, or working for the financial independence of developing countries, when he wasn't doing face time on TV as an analyst, or running his firm, Cumberland Advisors, which manages over $2 billion in assets, David Kotok was fly-fishing.

"Right! I've seen him on TV!" Craig said. I went on to explain that much of Kotok's fly-fishing is done right here in Grand Lake Stream, and that he doesn't make the trip alone. In fact, he's responsible for the biggest sporting event and the biggest spike to local business in any given year. Coined "Camp Kotok," a term used by CNBC, Bloomberg, Yahoo Finance, and Fox Business News, it brings together an A-list of about fifty economists, Federal Reserve bankers, asset managers, financial writers, CFO's, CEO's, and CIO's for an economic summit with a waiting list of over three hundred would-be attendees.

The size of the retreats has been growing for eighteen years, providing a boost not only for guides and local businesses, but creating, in essence, a second economy.

"So, how'd this guy get mixed up in the famous fish case?"

As we watched the chops sizzle and the potatoes and onions slowly browning in the Greenfield fry pan over the cook fire, I told him that besides the high finance, besides the fishing, besides the financial pundit powwows, there was something else that placed strongly in these fishing retreats. It was wine. An almost scholarly approach to, and appreciation of, wines of the world was a subculture within these economic summits. I told him I'd seen tables end-to-end stretching longer than a Grand Laker, completely covered with wines, some of them exceedingly rare.

"Then, about eleven years ago," I said, as I ran a spatula under the potatoes and onions and rolled them over, "the hosting lodge suddenly informed Kotok that they had applied for a liquor license. It meant that Camp Kotok would no longer be able to bring their special wines to the lodge. It was deal-breaker news. After some unproductive attempts to find a win-win solution to the impasse, Kotok, as one AP story reported, "responded by taking the group, their business, and their libations elsewhere."

"OK, but how—?" Craig stopped when I raised my index finger. I had to make some finishing touches to complete the lunch. I also knew approximately how long it would take to spin the whole saga, and I wanted to leave some of it to offset an afternoon fishing drought if necessary. After serving up our lunch on blue enamelware, we both tucked in to Josh Moulton's grilled pork chops with cranberry-apple sauce and Yukon Gold hash. Craig savored and devoured it, but we were neck-and-neck at the finish line. I poured our two tin coffee cups full to the brim and put a date square down for each of us.

I told Craig that a guide close to Kotok who had guided various members of his group over the years had, at Kotok's request, facilitated his transition to a different lodge where they would be welcome to bring their wines. It had all happened seamlessly. The large retreats, so good for local business, were saved, and were now scheduled to settle into what would become their new home, Leen's Lodge, historically beloved to a *Who's Who* list of fly fishermen topped by Ted Williams. Craig nodded with a thumbs-up. He knew the place.

I let that sit for a moment, then told Craig that about two weeks later, the same guide who had acted as Kotok's intermediary started receiving phone messages from Waitsfield, Vermont. A ski resort manager there wanted to book a trip with him.

"Dah dah dah daaaah," Craig sang, vamping the introduction to Beethoven's Fifth. "The plot thickens."

"You could say that," I chuckled, pleased to have Craig on a short line now. Even though I hadn't told him that this was the cover used by the warden, he'd figured it out for himself.

"OK, so it sounds like this thing was staged. Somebody felt slighted. Other guides maybe. Or the lodge. Sour grapes. Somebody thought they were going to lose money. They set him up."

"You could say that, too," I ribbed. "How 'bout this—you tell the rest of the story, and then I'll tell you how close you came."

As we stowed the last of the gear in the canoe, Craig picked up his baitcaster, smirking, "You talk, I'll fish."

I headed over to an area known to previous generations of guides as Mink Carry. It sports every kind of favorable habitat for smallmouth bass, besides being beautiful to behold for its jagged shoreline and natural granite castles. When I cocked up the outboard and began to take the slow paddle strokes that would give Craig time to cover everything, I picked up the plot right where it had thickened.

Even though I had Craig on a short line, I knew I had to play him in gradually. The fish were still not cooperating. I complimented Craig on his perception, saying that just like he already had, many people at the time suspected sour grapes. Still, it was the most compelling explanation for the timing and the decision to set up someone who had no history as a bad actor.

Craig wanted to know—was that possible? To set up just anybody that way?

"Just let me go on," I said.

On a beautiful Sunday morning, a month after the guide had unknowingly fished with an undercover agent, two uniformed officers pulled up in front of his home. It was a young, local district warden and his sergeant, who was also about to retire. The guide, who knew both men and had no clue he was about to receive a summons, welcomed them. They all sat on a deck overlooking a vegetable garden, commenting on the progress of various plants while the guide's wife brewed and served them all coffee. The conversation continued on a friendly tack until, without segue or warning, all the socializing took a sharp turn.

The guide was advised that he had fished with an agent for two days earlier in the season. The result was a summons. The sergeant described it only vaguely as having to do with assisting or allowing a client to commit a violation. For a moment, the guide looked them over carefully, then smiled, convinced it was a prank. Which of his colleagues had been able to put them up to this?

Their faces never cracked. When they produced the summons and handed it to him, all of the blood drained out of the guide's face. They stayed long enough to see if he might say something they could use against him in court, but hearing nothing of note from the dumbfounded guide, they made an exit much less cordial than their entrance.

The guide sat stunned on his deck. His wife came out and asked him what the visit was all about. He held up the summons. She took it and read. Then the blood drained out of her face, too.

"This guide told you all this?" Craig asked, making frustrated casts to what seemed like barren water.

I shifted my broad-brimmed hat. "Yeah."

I told him that for the guide, it was a moment of soul-searching, sitting there with the summons. He knew there'd been no changes in his guiding ethics. Even if he'd had some warped motive to suddenly become an outlaw and poacher, his clients would never allow it. They were all catch-and-release fishermen who enjoyed a taste of fish now and then if one or two came along within the slot limit.

Looking at the summons, his mind raced aimlessly until he seized on something—*yes!*—the wardens had given the dates he'd fished with the agent. He ran inside and looked them up on his guiding calendar. Right! Solo job—Vermont—fished with him in the morning—loon—forgot his camera—Montana—elk. Nice guy. Tiny bits of memory swirled in his mind like garbanzo beans in a blender.

He'd guided every day before those dates and since, but still, he tried to reconstruct the two days with the new sport. The first thing he remembered was that when they met at The Pine Tree Store, they were wearing identical shirts. He'd joked that they should be brothers for their two days together, since they dressed alike. The new sport agreed and they shook hands.

More and more came back. Of course, the memory that stood out most was that the man was a new sport. Most of his clients were longtime, repeat customers. With a new fisherman, job one is to assess skill levels. Now, with the benefit of hindsight, maybe the client was better than he let on. Maybe his fishing skills were undercover, too. As it was, they still-fished with live bait. To help attract bass, the guide had him free-swim some golden shiners while he cast a noisy, flamboyant lure all around the canoe—a tactic that's usually effective.

That's when Grand Lake Stream's most famous fish first took the stage. The guide caught it himself and slipped it onto the stringer in case the man's skills didn't match his declared desire for a taste of fish. A happy sport is the number one priority for the attentive guide. The guide was well within the law to keep not just one, but two legal fish, if he chose.

By the time they'd caught and released around twenty-five fish that morning, the "ski resort manager" had added two legal fish of his own to the stringer. At the selected lunchground, there was a mother loon hunkered over a nest off at one end of the landing. The sport wanted a picture but announced that he'd forgotten his camera. That day and the next, he talked about his elk hunting trips to Montana.

Once the man seemed to get the hang of hooking and landing fish, the guide stopped fishing, far too busy with the net and disgorging hooks to fish, himself. The rough count for the first day was around fifty fish released, three cleaned and eaten. Day two was nearly a carbon copy of the first, except that there was no need for an insurance fish. The sport was happy with the hundred or so fish he'd played to the net during his two-day trip.

"I would be, too!" Craig inserted, not without a teaspoon of sarcasm, which I pretended to ignore. I told him that sitting there on his deck that afternoon, the guide remembered a tidbit that suddenly seemed significant.

After returning to town, the "ski resort manager" announced that he'd left his wallet was in his truck. He went to it, and returned with the right amount for the guide's fee, but then paused and said, "Hold on a minute." He then went back to his truck and returned with a tip.

"A tip!" the guide exclaimed to his wife, who had been listening carefully to everything her husband remembered about that day.

"He tipped you? The State of Maine tipped you for being an outlaw and a poacher?" This man knows nothing happened, the guide's wife consoled, "He must've been under tremendous pressure from someone to come up with something."

"But why? Why me?"

"It's going to be all right," she told him. "But we've got to fight this."

"OK," Craig called back, obviously at the end of his patience with the fishing. "What would've happened? I mean, the worst thing if he didn't fight it?"

"Hold on, Craig!" I teased. "He did fight it, and you'll find out what happened." The fishing, unbelievably, was still flat, and I sympathized. I was, however, eyeballing a change on the southwest horizon.

"See that?" I said, pointing to the cloud bank.

"Yeah? So?" Craig challenged. I decided to go out on a limb. With Craig, there'd be no downside to making a prediction. We'd turn a false prediction of mine into a joke anyway, and get lots of mileage out of it on future trips.

"Things are going to change shortly, so be ready." Then, I said a silent prayer that they would. "To answer your question," I continued, "he'd be fined and lose his guide's license for a year. In other words, his livelihood."

"So he fought it?"

"Yup."

"Good. What happened?"

I told Craig that the guide and his wife quietly applied themselves to the work and the expense of finding a lawyer. Once they did, and entered their plea of not guilty, they were able to obtain discovery.

"What's that?" Craig asked, now sitting up on the bow, apparently on break from fishing.

"No, keep casting Craig. I'll keep talking." The cloud cover was closer now, and thickening. Craig made a dutiful sidearm pitch with his baitcaster, but rolled his wrist for the story to continue. I thought, something better happen and soon, as I wouldn't be able to stretch this story out much longer.

"Discovery is basically the other side's case. What they've got against you to take to court."

"So what'd they have?"

"That's the *really* bizarre part. Nothing! It was as if they'd never expected it to go to court. That he'd just pay the fine and willingly give up his license for something he hadn't done. Someone from the Advisory Council—a panel that helps inland fisheries and wildlife with regulations and policy—wrote a letter for the young district warden who at some point must have made the realization that he had nothing to go on. In it, the Councilman mentioned complaints he'd received about this particular guide. That was it. There was no explanation of what the complaints were, or who they were from."

"And they used *that* for *evidence?*" Craig barked.

"Well, it was all they had—this letter from a guy who lived fifty miles away. That, and the bass the undercover agent was allegedly allowed to keep over his limit. Except that they didn't have that, either."

"Right. He ate it."

"Right. And then, he tripped over his tongue in the courtroom saying the guide had caught it. And get this—the Advisory Council guy who penned the paragraph in support of the warden owned a sporting lodge himself, one that used guides who also happened to work for the lodge that David Kotok had taken his business away from."

"Ohhhhh," Craig called toward the clouds. "No wonder the press had a field day with—"

Before Craig could finish his sentence, his rod bent double. For an instant, he looked lost, it had been so long since he'd felt a pullback. He was using a #4 Mepps Aglia, Craig's go-to lure, especially when the odds were long. I instinctively looked up. The new system was right on our heels, which meant that the barometer was already dropping. Craig's rod tip told the rest of the story. The drought was over.

Mink Carry came alive. The contrast to the long lull was dramatic, and heartily welcomed. Any wildlife for miles around heard human caterwauls for the rest of the afternoon. In one quiet cove, a stream entered the lake, babbling over the rocks onshore. In the middle of the cove was a raft of weeds no bigger than a king-size bed. I suggested casting to its edges. Craig's first lob produced a seventeen-and-a-half-inch smallmouth. "Now try the other side," I whispered. That produced its older brother.

"Look at that!" Craig cried. He was leaning over the gunwale of the canoe so much that I had to counterbalance his weight by leaning the other way. When I followed his eyes and looked where he was looking, I nearly dropped the paddle. Below us was a school of smallmouth bass, which is a nonschooling fish, every one of them a monster. I told Craig I'd never seen anything to match it. They were aggressive, too, searching out the culprit for the commotion caused by Craig's catches. Now, he couldn't cast fast enough to keep up with the willing brigade of bass whose appetites had just switched to on. Their strikes were not curious, or probing; they were declarative and full of resolve.

The conclusion of the story could wait for the ride home. In the meantime, the wind went flat until the lake mirrored the cloud cover, which was now complete. We both felt the air change. Fish were swirling on the surface, causing hair-raising splashes that pulled our attention away from the fish Craig was playing. Craig pleaded with me to fish, saying he'd release his own, but I wanted to keep maneuvering the canoe to line him up with fish that were showing.

Two hours passed in a blink, and when I finally asked Craig, whose father was to meet him in town at a specified time, if we had to go, he said, "Yes," but there was a lot of "No" in his voice.

Fishermen know about afterglow. The feeling that follows such an experience can last and last. It is then transferred to the mental logbook of epic fishing moments. We'd both be copying this one into that archive.

"All right," Craig said, settling into the bow seat for the ride downlake. "Let's have it. What happened to our hero?" I relaxed, no longer under pressure to salvage the day.

Shouting over the outboard to Craig up in the bow seat once we were underway, I told him that through local contacts, David Kotok got wind of the case and the subterfuge surrounding it, learning that it might just relate to his decision to move his group.

Kotok's reaction was swift. He published the story with the heading "Abuse of Power" in his newsletter, read by some 30,000 subscribers. He called on readers to help him launch a letter-writing campaign to Maine's governor, protesting the case, the squandering of state funds, and the frivolous use of law enforcement.

Subscribers took Kotok up on his proposal, writing letters in large numbers. Once David Kotok's support of a fishing guide in the boondocks of Maine got out, news outlets that knew him picked up the scent. Many of the articles were either titled, or led off with the words "One Fish." The eleven-inch bass became a sensation.

The next thing Kotok did, along with another group of sports who had a long history with the same guide, was to start a legal defense fund. Before it was over, the guide's expenses to defend himself would reach $28,000. Money poured into the fund from all over the country. The guide and his wife, who were sure they'd be hocking their future to fight the case, suddenly looked around and saw a world of support from friends and complete strangers alike.

"Wow!" Craig shouted from the bow as we cut a seam across the glass-calm lake. "Twenty-eight thousand dollars! There should be a statue of that fish in town!"

As the calm lake and the afterglow cushioned our ride home, I told Craig that the real juicy stuff didn't come out until the dust had settled. That it was all in the court record now. Apparently, the so-called complaints alluded to in the Advisory Councilman's letter were either fictitious, or, if someone had actually made a complaint, they weren't willing to admit it in writing. So, the Advisory guy stepped up to provide one, was solicited to write one, even though he had no idea if any of it was true. The State had taken the whole case forward in full awareness of this, and its lack of evidence.

"Good Lord!" Craig called as the town dock came into view. I slowed to steerage speed so he'd no longer have to shout. "But he won. Justice prevailed. What about whoever cooked this thing up? Anything happen to them?"

I said it was probably they who ended up with the taste of sour grapes in their mouths. As for the Chief warden who had given the thumbs up to the one fish case, he was busted the following year while moonlighting as a lobsterman. Marine wardens met him at the dock for a routine check, and found nine lobsters below the legal length limit. It cost him his career.

"No way," Craig quipped.

I told him that the Advisory Council guy was gone soon after, too, but, amazingly, reappeared when a new administration came in. No one knew if the department had developed amnesia or all was simply forgiven. The warden sergeant and the undercover officer both retired. And the young district warden—well, he was still on the job. I said he was probably a better warden now, much more cautious and discriminating, especially when the smell of sour grapes came up.

"And how's the guide doing?"

I told Craig it was all good in the end. His very wise wife told him that they'd been right to fight, that sunlight was always the best disinfectant, that she knew the truth would be revealed in the end, and it was.

"And he's still guiding?"

"Well Craig, how'd your day turn out?"

"Great . . . Whadaya mean?"

"I mean, yeah, he's still guiding."

Craig gave a blank stare, then his face stretched into a wide grin. He sat straight up in his seat, slapping the gunwales of the canoe with the palms of his hands.

"You! How come you never told me this before?"

"Never had to."

Author's note: The satirical slant of the "One Fish" story certainly existed at the time, but so did the costly side. It is humbling to witness an army of supporters demonstrating that no injustice is small. We, in our tiny corner of the world, believed the matter was too obscure to garner a second look. Oddly, it wasn't the injustice itself, or the ill intent of a few that proved memorable. It was the outpouring and acts of kindness from several hundred friends and perfect strangers that produced an afterglow all its own.

A Note from Dave Kotok:

"Camp Kotok" was a nickname originally given by Becky Quick of CNBC to our gathering in Grand Lake Stream, Maine.

The history of this gathering can be traced back more than twenty years to a handful of men who were looking to get away from the hubbub of financial markets, economics, cities, and routine meetings and conferences. They wanted to get into the woods and spend a weekend in a quiet, inspiring environment. The gathering remained very small until September 11, 2001.

After the World Trade Center's destruction, the number of people who wanted to join our gathering grew exponentially. There was a need for processing, and for a quieter place. At that time, though, it was just men going into the woods, talking, and fishing in Grand Lake Stream. We were missing valuable perspectives.

We started to invite women to join us. For several years none accepted, for one reason or another. They were always polite, but rejected the invitation. Finally, a gender breakthrough occurred with Kathleen Hays of Bloomberg Radio and TV and her producer at Bloomberg, Margaret Popper, who is now at CNBC. Both remain invited participants in the gathering to this day.

Today, about one-fourth of our group is composed of women. They fish and talk economics along with the men. The gathering has become indifferent to gender.

All of this comes together in the pristine surroundings of Grand Lake Stream. We gather with the full support and energy of guides, our host, the lodge owner, and a welcoming town.

Behind the scenes, contributing in a diplomatic and sensitive way, is Randy Spencer. He rarely evidences a directive or forceful leadership style. Instead, he is a diplomat, and an organizer by suggestion. Randy seeks and builds consensus. He does so with the respect and the admiration of peers.

I, too, have relationships with other fishing guides in the neighborhood. Some of those are longstanding. Yet my feeling about Randy is one of camaraderie, friendship, and trust. I have a sense that in a pinch I could count on him. He would be there if I needed him. And I feel that if there were a reason, he would feel the same sense of bonding when he thought about me. At least one day a year we find a date and spend a few hours fishing together. I hope that never changes.

Sooner or later there will be another book. And we'll have another meal at a site with pristine water and enticing green scenery. Another bald eagle will soar above and remind us of the greatness of America. We will again step into a canoe, catch another fish, converse about life, philosophy, the outlook for the world, and we'll swap a joke or report some small anecdote that reflects the character and appeal of a village called Grand Lake Stream. Randy is an ambassador for this village. For me, it is an honor and pleasure to count him as a friend.

Three Days with an Old Warrior

In the State of Maine, general law open-water fishing ends September 30. I had already been noting for a week or more that the summer weeds were dying back in the shallows. There was a different feel to the air each morning. The maples along the lakeshores had made a strong start toward the colors that would soon draw the fall leaf peepers. Nearly all of my loyal, repeat customers had come and gone by then, adding to that fattening cache of fishing lore that helps warm a guide's winter.

This season had begun a little earlier than usual. Ice-out happened the first week of April—almost a record. No news travels any faster than fishing news, and when the ice goes out early, the toll booths at Kittery, near the New Hampshire border, start hauling in cash before sports in Grand Lake Stream start hauling in fish.

As usual, the season had gone by so fast that when late September came with its 40-degree mornings, it took me by surprise. Just like John Jewett did. We were on our way to meeting each other without either one knowing it. That's what a phone call can do when you're a guide. It came from Leen's Lodge, the sporting lodge Stan Leen built before he made a bid for Governor of Maine, before he hosted and befriended Ted Williams, Norman Mailer, Curt Gowdy, and a host of other noted salmon fishermen. Stan was long gone now, but things were substantially the same around the lodge he left behind in Grand Lake Stream.

Laura, a dark-eyed, beautiful Passamaquoddy woman, functions alternately as Leen's maître d', cook, concierge, and hostess, as well as the person whom Leen's clients, along with its owners, regard as the heart and soul of the lodge. It was Laura who introduced me to John Jewett and his friend and fishing partner, Norm Bietsch, having breakfast in the dining room. John rose from his seat, extended his hand, and announced, "Good morning sir. I've fished forty-nine states and now I've come to fish the fiftieth."

Hearing my cue, I hit the ball back with, "So you saved the best for last!"

We were going to get on well. John and Norm had come from Petersburg, Illinois, "to fish three days, in three different bodies of water, for three different species." That's good news to most guides, especially at the end of the season. The spice of guiding—and fishing—is variation. Long accustomed to taking fishing trips together, they'd been ranging around for ideas when Norm saw an article on Grand Lake Stream in *Field & Stream* magazine. That sealed the deal.

I chose West Grand Lake for our first day. It was its characteristic autumn color—dark blue. It had already turned over several times with big blows and cold snaps, so that the surface temperatures were much more inviting to salmon now than during August's dog days. The thermocline had ascended once again, and with it, the game fish that have ruled the waves here without much competition since the late nineteenth century—landlocked salmon. If the pilot on one of the many New York or Boston-to-Europe flights we saw flying over at 38,000 feet had telescoped West Grand Lake that morning, he or she would've seen just one green speck. That was us, with the whole, 15,000-acre lake to ourselves.

We rigged fly rods with fast-sink lines. We used nine-and-a-half foot leaders and selected from the classic catalog of smelt-mimicking streamer flies—Silver Doctor, Governor Aiken, Gray Ghost, Black Ghost, Joe Smelt. It was all new to John and Norm, both of whom negotiated this leap of faith as sportingly as I imagined they had in the other forty-nine states. Then, on the run between Kole Kill Island and Norway Point, John hooked and played a landlocked salmon up to the canoe. When everyone saw sunlight glint on its lustrous silver sides in the rubber mesh net, the canoe went silent.

No matter how many times I witness this moment, its power still rouses my curiosity. Once this happens, the conversation changes. When Herman Melville, author of *Moby Dick*, wrote "water and meditation are wedded forever," he might have substituted "salmon fishing" for "water" and still have been right on the mark. What is it that the salmon brings up to the surface that so beguiles people, casting them into a contemplative mood? True to form, it was after this salmon visitation on that first morning that a book opened— John's book. And he's not alone. Under these circumstances, anyone can suddenly find themselves leafing through the pages of the past so openly, so willingly, it may startle them later to recall how forthcoming they were willing to be.

John had recently returned from a reunion in Santa Fe, New Mexico. When I asked whether it was a high school or college class reunion, he replied, "Neither." It was a reunion of his old outfit— the 187th Assault Helicopter Company (AHC). John wasn't the first Vietnam-era combat helicopter pilot I'd guided. Just two years earlier I'd fished with another, but any reflections that floated to the surface for that aviator were still under lock and key when he left. Prying is not the province of a fishing guide. Good listening is. I therefore asked John about the reunion, not the war. His reply: "I find comfort in talking with old comrades."

I let that drift along with us under the azure sky all the way to The Narrows, leading into Junior Bay. I was thinking that John's point of view in these situations must be similar to that of an astronaut returning to earth. What could someone who has seen our planet from space say about the experience to do it justice? It might as well be arctic explorer Admiral Peary describing trains and trolleys to Greenland's Inuits. As I thought about it, John's simple statement meshed perfectly with things I'd heard from others who had experienced momentous, life-changing events. Another veteran had told me that the effect of having been part of something painfully extraordinary, but known only to a few comrades, seems to confer its own special kind of loneliness.

That first day, we lunched at my camp on West Grand, fished Whitney Cove and The White Horses in the afternoon. While John spoke, Norm, trolling from the bow, and I, steering the outboard, let his stream of consciousness unspool.

The story began with a childhood passion for flying. John said it's that way for many aviators. How it happens is less important than making sure it happens. Reading, watching movies, building models, trips to the airport—anything to do with flying was a theme to growing up.

The name Robert Mason came up a few times in our conversation. He authored the national bestseller *Chickenhawk*. Mason probably spoke for John and many others when he wrote: "I joined the army in 1964 to be a helicopter pilot. I knew at the time that I could theoretically be sent to war, but I was ignorant enough to trust it would be a national emergency if I did go." He wrote that he knew nothing of Vietnam or its history. He didn't know that Vietnam under Ho Chi Minh had been an ally in the war against Japan. He didn't know that Ho's model for a Vietnamese constitution drew heavily from the US Constitution. Nor did he know that free elections in Vietnam, to be overseen by the Geneva Conference in 1956, were blocked because of Ho's inevitable victory. "I did not know that our government backed an oppressive and corrupt leader, Ngo Dinh Diem, and later participated in his overthrow and his death, in 1963," Mason wrote. "I did know I wanted to fly. And there was nothing I wanted to fly more than helicopters."

It led both Mason and John Jewett to the same eventual realization: "I owed the army three years of service for teaching me to fly helicopters," (from *Chickenhawk*). It also led them both to Fort Wolters, Texas, for primary flight training, and then to Fort Rucker, Alabama, for advanced training, including over one hundred and ten flight hours. Lyndon Johnson had announced the deployment of the Air Mobile Division on July 28, 1965. By the time John completed flight training in 1968, the helicopter war in Vietnam was at full pitch. John, then twenty-two years old, was shipping out to Tay Ninh province, headquarters and base camp for the 187th AHC, "The Crusaders." Tay Ninh is located about ninety-six kilometers northwest of today's Ho Chi Minh City, the former Saigon.

When you have a book like John's, it falls open at any time to any page. Then there are interruptions. We have to play a fish, get unsnagged, change flies. Apropos of nothing, the book falls open again, and just as spontaneously, it shuts.

Once, it fell open to the topic of triggers. John said that anyone who's been treated for post-traumatic stress disorder (PTSD) is familiar with triggers, which can produce flashbacks and anxiety attacks disproportionate to the source. Triggers, he said, are alternately known as "Demons" (always with a capital "D").

The smell of charcoal lighter fluid at a backyard barbeque can conjure the smell of JP-4 jet fuel. A sudden movement in the peripheral field of vision—like a raven soaring from a tree on the riverbank—can conjure an ambush. A loud sound—like the Johnson 9.9 horsepower outboard backfiring—can conjure a rocket-propelled grenade. I shuddered to think how heightened the senses must be for a combat helicopter pilot.

The flashback effect from triggers is "very unpleasant," John says. Understatement is supposed to be the true mark of a Midwesterner. I knew this was the understatement of the morning so far.

John and his Crusader colleagues became used to a level of stress most of us never experience. But what happens when one day all that stress disappears, as though it had never happened? When you're suddenly back "in the world" and, instead of wondering whether you and your crew might be incinerated by the next rocket-propelled grenade, the most taxing thing to think about might be a busy commute, or the next mortgage payment, or a relationship? How do you go from being constantly shot at and seeing comrades killed to behaving and looking like all the people around you?

John told me that the timing varies from person to person. "It might take six months, it might take forty years," he explained. The Demons, just like the enemy back "in country," might strike all at once, or bide their time only to come calling during points of weakness, or loss, or crisis later in life.

John spoke of brothers who were able to successfully postpone this reckoning by throwing themselves into a career arc, keeping their plate overflowing with business, family, tasks, and hobbies as if to disallow the slightest crack in their armor. "It comes," John says, "no matter who you are." It might happen soon after getting out like it did for John's door gunner, Nick, who was dead from drug-related causes within a couple of years of discharge. Then again, it might happen when someone is downsized from their position, or during empty nest syndrome when the kids have grown and gone, or after a marriage has dissolved. The Demons, John said, can even be patient enough to wait until retirement. "Your vulnerability increases when the velocity of life slows down."

John emphasized that it can be negotiated. For him, it's been a long road, but one that includes reuniting with brothers who share the same history, speak the same language. Only they fully understand. He told of repeated incidents when a former Crusader might be undergoing his second baptism of fire, this time the hellfire of PTSD long after his service. A fellow Crusader from across the country would rush to his side to help him through it. "When someone has been willing to lay down their life for you countless times," John said, "you don't forget it."

For me, the evening after my first day with John and Norm was one big flashback. John had kick started some engine that now was thrumming away in my head, threatening to cancel any prospects of sleep. When sleep finally came, it only provided the theatre for dreams that that took their cue from John's story.

When I greeted John and Norm in the Leen's dining room the next morning, Norm brought up the St. Croix River. He'd read about it in the *Field & Stream* article. "Any chance we could fish there?"

Earlier, I'd heard the NOAA forecast on my battery-op weather radio. We had another gorgeous day in store, but with a pretty brisk west wind. The St. Croix offers not only protection from that wind, but also the prospect of some very busy fishing for large smallmouth bass. "I guess great minds think alike," I told Norm, whose face lit up.

We were up close to the whitewater on the St. Croix when I about-faced the canoe and ruddered us down current, Canada to port, America to starboard. A fish was being boated on one out of every three casts, and Norm was in his glory in the bow. It was a perfect diversionary activity to enable the past to once again take the stage.

John said the military was full of jargon, acronyms, and abbreviations, but that helicopter pilots used more than most. It was essential for getting messages across clearly and quickly. Thus, an AO was an area of operations. The AC was the aircraft commander. Oh Dark Thirty was any hour before dawn, and the alphabet used was phonetic: Alpha, Bravo, Charlie, Delta, etc., for clarity. The grunts, or combat infantry, were known as Manchu's, a handle used with the utmost respect by helicopter pilots.

The AC; his Peter Pilot, or copilot; the door gunner; and the Crew Chief comprised the whole crew. The helicopters often flew in formations of ten, so close that their blades overlapped. The Flight Lead was at the head of the chevron, responsible for the entire flight. The Trail was the last to land and the last to leave.

"Speaking of landing!" Norm called from the bow. He had hooked a seventeen-inch smallmouth about halfway to the lunchground I had in mind. The water was so clear that we could see every move the fighting fish made. After releasing it, Norm said, "It happened just that way in the *Field & Stream* article!" Without missing a beat, John's memory immediately switched to an old friend and mentor who had helped him along the way.

Bob Bess had the nickname "Papa" from the day he entered the Army. He was twenty-four years old and surrounded by eighteen- and nineteen-year-olds. Papa hailed from Cedar Grove in West-By-God-Virginia and grew up in coal country. He was shy of six feet, barely 140 pounds, mean as a snake, and didn't trust anyone who wasn't born in West-By-God-Virginia. He was also a fiercely loyal friend, and a warrior who showed no fear in combat. He was the best natural Huey pilot I have ever flown with. Papa simply didn't believe there was anything a helicopter under his control couldn't do. He attempted maneuvers that seemed, if not impossible, at least foolhardy to me. We flew together regularly and he was without question my favorite stick-buddy.

Once I woke up to Bob Bess shaking me in my rack. "Grab your gear and go by Operations and pick up the mission maps. Meet me at my aircraft! Something is seriously wrong to call us out at this hour." He was right. Something was terribly wrong out in the boonies and we were expected to get there, and fast. Papa had the helicopter up and running by the time the Operations Jeep delivered me to the revetment. The gunner had my door open, shoulder harness in hand, ready to expedite our departure. He grabbed my helmet as soon as I climbed in; he plugged me in; and as soon as I buckled in, slid the armor forward, secured the door, and climbed into the gun well, he handed it back.

We had an LRRP (Long Range Recon Patrol) about forty kilometers southwest of Tay Ninh Base Camp, west of GoDaHa, a little river crossing the border from Cambodia—really not a friendly piece of the country at this time of the night. The LRRPs had probably waited for dark to sneak back in country, and after completing a long mission on the other side of the river they didn't want to spend another night in the boonies. It was a moonless night, black and featureless.

We were having difficulty hearing communications from the LRRPs. We heard just enough to establish that they would contact us when they could hear or see our aircraft. There was no way to tell how close we were to the border or if we were actually going into Cambodia to pick these guys up. Regardless, we would pick them up. All of their transmissions were soft, broken, and barely audible. We assumed that they were working with weak batteries. Finally, they said they would turn on a rescue strobe when we were ready to turn inbound.

It was then that we realized these guys were in a running gunfight and were trying to run, talk, and shoot—that's why we couldn't make out what they were saying. They were afraid that if we knew they were in contact with the enemy, we would not come in for them. We finally got a count of the number in the patrol and shot the approach far enough ahead of them. We started receiving fire as Bob landed light on a dirt trail. Within seconds, four tired but very grateful grunts lay belly-down in the cargo compartment of Papa Bess's Huey. When the last LRRP was onboard, Bob pulled pitch and cleared his Crew Chief for full suppression, silencing the hostile fire.

As we gained altitude, the lights of Tay Ninh appeared faintly near the horizon. Turning north, we ferried the exhausted warriors back to their base to sleep warm, dry, and safe. In a few hours we would be back up at Oh Dark Thirty ready for another day of flying.

The St. Croix was good to us that morning. Onshore, fish sizzled in the pan as we watched a few Canadian fishermen navigate upstream in small, open boats, each one with a Golden Retriever in the bow. Letting his book rest, John took it all in, joking with Norm about how he was getting to all the fish first since he was in the bow. "Let's switch," Norm said, but we both sensed that John was on a roll of his own.

After lunch, we caught golden shiners in a backwater choked with protective weed cover. In minutes we had a bait bucket full of them. Out in the middle of the slower water, we anchored. John and Norm free swam the baits in the current. In Crusader parlance, this was sure to draw fire. A muscular river bass with broad shoulders slapped a shiner so hard from below that it flew into the air. When it alighted, there was a violent, swirling eruption right next to the boat that jarred all three of us. It even splashed water in John's face. For a moment, no one knew whose shiner the bass had raided. Then John's rod nearly flew out of his hands. When the nineteen-incher was measured and released from the net, we all let that special silence come, the one that always follows great catches.

With some difficulty, I freed the anchor from the pulp logs on the river bottom and once again ruddered the canoe downstream with my paddle. The things John now felt free to share had been the very things he'd built ramparts around throughout his whole adulthood, things he'd made it a personal commandment to never speak about.

When he'd only been two months "in country," his unit had not yet lost an aircraft to hostile fire, nor had the Flight taken any casualties. Typically, they flew twelve hours a day beginning, of course, at Oh Dark Thirty.

"While it does become routine flying supertight formations with very close gunship support, flying into the unknown of an LZ with trees, snags, elephant grass, who knows what else—does keep both pilot and crew on top of their game," John said. During his first two months, his ship had taken some fire, though nothing serious. "Nothing serious" was how the Midwestern veteran understated those times when people were shooting at him but missing. All of that was to change, he said, and all too soon.

> *I remember it had been an easy morning and the Crusader flight was heading back to Tay Ninh to refuel and rearm. The Flight might actually get lunch in the mess hall this time rather then cold C rations on the aircraft. We were twenty kilometers east of our base camp at Tay Ninh when a voice crackled over the radio.*
>
> *"This is Flight Lead! The Manchus (grunt unit) need a medevac. Does anybody have enough fuel to take it?"*
>
> *They had a wounded boy who was bleeding out. He needed to be pulled now to even have a chance. They were ass-deep in NVA and there was no landing area.*
>
> *I told my crew we were going in without the gun team. We'd have negative suppression unless they could identify individual targets. I told them to stay on your gun, but be ready to help load the wounded grunt if necessary.*

Then, I got on the intercom . . . "Hey guys. Look on the bright side. If we go down, we have two fully armed cobras inbound to get us out or make them pay for shooting down a Crusader ship."

The grunts really gave us all they had as we made our fast low approach. We terminated to a hover with left skid against a broken tree to stabilize the aircraft. At that moment an entire Infantry company broke cover, stood up, and flipped the M-16 selector to rock and roll (full auto). They filled the air with hand grenades and automatic weapons fire. Below us, the Manchus struggled to get their wounded onboard. Dean left his gun well, crawled out on the skid, and lifted the wounded boy the last bit into the aircraft. The ground commander waved us off with a big salute.

The trip back to the Surgical Evac Hospital was fast. We were very low on fuel, which made us lighter. I put everything to the red line and flew as hard as that UH-1H Huey would fly. The boy was still alive. I have no idea how he managed from there; only that we had done everything we could for him and kept faith with the brave infantry, who were our whole purpose for flying.

John left me on the edge of my guide's seat in the canoe, not only because of his skill in recounting the story, but also because of those unknown outcomes. How had the Manchus fared following the extraction of the boy who was bleeding out? What happened after the Cobras arrived? Did the boy live? I was slowly learning that unknown outcomes were a routine part of the service the Crusaders performed. To do their best and then quickly move on to the next crisis was evidently their stock and trade.

Late in the afternoon, the wind laid down. The last casts of the day were made in silence, as if there were too much to think about. Any conversation would intrude on our private dialogues. I'd seen this before. It was the power of the river, and the scenery, and September that had fleshed out this remarkable biography, ripe to be told in safe surroundings. We had only one day left, but I sensed much still untold.

The St. Croix River had been good to us on the second day of John and Norm's fishing adventure. Could we squeeze out just one more day when the wind was down and the sun high?

The next morning, in broken, garbled static, my weather radio delivered its good news. The light was green for my first choice, Third Machias Lake. Both John and Norm had mentioned their fondness for crappie fishing in Kentucky. I knew that if they liked that, they'd love a white perch frenzy if we could find one.

When I walked into the Leen's dining room at 7 a.m., there sat Norm and John in front of the bay window looking westward toward Munson Island, Kole Kill Island, and Big Mayberry Cove. It was just as beautiful as it had been on our first two days.

Ten miles out of town on rough dirt roads, John and Norm began to wonder where in the world I was taking them. I told Norm to reach under the seat and pull out DeLorme's *Maine Atlas and Gazetteer*. "Page 35," I said. When he had it open for both him and John to see, I pointed and said, "See the lobster?" I told them about my annual fall trip to the lobster-shaped lake with Shelley. "That's one helluva girl," Norm said. "I couldn't get my wife out here on a bet."

The boat landing is just above the bridge over the outlet from Third Machias Lake. Getting up through the narrow passage into the larger lake was more easily accomplished by standing in the stern of the canoe and poling with the paddle. Barely a breeze blew across the water. I told my party these were the best three days in a row of the entire season as far as the weather was concerned, and that the company wasn't too bad, either. I wanted everybody in good spirits in case the perch proved timorous.

It seemed to take only minutes before Norm had a fish on, one whose pulling power was far more than he'd bargained for. It was an adult white perch, fourteen inches long. "They fight like crappie!" he exclaimed. Fish then started coming aboard in rapid succession, in true frenzy style, and it lasted most of the morning. The mood was jovial, as it always is with fast-action fishing. Even when a three-foot eel showed up and I snipped the monofilament, we all had a hearty laugh.

Often, when I come to a lunchground with sports after a morning of guiding, I have some time alone. They might grab a rod out of the canoe and wander off on their own, casting from shore. They might find a rock or stump with a view and spend some time with their own thoughts. Meanwhile, I'm getting a cook fire going, peeling potatoes, slicing onions, making coffee, racking up some steaks or chops, or preparing a fish chowder.

It was Norm who wandered down the natural sand beach, making random casts, while John helped me get all the gear we needed up to the picnic table. I could tell he was ready to talk. "Those missions I spoke about—they aren't the ones that produce the Demons," John began. "It's the darker ones."

One morning, I was at the controls on a routine Flight mission, flying Chalk Seven in a ten-ship formation with Frank Cozart, who was one of the top Crusader pilots. The Flight hovered for a vertical landing, which made it a sitting duck. The enemy held their fire until the Flight was down.

I had already landed my aircraft when we started taking hits. Then a burst of automatic weapons fire came through my side of the windscreen. I felt impact to my face and shoulder, while bullets passed close enough to my face that I could feel the shock wave. Bullets were hitting all around me.

Frank Cozart dealt with fear by giggling. But when he turned and looked at me, he stopped giggling. His face turned white. Frank said, "I have the aircraft!" Then I was really worried. Touching my face caused sharp pain. Pulling my hand away, I saw blood. I got back on the controls, waiting for the Flight Lead to call the Flight out.

"Lead! This is Trail! You are down with ten!" Right after that call, an enemy rocket-propelled grenade hit Trail.

"Flight! This is Lead. Pulling power!" It was the order to depart the landing zone. He didn't know Trail had been hit. I stayed on the controls as we started climbing.

But Frank Cozart made the snap decision for Chalk Seven to help Chalk Six extract Trail's crew. I couldn't believe we had made it out and now we were going back in! I was thinking—we can't make it in and out again. The NVA guns are re-arming, and we have no gun cover. We're dead. Trail was now almost fully consumed by fire. We were just ready to terminate our approach when Chalk Six began coming up. Frank pulled us up along its starboard so that we flew formation with him as we started climbing out of the LZ for the second time.

At about eight hundred feet above the river, Chalk Six's engine began shooting craps, and the engine came apart. Entering autorotation, we followed it down, landing at nearly the same time. Chalk Six had twelve souls (in addition to its crew of four) and got out of the LZ before its engine quit—an amazing accomplishment.

A second ship landed on the port side of Chalk Six. I don't know where the hell he came from, but it would have been impossible to get the load and crew from Trail without his help. It loaded quickly, taking the burned crew and heading back to the Medevac hospital twenty minutes away. We loaded the door guns and radios from the burned ship, as well as everyone that had been onboard.

The brief look I had of the Aircraft Commander and his Crew Chief was horrifying. They were burned black. Their skin was charred with whitish fat, visible through cracks. They were walking, but shaking, either out of pain, or cold, or both. It was a terrible sight. The flight back to Tay Ninh was mostly quiet after we determined that the crew had all survived.

Luckily my wounds were basically Plexiglas and shrapnel, nothing serious. The doc said that if my clear helmet visor hadn't been in place, I would have lost my eyes. My shoulder was also cut, but that was very minor. My aircraft had thirty-eight bullet holes in it.

That evening, the Flight crews and pilots assembled in the Officers Club, where we listened to the remaining hours of the battle on a radio. We were just beginning to feel that we had gotten off pretty easy, with a limited number of casualties, when someone yelled, "Shut up!" and hiked the volume on the radio.

The flare ship had taken a hit and was burning with a full load of aerial flares. Discipline went to hell. The radio was a garble of screams. "Flare ship going down! We're on fire! We're burning!" Then came a report from the ship following the flare ship. "They flew into the ground at over three thousand feet a minute. The ship is fully involved. All the onboard flares burning. No possible survivors. Ashes to ashes." A hush fell over the entire Officers Club.

It was too much after all we had been through that day. All five aboard the flare ship were dead. For the day, that meant six comrades dead, thirty-six casualties, including two pilots very critically burned and not likely to live.

Afterward, we went down and saw Trail's Aircraft Commander, with over 60 percent third- and fourth-degree burns on his body. Right there and then, three of us made a death pact with one another. Should any of us get burned like him, the others would make certain that the victim got helped to opt out. Later, we each bought a 9mm sidearm. We were not going home like that.

It's a good thing I've been able, like most guides, to commit the chores of preparing and cooking a meal to muscle memory. My mind was nowhere near the Third Machias Lake lunchground. It was in a tailspin with the lost Crusader crew. Not usually at a loss for words, I could think of nothing to say that didn't seem absurd before uttering it. My silence launched John into another reminiscence.

On one mission, John and his crew had to land under fire to extract a dead Crusader pilot hanging upside down in his harness with a .50 caliber bullet hole in his head. Wounded crew on the same ship also had to be picked up. Miraculously, the extraction went off without further injuries. Later, in the Officers Club, John and his colleagues raised a glass to toast their fallen brother. They would never mention his name after that. "Just too many dead and wounded to live with when you have to fly the next day," was how he explained the custom.

John, Norm, and I finished up our day on Third Machias Lake with the sun shining lower in the sky, but just as brilliantly as it had for three full days. The afterglow of good fishing buffered the twelve-mile ride back to town over rough roads. I don't think any of us wanted to see the trip end. Nevertheless, we shook hands outside Leen's Lodge, exchanged email addresses, and pledged to keep in touch.

That night, after dropping my sports off, I tried watching TV, but switched it off and turned on the radio. Then I turned that off too. I was preoccupied with images I knew would stay with me for a long time.

Lying in bed that night, I was aware of confused feelings of indebtedness and unworthiness. John Jewett had entrusted me with the truth of the most critical year of his life. A show of trust of that magnitude had not been earned.

No one who had been to war, including my own father, had ever taken me into his or her story as deeply as John had. Long into the night I did my own mulling.

Everything John had said kept circling back to the same thing: that for those who were there, the horrors of war make their mark in the mind, in the memory, some might say in the soul. His struggle is like a simmering pot of water that is always on the verge of boiling over. And the process of maintaining that simmer is one that is ongoing for John and many of those comrades in whose company he is most comfortable these days. "It can be negotiated," he insisted. That surely was John's biggest understatement of them all.

Petroglyphs

A beautiful Indian Summer morning in Grand Lake Stream pulls a pleasant veil over the senses, as if to debunk the rumor of winter. It's October 5, and fall salmon fishing is at full pitch. Now the stream is swelling with new arrivals every day—fish and fishermen.

Spawn-ripe salmon are dropping in through the fishway from West Grand Lake, while others are swimming up the three miles from Big Lake. When the light is right, you can see them in their lies, feathering tail and fins to stay in the spot they've laid claim to. Mounded redd pillows will take shape there by early November. In the shallows in front of West Grand Dam, you can see salmon darting about, dorsal fins sometimes breaking the surface, some of them wearing jousting wounds. The eagles certainly know they're there. Their screeching begins at daybreak and doesn't stop until dusk. They are hunting the river, sometimes resting on tall pine perches overlooking likely killing lanes.

Bob and Sandra Lloyd had checked in at one of the local lodges the night before. The night before that, they stayed at another lodge in Lincoln, Maine, about an hour and a half's drive northwest of Grand Lake Stream. The night before that, they were at home in Florida. The long and the short of why and how they ended up in Grand Lake Stream was simple: their Lincoln host had told them about landlocked salmon.

When their equipment came out, I saw that they might be new to this particular fish, but not to fly-fishing. Both had embattled nine-foot Orvis rods. Sandra, an accomplished artist, is at the forefront of a relatively new women's movement—a movement toward fly-fishing.

At the first pool on her first afternoon of fishing, she was one of two women in the rotation. Fifty years ago, there was a better chance of seeing a leprechaun in that rotation than two women.

We had spent the morning scouting the river, chatting up fly fishers, looking over the fly selection at The Pine Tree Store, and having a shore lunch under two maple trees that seemed to be turning redder by the minute. After lunch, we took the path leading to Big Falls. There, between the tail end of the Cable Pool and the rightward sweep of the swift current just before it cascades over the falls, I showed Bob and Sandra the etchings on the exposed Big Falls ledges. Sandra dropped to her knees. The artist's eye followed the chipped indentations, as though reading a language some ancient artist put there for some future artist to decipher. She was right.

The petroglyphs of Maine—a language of images carved in rock— range in age from five hundred to three thousand years old. They were typically carved into ledges along waterways where Native people gathered, fished, worked, and lived seasonally. This was one of those places. The artists were the tribal shamans, alternately known as medicine men, healers, seers, visionaries, or spiritual leaders. The Grand Lake Stream petroglyph site is small in comparison to what is now known as The Picture Rocks Property in Machiasport, a small town of about 1,130 residents located thirteen miles east of Machias. In 2004, that site—the highest concentration of authentic petroglyphs in the eastern United States—was set aside as a historic preserve.

Malusah'ekan is the Passamaquoddy term for "picture rocks on the shore." Most, but not all of the drawings tend toward the abstract. They were intended to symbolize tribal beliefs and values. Some, however, are more graphic and realistic, depicting, for example, the ships that may have been seen when the first European explorers and settlers arrived off the coast of Maine. One etching seems to show the heads of the ship's crew on fire. It has been speculated that this conceptualization arose from sightings of Viking ships.

The glint of the sun on metal helmets could have produced such an impression.

The sea life, as well as the upland animals, so vital to the survival of native peoples, is also represented in the Machias Bay petroglyphs. Canoes, serpents, eagles, even sexual images reminiscent of the second century Sanskrit texts, the *Kama Sutra*, can be found. In some cases, it is believed that visiting shaman/artists traveling extensive trade routes added to the body of work on the ledges.

At the beginning of the petroglyph period, just over three thousand years ago, Maine's climate had not yet advanced into the Little Ice Age. The Gulf of Maine was still warmer, with large areas of shallows offshore. A wealth of sea life made certain coastal areas favorable for Native encampments. Thriving oyster beds, clams, and muscles available from mud flat expanses contributed importantly to tribal life. These shellfish gardens, in turn, attracted waterfowl. Swordfish, cod, and halibut could be hunted from dugout canoes. The Native diet was therefore diverse and conveniently accessible. All of that was to change, giving way to a period known in Passamaquoddy oral history as the "time of stress." The petroglyphs reflect the changes that impacted the tribe over millennia, and the millennia altered sea levels. Today's vertical tide at Machiasport is seventeen feet. The lowest petroglyphs can be found four feet below the high water mark.

The relatively small sampling of etchings at Big Falls is only a microcosm of the body of work left to posterity from the ancients. Almost universally, they are at their peak of visibility early in the morning and again at dusk. The sun's angle at those hours highlights the figures, occasionally creating the optical illusion that they were etched in relief.

The focus of shamans on the spirit world is evident in many petroglyphs. Vision quests seem to have been undertaken at the rock ledges, which were considered lodges that welcomed spirits. Not only human spirits were drawn there. Drawings of bird men with prominent beaks and a human torso might represent spirits of the sky, while salamander spirits were of the earth. Sometimes a human figure has antlers, sometimes a triangle for a head, or no head at all. It is believed too that dreams and visions were translated by shamans using this art form.*

More recently, a petroglyph has been discovered in the ledge rock of Machias Bay that depicts a Basque ship with Native people aboard. The drawing is thought to have been etched there between the years 1500 and 1550. The Basque, an ancient, pre-European people already known in Roman times (second century), came from an area that includes today's north-central Spain and southwestern France. Today, over two million Basque live in the same region, now known as the Basque Autonomous Community. Like the Passamaquoddy people, their language and culture is being excavated, explored, and celebrated. The petroglyph discovery suggests that these two cultures knew each other six centuries ago.

Sandra, the artist, is riveted to the drawings at Big Falls. It's time to fish, but she wants to know more. How old is this culture? How much of it survives today? The answer to that question changed overnight in 1999.

The improbable tale brought together a fugitive on Maine's Most Wanted list, a bulldozer, and the US Environmental Protection Agency to accidentally cause one of the most important archaeological discoveries in Maine's history. It all unraveled near a lake just fourteen miles southeast of Grand Lake Stream.

Meddybemps, in the Wabanaki family of languages, which comprises Passamaquoddy, Abenaki, Maliseet, Mi'kmaq, and Penobscot, means "plenty of alewives." Alewives, first cousin to the blueback herring, are anadromous. The Meddybemps alewives historically swam the seventeen miles from Dennys Bay to the Dennys River outlet at the

---

* In 2003, two professors brought the petroglyphs of Maine to light in the first film documentary of its kind on the subject. Mark Hedden, an archaeologist with the Maine Historic Preservation Commission, teamed up with Ray Gerber, from St. Joseph College in Standish, Maine, to research, film, and produce the groundbreaking documentary. Their partnership resulted in *Song of the Drum*, an in-depth look at this language of rock imagery.

south end of Meddybemps Lake in order to reproduce in freshwater. It is said in tribal oral history that the river "ran black" with them.

For modern-day Passamaquoddies, the location has long been considered a place of interest. The intersection of a bountiful river with a lake that provides for a southeasterly-facing encampment are attributes that have proven, over and over again, to have been sites that ancestral people sought. "It would have been the heart of an important network of canoe routes, with short portages to many streams," according to tribal historian Donald Soctomah. The problem was, the area had been a junkyard for nearly fifty years. Harry Smith Jr. owned Eastern Surplus, a salvage operation, along with two companion sites, Smith Junkyard and the Green Hill Quarry. The chances for in-depth research and on-site archaeological study seemed remote.

Then, in the late 1990s, the fortunes of Mr. Smith took a dark turn. It was discovered—by accident—that most of his five-acre parcel was in use not just as a junkyard, but as an above-ground storage dump for hazardous waste.

According to Soctomah, who at the time was serving as the tribe's legislative liaison to the State Legislature, Smith had brought tons of surplus materials to his salvage yard from Loring Air Force Base in Limestone, Maine, when the Base's closure was announced. "Trucks, trailers, some of them filled with barrels of contaminants, some with live ammunition, along with other surplus items, were purchased by Mr. Smith at the Base auction and brought to Meddybemps," Soctomah said. Silently and over several years, drums of dangerous compounds started to leak from corroded barrels.

Local fishers and hunters were the first to notice oddities. Some spoke of unexplained diebacks of fish populations, others of fish deformities. Still others observed off-color liquids leaching into the ground. Some of them contacted Maine's Department of Environmental Protection. It was the proverbial tip of the iceberg. The results found were shocking: PCBs, leaking electrical transformers, chlorinated organic compounds, and calcium carbides were all found on the property. It was the poisoning of an entire local ecosystem so profound, its siren call was answered by the US Environmental

Protection Agency, which promptly declared the five-acre Smith Salvage operation Superfund Site 96.02.

Cited for numerous criminal violations and then for ignoring court orders, Smith, the alleged felon, went on the lam. Meanwhile, the digging and the cleanup went into high gear. By 1999, EPA excavators were immersed in trying to reclaim what had grown with each new discovery into a nightmare. One tractor-trailer full of dangerous acids and chemicals spontaneously melted. Poisons had leached into area wells and groundwater. US taxpayers were paying $20 million for the Superfund cleanup while the culprit was rumored either to be living in Central America or fishing in Argentina.

In the midst of the environmental catastrophe with the ignoble name—96.02—Donald Soctomah had a premonition that history might be stirring in its grave. As bulldozers peeled back layers of topsoil, he contacted archaeologist Rick Will from Ellsworth, Maine, asking him to accompany Soctomah to the site so strategically located to the probable advantage of ancient peoples. Meanwhile, Soctomah invoked the National Historic Preservation Act and several other federal laws pertaining to consultation with the tribes in special circumstances, and managed to win the full support and cooperation of the EPA for an archaeological undertaking that would last for the next three years.

When Rick Will arrived at the site, it didn't take weeks or months to make a determination as to whether there were ancestral footprints there. It took minutes. On the first morning of the first day, Mr. Will found chert. One of the rare, but preferred, materials for tribal tool and weapon making, chert is found in quarries of the Minas Basin in Nova Scotia. Will also found rhyolite, another tool and weapons-grade stone well-known to the tribe. It was quarried forty-five miles away on Flint Island, but also at Mt. Kineo on Moosehead Lake. All three sites were part of canoe trade routes strategically accessible from Meddybemps. The Algonquin tribes of northeastern North America, including all the Wabanaki tribes, used the routes.

Will, along with tribal members, developed a work plan, and launched into a full-scale dig. After the first year, the University of Maine at Farmington joined the project. Professional as well as student archaeologists were part of a once-in-a-lifetime opportunity. Not long into the campaign, much more than chert flakes were excavated. Bowls, tools, weapons, ancient crop seeds—relics from a developed culture—were being unearthed, first by the hundreds, then by the thousands. By the project's conclusion, over six thousand artifacts would reside at the Abbe Museum in Bar Harbor, and Gunnar Hansen would be producing a film called, *N'tolonapemk, Our Relatives' Place* based on a civilization that was long suspected, but never before proven to exist. Carbon dating put objects from Meddybemps in a period from roughly seven thousand to possibly nine thousand or more years ago. The fully functional, well-equipped, working village of Native people predated Christ, the pyramids, and the Mayan temples by thousands of years. Donald Soctomah's premonition paled compared to what had actually been sleeping beneath the soils and detritus built up since the last glacier.

The Meddybemps excavation revealed important information about the tribe's lifestyle, including diet, fishing, hunting, and a broad range of travel. Plant and vegetable evidence was found, along with the remains of clay-fired cookware. These ceramics were used by the tribes from thousands of years ago right up to the time when trade with the European settlers began. Unexpectedly, the dig revealed swordfish remains. Apparently, the tribe hunted and killed them off Passamaquoddy Bay, then brought the dried, preserved food far inland to their seasonal encampment.

Weights used to hold a form of weir net below the water's surface were also excavated. These were probably employed to capture alewives by the tens of thousands. Alewives were prepared similarly to swordfish, but when the weather allowed for freezing the fish were not cleaned or cut, but frozen whole.

I told Sandra that fortune smiled for me the day I was invited to the screening of Gunnar Hansen's film. As the world of these Passamaquoddy ancients emerged on the screen that evening, the hush that fell over the audience was absolute. Here it was, in shape and form, attesting to a people who may have actually been around to see the rivers run opposite to their flows today. The explanation: the weight of half-mile thick ice sheets had depressed the landscape for thousands of years. Once relieved of this weight, the land rebounded, perhaps as much as seventeen feet, according to some geologists. Rivers, seeking the path of least resistance, would respond to the rebound by moving in one direction, and then respond again by reversing when the land settled. Evidence of a society in this region present to witness this phenomenon was not seriously contemplated until the Meddybemps discovery. Evidence of a people, seven thousand or more years ago, organized to some degree around trade routes stretching halfway across North America now compelled a deeper, broader study of this heritage.

When Richard Stevens, tribal governor at Indian Township, spoke at the first public tour of what had been Superfund Site 96.02, but was now renamed N'tolonapemk (our relatives' place), he said, "Our ancestors are happy." He was referring to the traditional tribal belief that "the old ones" are never far away, and the separation between their world and our world may be as thin as the wind. Governor Stevens said that the ancestors were happy because fifty years of poison that had been covering up tribal heritage was now removed and the Passamaquoddy people could embrace their own.

"What about Harry Smith?" Sandra asked. "Was he ever found?" Yes. Not in Central America. Not in Argentina—he was apprehended in a much less romantic setting. Authorities caught up with him working—where else?—at a junkyard in Everett, Massachusetts. He was extradited to Maine, stood trial, and was sent to federal prison.

Bob already had a salmon hooked as Sandra took a last look at the petroglyphs at Big Falls. She recovered from her meditations in time to cheer him on. It was a male fish, golden-gray with an impressive kyped jaw. I held up Bob's net just far enough to look for fin clips— the age indicator if it was a stocked salmon reared in the hatchery. No clips! Bob's first-ever landlocked salmon was a wild fish, one of only five percent of the total population. He was using a Black Ghost streamer fly.

I took Sandra thirty yards upstream and tied on a Barnes Special streamer for her. Most of the people we'd talked to on our morning chat tour were using weighed nymphs, but the results weren't compelling. If there are a couple of gates open at the dam and good flow in the stream in October, a return to streamers can be just the ticket. I stood back and watched Sandra's practiced arm, a joy to behold. When the bright, colorful hackle scribed its arc and straightened out, it was only twenty feet from Bob's waders. A fish came up and swirled behind the fly, causing Sandra to respond with a yank. "Short strike," I offered. "Let's see that fly."

When she'd stripped her line in, we saw that the Barnes' wet feathers reached almost a full inch past the bend of the hook. I suggested a haircut. Out came Sandra's snippers from a retractable case pinned to her fishing vest. She lopped off the perfect amount, sacrificing no attractiveness while ramping up its allure. Switching to a smaller version of the same fly pattern after a missed strike is a fairly accepted practice among salmon fishers. In effect, that's what Sandra had just done. We both may have been holding our breath as the leader swept around in the same place and the Barnes darted toward us when the line straightened out. This time there was no swirl, and no miss, either. It was all crashing and thrashing and enough commotion to jolt Bob's head around. "Hold on, honey!" She did, and all she needed a guide for was to complete the cheering section. Picking her moment, she raised her rod tip, shortened her line, and walked the fish into her net.

It happened three more times, twice for Sandra, once for Bob. By that time, we felt that the pool had been kind with its gifts. Walking out the way we'd come in, Sandra stopped once more at the smooth ledges, kneeling down on one knee. "Look!" In the light and shadows of the late afternoon sun, it was as if the drawings had suddenly leapt into full focus. In three hours they had taken on a completely new aspect, appearing almost animated. We all stared at them for several minutes, but Sandra lagged behind longer. I imagined her complimenting her ancient colleague whose work had reached forward hundreds of years to stir reverence in Sandra Lloyd, an artist poised in admiration at Big Falls.

NINETY-TWO AND GROWING

Many guides, game wardens, and tackle shop owners are former fishermen, hunters, and outdoorsmen. It is too often the result, when an avocation becomes a vocation, that the juice for one's passion is sapped by one's job. I never wanted that to happen to me. I decided at the beginning of my guiding career to plan a fishing trip of my own at the end of each season. Its purpose would be to replenish the well and to rekindle the flames I first felt as a child learning to fish in the Sebago, Maine, region. The added benefit would be a renewed commitment to my guiding work in Grand Lake Stream. As I ranged around for ideas, my lifelong friend from those days in Sebago came up with the perfect solution: Atlantic salmon fishing.

Unfortunately, opportunities in Maine were shut down in 1999 when Atlantic salmon were listed as endangered, and fishing for them was outlawed in all Maine rivers. It was a blow to many seasoned anglers, whose sporting approach to Atlantic salmon fishing put no fish at risk. In fact, they reasoned, if more people like them could be attracted to the sport, more champions for conservation initiatives would be created. Instead, the fishery was closed and a resource that might have been mined to further the cause of restoration was left to its disillusionment.

I came to the Atlantic salmon party late, and by the time I was ready to jump in with both feet I had to leave the country to do it. Frank "Skip" Burnell, who, for many years held the Veazie Salmon Club record for the largest Atlantic salmon caught by a club member on the Penobscot River, put forth a proposition. He offered to take me with him to Cape Breton, Nova Scotia, to fish one of the world's most storied rivers, the Margaree.

Skip and I had plied trout and salmon waters together since the light of consciousness dawned and our fathers first put rods in our hands. He had long preceded me with his own leap into Atlantic salmon fishing, right out of college. In the 1970s and '80s, every serious salmon angler along the Penobscot River knew the name Frank Burnell, the name Skip was born with. In those early days of Skip's forestry career, he burned midnight oil at the fly-tying vise and wasted no dawn's early light getting out to the river. Then, in 1999, like a prospector whose claim had been taken over by the government, he had to sever those ties and make new ones if he was going to continue his passion. Long before inviting an old friend and an Atlantic salmon newbie along, he had learned the pools and the changeable personality of the Margaree River. I therefore had a guide on my first foray into this world so new to me, and yet so very, very old.

The first legislation to regulate Atlantic salmon fishing was passed in Scotland in 1310. By the 1400s, fairly sophisticated laws were in place to ensure inward and outward migrations of salmon in the Tay, the Spey, the Tweed, and the other fabled salmon rivers of Scotland. Societies, clubs, culture, etiquette, and even a literature grew up around the sport. Small wonder, in consideration of the Atlantic salmon's status as "King of Fish," as proclaimed by Isaac Walton in his *Compleat Angler*, published in 1653. By any scientific or aesthetic measure, *Salmo salar* is one amazing fish.

The *salar* comes from *salio*, which means "the leaper."The name was given the fish by conquering Roman legions in 100 BC. Returning to their rivers of birth after years at sea, and covering almost three thousand miles to do so, Atlantic salmon still have the strength to leap obstructions as high as three and a half feet. In the 1950s, with the aid of submarines and sonar, it was discovered that populations of Atlantic salmon that were birthed in American, Canadian, and European rivers congregated at feeding grounds off the west coast of Greenland and near the Faroe Islands. It was an epic moment in both the study and understanding of the species. It was also fateful. Drift nets and trawling began to take devastating tolls on these newly mapped gold mines of fish flesh, inaugurating a historic decline and crash of the fishery. Since that time, loss of habitat, acid rain, hybrid fish escaping* from aquaculture pens, and overfishing have contributed to the decline. In recent years, overfishing has been less of a contributor.

Being anadromous—spawning in freshwater but living at sea—an adult salmon must repeatedly adjust its tolerance for freshwater after becoming acclimated to the salinity of the ocean. Its stages of growth—from egg sac, to alevin, to fry, to parr—all occur in freshwater rivers, while the smolt stage involves out-migration to the sea. There, if the salmon can survive predation from sharks, cod, halibut, grey seals, and ocean trawlers, it becomes a grilse—sexually mature enough to return to its river of birth to reproduce. Not just to the river, but to the exact spot in the river. It travels thousands of miles, apparently using celestial navigation, to come to that one river that emits a chemical signature that can be read by that one salmon. This immediately triggers a fasting diet right through reproduction.

The various salmon sportfishing traditions that have evolved over centuries in the British Isles, US, and Canada carry a common ethic—respect for the miracle of the species. In the stream of fly-fishing consciousness, Atlantic salmon exist in a class by themselves, and therefore, the thinking goes, so should fishing for them. You stand on a shingle (a cobble of aged, marbled stones washed smooth by the current) and you fish a beat (a particular pool or "lie" of salmon). Depending on where in the world you're doing it, you may hire a guide or gillie (Scottish), and you may even fish with a two-handed Spey rod (a long rod for longer reach) named after the Spey River in Scotland.

---

* Salmon pens used in the aquaculture industry off the coast of Maine are sometimes susceptible to storm breaches.

On the Margaree, where the sport began in earnest in the 1860s, salmon fishing draws an uncommon number of anglers in their nineties. One can observe these seasoned sports bent slightly forward, almost on point, watching with a studied intensity as their fly completes its drift. They may be casting one of the standards: a Cosseboom, a Rusty Rat, a Blue Charm, or some inventive permutation from their own fly-tying vise. "Why so gaudy?" asks the newbie, seeing how flamboyant these flies can be. For first-time fishermen like me on the Margaree, the news that these fish are not feeding takes some wind out of the sails. "Drawing a reactive strike" more aptly describes this type of fishing, since it is not a question of matching a hatch or imitating something they're feeding on. Colorful flies and a positive attitude, Skip assured me, are the best gear to bring.

Skip schooled me in knots that were new and exotic to me, techniques that tested not only my patience and stamina, but also my resolve to broaden my own fishing horizons. We hiked for miles and miles each day to reach pools that he had known to be productive in the past. We lashed those scenic waterways from first to last light each day, stopping only briefly for a lunch break.

On the third afternoon, I watched as he hooked a bright fish just downstream from me. "Bright" is the term given to fish that haven't been in the river too long, for they darken a little with each passing day in freshwater. He braced the butt section of his nine-foot fly rod against his chest, holding the rod straight up, but it was still bent double. At this point it was the salmon, not Skip, in control. Then a tremendous, sleek mass of silver and crimson launched itself out of the river and hovered there as if posing for a picture. My abiding love for Atlantic Salmon fishing dates back to that very moment.

I've remained faithful to my inner fisherman in the twelve years since that trip. I've returned to the Margaree every October since my friend first brought me there—each time watching, listening, learning, and gaining greater appreciation. It has been a transformative experience to be among fishermen not as a guide, but as a student. Many experienced Atlantic salmon anglers whom I've never met have had something to teach me. Every one of their rotations on a pool, unbeknownst to them, has been a learning experience for me. Of all those time-tested salmoners I did have the good fortune to meet, one stands out today as much as he did the first day I met him eleven years ago.

It was a busy day on Hart's Pool. The etiquette of salmon angling suggests a method of fairness when numbers of fly casters wish to fish the same pool. "Two casts and two steps" keeps the group in a rotation so that every angler gets the same chance at all the best water. On some pools there are benches where fishermen wait their turn, and, inevitably, socialize.

That morning, I saw an older man explain and then demonstrate a nonslip knot to a younger fisherman who'd never used one before. The older man's legs were apart, feet firmly planted in the cobble, wading stick looped around his belt—he had obviously been there before. He stood alongside afterward while the avid young sport made a cast and let his fly line unfurl across the breadth of the pool. The older gentleman looked as if he were listening to the river, anticipating the strike that came when the line straightened and the fly took off upstream. He coached the fish fight all the way to the tailing, then stood for a long meditative moment after the young man released the fish. He looked as if he were in prayer. Later, when we wound up on the bench together between rotations, he reached out his hand, and full-voiced, said, "How do you do? I'm Ray Plewacki."

Ten years later, I'm seated on another bench at a different pool on the Margaree. Ray Plewacki is beside me, and at ninety-one, he is as broad across the chest and shoulders and as flat across the belly as he was at eighty-one. This is his favorite pool on a salmon river with seventy-three pools. It is called Chance Pool.

I tell him I've learned so many things from him over the past ten years, and he ducks the compliment, editing it instead to say, "We learn from each other."

Ray had been retired for less than seven years. It wasn't a cushy desk job that allowed him to keep working until he was eighty-five. It wasn't one of those overseeing positions where the elder sage drops by the office to remind everyone how and why he or she has come to be there. And it wasn't one job that Ray retired from, but two. He was a Montana trout guide by summer, and an upstate New York ski instructor by winter. There are men I know thirty years his junior who would trade the shape they're in for the shape he's in today.

As someone who's been true to his own inner fisherman, despite the decades he logged as a Montana trout guide under the business name American Eagle Outfitters, Ray serves as a model to me. He has kept his passions alive by immersing himself in them in every conceivable way. He migrates to the Margaree each fall with the same punctuality as those wild Atlantic salmon from Greenland. When Ray stands waist deep in the Margaree River with a fourteen-foot Spey rod in his hands, he cuts the figure of a fly fisherman who knows the world and its waters because he has seen and fished so many of them.

The first thing Ray does at any pool where there are other fishermen is make sure to meet all of them. His expansive personality is infectious. It's clear Ray has not yet met everyone he wants to meet in this world, and as he says, "At the end of the day, it's not how many fish you caught, but who you fished with that matters." When he lays out a fly line with the Spey rod he made himself, it is a grace to behold. And when he takes his turn on the bench, resting from a rotation, Ray holds court to rapt audiences until it's time to fish again.

He arrives each year the Saturday before Canadian Thanksgiving, in order to make the annual meeting of the Margaree Salmon Association. He remains an active member of the club, the purpose of which is to foster the health and well-being of the river and the salmon.

Over the ten years I've known Ray, chapters in his extraordinary life have spilled out on those salmon pool benches. It's a life story that contains World War II Bronze Stars and a long list of near-miss scrapes that led Ray's late wife to proclaim him "two lives past the feline nine." She passed away at the early age of forty-eight. He has been a widower for almost forty-five years! With time, I've come to agree with her assessment.

Ray was shot down over Guadalcanal on the same day and on the same mission with famed Black Sheep Squadron aviator Pappy Boyington. "I often marvel at the luck I've had," said Ray. "After ditching my plane and spending forty-eight hours in a tiny raft, I was rescued by an American destroyer. Pappy was picked up by a Japanese submarine and beaten with baseball bats." Though he downplays the incident, Ray froze at night alone in his raft, and roasted during the day, not knowing if he'd ever be found—or if so, by whom. Ray firmly believes in predestination. "It wasn't my time," he said, wryly. His life is a compelling argument for that theorem.

While still an aviation cadet, Ray was flying backseat, with his instructor occupying the front seat of an open-cockpit trainer. When the instructor went into a barrel roll, Ray found out too late that his safety belt had not latched. He fell out of the plane. Completely unaware of this, the instructor flew on, returning to the base without his student sitting behind him. Fortunately Ray was wearing a parachute, which deployed, delivering him to a farmer's field covered with a foot and a half of snow. The farmer had a surprise that day when he answered the knock at his door. "Do you think you could give me a ride back to the airbase?" Ray asked. "I fell out of a plane."

Another time, Ray crash-landed a Navy jet when a tire exploded on impact with the fiery-hot runway. He finished that story, too, with, "It wasn't my time." I once pressed him about predestination. Without hesitation he said, "When you're put on this earth, there is a time and a place at which your designated time will be up. You will be at that exact place at that exact time to fulfill your destiny."

Back home near Buffalo, New York, Ray was hit by a train during a blizzard because the railroad's track warning signs had been misplaced. The train hit Ray's car while he was still in the driver's seat, and he walked away. "It wasn't my time," he laughed.

Ray has a season pass to his home mountain in the Buffalo area of New York, where he taught skiing for so many years. There, even now, he's the first one up the lift four days a week, Monday through Thursday. He says he likes to avoid the weekend crowds. When he travels, he's allowed to ski free at most mountains because he's over seventy. He once quipped to a lift operator that since he's over ninety, *they* should pay *him* to ski!

Three times a week, Ray rides his mountain bike twenty-seven miles, and if you've ever shuffled through Buffalo, you know it isn't exactly flat. He once offered that the reason he feels younger than his years is his constant association with younger people. He includes me in that group.

Ray not only makes his own rods, which have been sold around the world (all of them carry a lifetime guarantee—his lifetime), he also ties his own flies. That's something of a feat in itself for ninety-two-year-old eyes. Last year, just before leaving the Margaree, Ray gave me a salmon fly called The Kilberry Spey. It has a black body wrapped in foil, with an orange tail hackle, and a bucktail tuft around the head.

When Ray left before I did last year, I felt a sudden sadness steal over me as I hiked out one evening to a favorite pool. I thought about it as I sat alone on the bench, rigging myself up to fish. Without Ray there, observing, commenting, and sharing the experience, it was suddenly diminished. I'd been befriended these last ten years by someone old enough to be my father, someone who might've chosen to be among people his own age, but hadn't. His reason: "I don't feel as old as they seem to me." He went on to say, "I savor every moment. I look forward to each new day. I have the luxury of being under no time pressure, and I wouldn't have it any other way." Even as I contemplated this, Ray was on his way back home where he would begin work on the rod orders he had for the year, each one taking sixty or more hours to make.

With no witnesses that evening, I was able to practice my Spey casting with abandon and without risk of embarrassment. The river level was up from a good rain. I liked the sweep and drift of the line in the new freshets. The leader and fly were unfurling just where the riffles smoothed out at the tail of the pool. When the evening light dimmed enough to eliminate the need for polarized sunglasses, the time seemed right to tie on Ray's Kilberry Spey.

It was there, a few casts later, that an Atlantic salmon, the fabled King of Fish, took Ray's home-tied fly and me for the ride of a lifetime. My inner fisherman was alive and well, but it was after releasing that fish that I realized Ray was right about something else, too.

At the end of the day, it's not about how many fish you've caught. If anything could have made that moment sweeter than it already was, it would have been a fishing party of three instead of just one. And yet, perhaps unbeknownst to them, those other two were there as kindred spirits just the same—Skip Burnell, the person who taught me it's never too late to discover a new passion; and the guide I'd like to grow up to be one day, Ray Plewacki, ninety-three years young.

Author's note: Weeks before *Wide and Deep* was sent to press, I received the sad news that Ray Plewacki, a guiding colleague and someone I was proud to call a friend, died suddenly and without suffering at his son's home in Fairfax, Virginia, two days before Thanksgiving in 2013. We had just fished together in Canada the month before, and he'd shown me three of the six custom rods he had built over the winter, in his 93rd year. Ray was memorialized at Arlington National Cemetery for his military service, and his ashes will be committed, by family, friends, and admirers, to his beloved Margaree River in Cape Breton, Nova Scotia. As I imagine he'd have said it himself, it was his time.

Moose and Cranberries

Naming is important. Native people, who believe that all of nature is animated, let the woods and waters speak. In this way, their names become a manifestation of their uniqueness. Hanging a convenient label or number on natural beauty would have seemed to them an indignity.

When you stumble across a river or lake in Maine with a Native American name, it is almost always a toponym. Some characteristic of that body of water was responsible for its name, even if that trait is not immediately obvious. When, instead, you stumble across a lack of imagination in place names, it tends to be the legacy of the newcomers for whom nomenclature served a more bureaucratic purpose.

There is only one Sysladobsis Lake, one Pocumcus, one Wabassus on the Maine map. But tally the Long Lakes and Long Ponds, Pleasant Lakes and Pleasant Ponds, Pug Lakes and Grand Lakes, Little Falls and Big Falls, and you may have a life of work ahead of you. When several lakes calved off of the same glacier or perhaps derived from a common river, the new namers resorted to numbers. If there were two ponds situated close together, perhaps sharing a stream, a favorite last-ditch handle was Upper this and Lower that, or Big this and Little that. The Geodetic Surveyors, followed by the US Geological Surveyors, had to put something down, and too often they stirred the same barrel to see what floated to the top. The proof is in the sharp contrast of place names on any Maine map. Run through a list of flowages, gorges, estuaries, bays, rivers, and lakes, and it's easy to see which place names left a lasting impression and which might've found a better home on a ledger in a desk drawer.

The river that took its name from the "bad little falls" at its mouth finds its headwaters five lakes and seventy-seven miles upstream from those falls. The flow that ultimately becomes the Machias River, after passage through all five lakes, begins at the outlet of Fifth Machias Lake in a remote, unorganized territory with the negligible name, T36. The layout of the five lakes from Fifth to First forms a circle with clockwise-flowing water.

Fifth Lake Stream runs its eight-mile, irregular course due north to Fourth Machias Lake. It was made famous in the pages of the *Saturday Evening Post* in the 1950s by Edmund Ware Smith, guided there by Sonny Sprague from Grand Lake Stream. Fourth Lake, though glacial like the others, somehow was the "black sheep" of the lake litter. It was not dredged out by the retreating glacier in the same southeast-northwest trend seen most commonly in the region. Fourth Lake Stream flows southeast into the lake that looks so much like a lobster that some of its landmarks are named after lobster body parts. The Eastern and Western arms of Third Machias Lake are the left and right claws, which seem perfectly poised to reach for and engulf Second Machias Lake just a few miles downstream. Second and First Machias Lakes are the smallest of the five. First Machias looks more like the widening of a river, a long deadwater that might have qualified as a flowage had that name come to the top of the barrel instead of "First."

The most popular river trip, fifty-one miles long, begins at the Third Machias outlet where a dam existed until the mid-1970s. It was the last obstruction on the Machias to be removed, and when it was gone, it was clear sailing all the way from the Machias Lakes to Machias Bay and the Atlantic Ocean. Since the demolition, evidence of Atlantic salmon has been found once in Fifth Lake Stream by fish biologists. The finding inconclusively suggests that Atlantic salmon once migrated for spawning all seventy-seven miles to the Machias headwaters, not uncommon for the species.

Highwater canoeing the Machias is not for novices. Lacking those earned stripes of experience, better wait for the sluggish flows of August to make it a learning experience rather than a brush with mortality. Wigwam Rips, Holmes Falls, and Little Falls can all make mighty showings of Class III whitewater and tall rooster tails. Along the way there are drops drastic enough to require portaging, and other runs that beckon a good scouting on foot rather than shooting blind.

The removal of the dam in the 1970s caused a near fishery crash on Third Machias Lake. Already well-established by that time as premier bass water, the prime spawning habitats around the lakeshores were suddenly high and dry. The lake has been rebounding ever since, sometimes with the aid of a restocking program. In the late 1990s and early 2000s, fish from other, more bountiful fisheries were caught by guides and volunteers and transferred to Third Machias to jump-start its recovery.

Considered by many to be the diamond in the Machias lakes necklace, Third Machias offers its gifts up gradually from the boat launch in the left claw all the way to where Fourth Lake Stream tickles the tail end of the lobster. Just behind the lobster's eyes, Trafton Rock towers above the landscape, in certain light and shadows looking more like a whale's head than a rock. There are narrow passageways and long expanses, compact islands and craggy shorelines, and natural sand beaches hundreds of yards long. With surrounding sedge meadows as well as high country, cedar swamps and hardwood ridges, conifer forests and cranberry bogs, it is magnificent moose country.

It was here that a guiding colleague guided a man from Ohio on his very first moose hunt, one neither guide nor sport will ever forget. They had spent two days before the opening of the October season scouting likely moose haunts around Third Machias. They quickly homed in on travel paths leading from the high country to the swamps and cranberry bogs (moose have been known to savor the tart treats in the fall). They followed these signs once the season opened. Naturally, the traffic on what had appeared to be moose highways abruptly detoured once the hunters took to the woods on opening day. Four days later they had nothing to show for all their traipsing but half an antler shed. There were just two days remaining.

When nothing materialized on his second to last day, the Ohioan, naturally transferring culpability to his guide, decided to go for broke. Perhaps he'd do better on his own, he reasoned. When he failed to make the first checkpoint outlined that morning in the guide's plan for the day, the guide searched for his client until he found his track. The webbing of his Muck boots left an unmistakable print in the mud. They led in the direction of a cedar swamp that bordered a cranberry bog. Just before descending into the low country, the terrain offered a granite outcropping with an overview of the bog. From that perch, the guide viewed the extraordinary events, which he later recounted to me.

The hunter, after slogging partway through the cedar swamp, came unexpectedly upon a very large bull feeding on cranberries. Shocked at the size and site of the monster, the sport crouched prostrate. After several minutes of trying to compose himself, the sport decided that the air must be in his favor, or else the moose would've already charged. Marshaling all of his courage, he decided to creep closer for a shot. Belly-crawling like a Dunkirk soldier, he misjudged and got closer than he meant to. When he picked up his head to look, the bull, paunch-deep in the soggy heath, suddenly picked his head up, too, making direct eye contact with the Ohioan. The sport knew he was well-within charging range and there would be no escaping. The long-legged quadruped would have every advantage in the floating hummocks of cranberries. From his perch overlooking the drama, my friend, the guide, was thinking, "Raise your rifle, raise your rifle!" so loudly, he hoped his sport would hear him.

Of the many possible outcomes, my friend couldn't have dreamed up the one that happened. Apparently, no early frosts had arrived to work their sweetening magic on the cranberries the moose was feasting on, for one look at the bull's face gave proof of a mouthful of sour grapes. The moose's lips were stretched angularly and awkwardly back, exposing his teeth and gums in a crooked, gaping grin. Moreover, those teeth and gums were blood red. This tuned the Ohioan's fear to a high-pitched panic. Was this a man-eating moose? The more he looked, the less he could believe his eyes. Had he been feeding on some other hunter?

When the guide's client began to back up, the bull stopped smiling. He turned fully toward the hunter as though weighing the energy expenditure of a charge versus wandering away to feed someplace without interruption. Making his decision, the moose burped once, snorted, and then ambled away, all hooves and elbows, leaving the disheveled hunter no chance to collect himself or even bring his weapon to port arms. The Ohioan stood stupefied until he heard laughter from a balcony seat on the rock outcropping above. Euphoric from what he saw as a close brush with his own demise, the sport laughed, too.

I shared that story with Shelley a week later as we began our annual October pilgrimage to Third Machias Lake. My final guiding days of the season usually coincide with at least one early frost, the kind that sweetens those berries enough to wipe the smile off any moose's face.

Sassamanash. That's the name those earlier Pilgrims learned from the Natives for the red bearberry that became an accessory to their biggest holiday meals. It showed up as "cranberry sauce" in the first Pilgrim cookbook, published in 1663. No one yet was calling it a superfruit. No one yet knew its power as a health food, able to help humans fight everything from dental plaque to E. coli. The fact that it was a powerball of vitamin C and antioxidants was not what sold it as a side dish to the colonists. It was the taste of the sweetened, dime-sized treats that grew wild and plentifully in acidic bogs and heaths.

From years of scouting, Shelley and I knew where to beach the canoe and set out with buckets and berry rakes. These ground rakes resemble a dustpan with spindly tines, and a reverse handle situated above for scooping. The rake can be pulled or pushed through the ground-covering vines, then lifted to separate the berries from the plant. In a good year, it may take only two hours to harvest enough cranberries for a year—a year in which they are used at our house almost weekly in various forms. Since achieving their new rank as a health food, cranberries have been promoted in many homes from a side dish at holiday feasts to a culinary mainstay.

After pick-poling our way in autumn-low water through the Third Machias outlet, we headed up the left lobster claw to a likely cranberry ground. Even before beaching the Grand Laker, it was already obvious it was a bountiful year. We settled into raking and picking, kneeling or sitting where it was dry enough, standing in calf-deep water or mud when it was not.

Content that we'd picked a year's worth, we headed for our favorite lunchground. Local guides maintain these lunchgrounds, raking them off in the spring, clearing away blowdowns, fixing up the fireplace. My son and I had lugged in a new picnic table for this site the previous year. Shelley and I would have to make just one important stop before reaching it—we had to catch lunch. Yes, my skills as a guide were on the line this day more than any other.

The fishery that didn't crash when the Third Machias Lake dam was removed was the white perch fishery. Most of the Machias lakes are known for excellent perching, especially in late summer and early autumn, when the perch school up for their migration to deeper water. Sport fishermen come from all over the United States and beyond to fish for landlocked salmon and smallmouth bass in Fisheries Region C, as the Maine Department of Inland Fisheries and Wildlife calls it, but when it comes to finned food, locals want white perch.

It's the main ingredient in most guides' fish chowders, as well as in almost every fall fish fry. We weren't long in boating half a dozen humpbacks—perch over a foot long achieve that characteristic along with the pulling power of a small dog at the end of a rope. That catch provided for twelve fine fillets, which would be dressed with Shelley's homemade tartar sauce. They'd still look lonely on the plate without those twice-fried potatoes. That's the trick Josh Moulton, my chef sport and friend, taught me when we fished together the previous June. "The world's best fried potatoes are always twice-fried," he told me. "Sear them first, then remove them from the oil, keep the oil up to temperature, then put them back in again for browning." Overnight, my once-fried potatoes were forgotten.

The final touch was Shelley's idea. We had sugar packets for coffee in the lunch basket. Why not prepare wild cranberries? Would they ever be fresher? She barely covered them with lake water in a saucepan, and in no time they were popping like popcorn. She stirred in the sweetener, then put them at a simmering distance from the flames for ten minutes.

Ready! Red cranberries, white perch, and blue enamelware put a Betsy Ross flair on that picnic table as Shelley and I marked the end of another guiding season in our traditional way. Well, almost the end. We tossed out the anchor one more time that afternoon, and left it there long enough to catch a Ziploc freezer bag full of white perch. Later, on the way downlake, the resplendent fall colors shouted to us from the shorelines. I was daydreaming that back when the Pilgrims were first discovering *sassamanash*, it coincided with the time of year when three- and four-foot Atlantic salmon would be entering "Bad Little Falls," fifty-one miles downstream.

The Fall Trip to Drummond's

E ach fall, the realization that the guided fishing season is over rolls over me like a slow-moving train. At first, it feels no different than a few days off. Then, the effects of two opposing lifestyles colliding begin to sink in. The next six months will bear no resemblance to the previous six. The constant camaraderie and high-spirited conversation will be replaced by too much solitude and quiet contemplation. There are, of course, the projects—the work of winter—that serve as lifelines connecting one guiding season to the next. Every guide needs them, not just for economic reasons, but also to fight the slump in morale that inevitably comes. But first, there's a period of something akin to withdrawal that must be reconciled.

As Shelley will often remind me, I mope around like an old salt whose sea legs don't work well on land. I postpone the fall duties that call me only faintly on those Indian summer days of October.

This fall, like most, it was a chilly snap that finally launched me into those end-of-season chores. First, I thoroughly washed out my Grand Laker canoe, the one Sonny Sprague built for me in 1987. I let it dry in the sun on its trailer, and then backed it into the garage where I gave the inside a light sanding. Too many heavy sandings, and the brass tacks that are clinched to hold the ribs to the planking would be sanded off and let go. These are things I learned from Sonny. I wiped the sawdust out with a tack cloth, ran a vacuum through after that, then brushed on a coat of a good spar varnish. I had great autumn drying weather, and was ready the next day to flip her over onto sawhorses.

Then came a light sanding of the hull, only this time it was fast going with the Makita palm sander. I inspected the keel for cracks and pronounced it healthy, admiring once again the strength and resiliency of ash wood. That keel had been raked over untold stumps; dark, subsurface boulders in tannin-stained lakes; and even an occasional deadhead—most difficult to see when the wind was up.

Last came a coat of jade Easypoxy paint, which Sonny Sprague swore by. "Poor man's fiberglass," he would say. Working on my canoe gave me the feeling of Sonny's presence right next to me. I think I might even have said some things to him out loud. I think he might have answered, too.

The Easypoxy took only a day to dry. With a little help from Shelley, the vessel upon which my seasonal livelihood rests was set upside down on its rack in my canoe shed for its long winter's sleep.

Just seeing it in that position at the end of the season struck a solemn note. Another page had turned; another chapter had ended in its life and in mine. If there's some celestial clock keeping track of exactly where we are in the big arc of time, I felt it advance just then.

Rather than wallowing in that sensation, I decided to take a walk—my antidote for almost everything. I took up walking as a discipline right out of college, after reading Emerson and Thoreau. In fact, Emerson once said of Thoreau that he never knew him to write on the days he didn't walk. Thoreau was a tireless traipser by all accounts, notepad always at the ready to record his keen, natural observations. I pictured an invisible drive belt that ran from Thoreau's legs to his brain: the movement of one activating the creative work of the other.

I know some people who walk with a purpose. They wear their mission on their faces with an expression of determination. Slowing down or stopping would, they feel, defeat this purpose. I know others who stop and talk to almost everyone they meet and probably get little or no aerobic benefit from the outing. I think they benefit, just the same.

As I stepped onto the only concrete bridge across Grand Lake Stream, I saw a blue heron standing on a rock on the downstream side. In eastern cultures, cranes and herons are drawn and painted in this very pose to symbolize tranquility or peace of mind. They are capable of maintaining this posture for hours. Viewed against the shore or a tree line, they can be virtually invisible, and sometimes the heron will turn his bill upward so that his entire body blends in with the understory growth along the shore.

When an errant fish strayed too close, the heron's reaction would have been missed if I had blinked just then. Here, in this ungainly, slender bird, opposites seemed joined in practical harmony. The svelte predator came out of a perfect stillness to attack and kill its prey with a swiftness that would leave even the fastest fish at a disadvantage. By the time you realized that these birds are a more lethal threat to salmon than eagles, lunch was over.

A freeze-frame of the image was still in my mind when I stepped off the bridge near The Pine Tree Store. Close by, I noticed a moose hanging from a stout tree limb in a neighbor's dooryard. It was a mighty bull, probably close to half a ton. I couldn't help walking over for a better look. A closer inspection revealed that in life—recent life—this bull was a fighter. He was bunged up from stem to stern with pocks, punctures, contusions, and abrasions; and his stunted eleven-point rack was all chipped and staved from jousting. As I surveyed all this, the man who bagged the bull came out. He said he took the monster on the first day of the second week of the year's split season. I snapped a photo, shook his hand, congratulated him, and walked on toward Middle Walk.

Middle Walk is a special place in Grand Lake Stream. It is the trail that connects town to lake, but along the way it parallels the stream on one side and the historic tannery canal on the other. One can imagine rafts of hemlock bark being floated down the canal into the tannery to make tannic acid, a century ago.

Toward the lake end of Middle Walk, the famous Dam Pool on Grand Lake Stream came into full view. In two weeks' time, the dark backs of spawning salmon would be stacked up here amid the redds: the mounds of gravel that they would build to protect their progeny. Eagles would soar overhead, or occupy perches on pine limbs, which for successful raptors would serve double duty as picnic tables.

As I stepped closer to the pool, I heard the increasingly deafening din of rushing water from the gates of the dam. The volume knob rose until it would have been difficult to carry on a conversation with someone standing right next to me.

Before I ascended the hill for a view of the lake, I noticed a nice play of morning light on the Dam Pool from the vantage of the first gate. There were only two fly fishermen down on the right side, and just as I snapped a picture, one of them hooked a fish! I watched until he brought it in close to his waders, raised the rod, and eased the eighteen inches of quivering liquid silver into his rubber-mesh net. I gave a wave and a thumbs-up, which was copied and returned.

On the way home, I stepped into The Pine Tree Store. Kurt Cressey was behind the counter. He asked me if I'd heard about the mishap up on the lake the previous day. "Oh no," was all I could say.

A father, his young boy, and their dog had been camping on an island in the middle of West Grand Lake, about five miles from the town landing. They came downlake Saturday morning for supplies and decided to go back, only this time, head-on into the substantial wind that had kicked up in the meantime. They were in an aluminum open boat with an eight-horse outboard. The north-northwesterly blow was producing three-to four-foot waves consistently. Suddenly, one of the even taller, dreaded, rogue waves overtook the boat when it lurched into a trough after negotiating the previous wave. It was too much. The boat instantly swamped and capsized.

The dog had apparently remained in the boat when it went over. Both father and son dove under to save it. The dog made its way to the upside-down hull and sat on it, while the other two clung to the boat's gunwales. The life jackets that they'd neglected to put on had been washed away. When the boat flipped, they were in the middle of the vast lake at a time of year when few vacationers were in their camps, and few fishermen were on the lake.

Against all probability, one of those few vacationers happened to look westward from the camp he was staying in on the east shore. He thought he saw a speck out on the lake at some distance. He picked up his binoculars and confirmed it was a boat. And then, while he had the craft in his glasses, it dipped totally out of sight, then emerged, upside down. The man got to a phone as fast as he could.

The Warden Services of both the State of Maine and the Passamaquoddy Reservation were contacted, as well as local EMTs. A boat was launched as the wind continued to build. The team battled a fierce, oncoming sea for several miles to the middle of the lake until, with field glasses, one of them made out an upside-down aluminum hull with a dog struggling to stay upright on it. Then, two heads came into view as the team drew closer.

They were alive! By the time the rescue boat reached the party, they had been in the lake for over an hour in fifty-five degree water. The life rings were thrown, and all three were brought aboard, taken downlake wrapped in blankets, and then brought indoors to begin the slow process of warming. The boat washed ashore and was later retrieved.

When Kurt finished, I sat down on the Liar's Bench and breathed a sigh of relief. Kurt and I then went over all of the what-ifs that didn't happen.

Here was a brush with mortality that should have ended much worse than it did. Surely, both father and son knew that some intervention of fate had occurred. Only that could explain such an unlikely outcome. We mused that it would become a life-shaping moment in the young boy's life, and a moment of truth in the father's, too.

After all, of the three of them, the best chance for survival belonged to the dog. Clinging to the gunwales in cold water, not seeing any other boat on the fifteen-thousand-acre lake, the awful truth of their situation must have dawned on father and son with horror. And yet, the one person in all that country who *could* see them, albeit from two-and-a-half miles away, *did* see them. Kurt and I agreed that it was proof that sometimes, new leases on life are miraculously granted against impossible odds.

That kind of story could make a train of thought take an unscheduled track, and that's what mine did. Hearing about something so harrowing, so narrowly escaped, ended any fall funk that might've been attempting to overtake me. Before hearing the story from Kurt, I was a moper trying to resuscitate flagging spirits. Now, heading over the bridge and up Tough End Road, my gait quickened.

Thirty minutes later, a pack basket stuffed with everything from gauze to garbage bags, from Cloverine to Q-tips, was sitting in the back of my truck. I thought I was ready to go, but as usual, I ran back inside one more time. I came out with my 20-gauge Savage Fox shotgun, a fistful of shells, and a Ziploc freezer bag full of white perch. The excitement I knew the perch was going to produce in a certain friend of mine put a smile on my face for the ride out of town.

It was the kind of crisp fall day that breathed ambrosia into the soul. Like many fellow northerners, how hospitable I am toward the cold depends on the time of year. The chill that lingers too long beyond winter is a rude guest that has overstayed its welcome. But then time, and absence, and the summer's heat make the heart grow fonder. In October, the prodigal chill is welcomed home along with wool and down to kindle the inner flames.

The cool temperatures balanced perfectly with the body heat produced by hiking. Conditions were perfect for a trip to Township Unknown. There were no biting insects. The hardwoods hadn't yet shed their brilliant raiment. All the round-shouldered melancholy of the past few days withdrew in defeat on that trail.

Better to say route than trail. I doubt anyone could identify it as a trail anymore. The route I travel into Drummond's place is determined sometimes by memory, sometimes by topography, sometimes by compass. The route I travel out has twice been determined by stars.

Drummond would be expecting me, for sure. Even though the exact day and time wouldn't be known to him, this was roughly a scheduled visit. For a full decade I'd made the fall trip after my end-of-season chores had been put to bed. At this time of year Drummond would be as busy as a red squirrel doing something interesting that helped ready himself or his humble abode for winter. He might be rendering fish fat for lamp oil, making soap, skinning some critter or larger game animal, culling berries . . . or processing his eel harvest.

I've helped him do all of these in the past and have learned things each time that almost no one needs or cares to know about today. As far as I know, only Drummond prefers to live as he does, at a safe distance from plastic, electronics, telephones, and technology. His is a world of cast iron and canvas, double-bitted axes and rawhide strapping, wrought steel and wool, cedar sinews and hewn hemlock, brass lamps and basswood furniture. To watch him move about in this world has shown me what it once literally meant to be a self-made man.

A half-mile in from the old logging yard where I'd parked the truck, a plaintive chorus of cries and yelps broke the morning's calm. Had it been closer, I would've instinctively shouldered the shotgun. It continued for several seconds, then stopped for a time as I advanced. In the mud, next to the first brook I had to cross, I saw the tracks: A yearling deer was being chased by a pack of four to seven coyotes. As I stood there counting them, the blood-chilling din resumed.

I knew the situation was dire. The howling changed pitch and intensity as the deadly drama progressed from the chase to the kill. The coyotes had in some way gotten the drop on the deer. Maybe it was already injured, or not traveling close enough to its mother to receive her signs and direction. The worst part of it would be the carnage and waste. Coyotes would often leave their prey only partially eaten, still conscious while the life ticked out of them in labored beats.

I looked again at the number of tracks, then broke open the double-barreled Savage Fox and looked at the measly two shells full of #8 birdshot that I'd chambered earlier. A nineteen-year-old woman hiking in the Cape Breton Highlands of Nova Scotia recently had been overtaken by a pack of coyotes the same size as this one and brutally killed. She was a folk singer. It made headlines all across the Maritimes and Maine. If I encountered the pack whose prints I now studied, still bloodthirsty from a fresh kill and willing to go for broke, I wasn't sure how I'd fare with such pathetic munitions. Taking out the lead dog is the conventional wisdom, but if that didn't turn the pack, I wouldn't have a prayer of reloading in time. With such thoughts now crowding out the meditations of a perfect morning, I plodded on, nervously fingering the trigger guard of the 20-gauge.

The incident brought to mind the tragic wildlife event known as the Rolling Tier Slaughter. While tending his trapline, a guiding colleague made a gruesome discovery that changed the hearts and minds of guides, sportsmen, game biologists, naturalists, and conservationists alike.

Up to the year before this event, local guides were signing on to help with the newly instituted Animal Damage Control (ADC) program overseen by the Maine Department of Inland Fisheries and Wildlife. Whitetail deer populations had been in decline since the late 1970s—when the first packs of coyotes had migrated eastward from the prairies and America's breadbasket. Just as the new predator was making its debut, new, faster mechanical wood harvesting methods overcut too much deer wintering habitat. It was a perfect storm. Almost thirty years later, the deer census in much of Maine was in a death spiral, and a coyote control bill was passed in the Maine Legislature. The wheels of government, though slow, were finally turning. Meanwhile, conservation groups were successfully influencing the forest products industry with sustainable forestry ideas designed to preserve habitat. Promise finally loomed on the horizon.

The ADC was going into its third year and had already logged impressive successes. Deer counts and tag station harvest numbers were sharply on the rise. Then, a task force opposing the program (citing the potential risk of accidental snaring of endangered species) threatened legal action unless the ADC was cut off. Political winds blew and the management program and all its gains were scrubbed. The wheels of government, so slow to move in the first place, had once again seized up. Around Maine, crowded halls of growling citizens protested loudly. "If it had been a new strain of potato bug threatening the harvest instead of coyotes threatening the deer herd," they said, "you can bet your bottom dollar we would've been allowed to manage it." They were referring to the economic losses being suffered by historic sporting destinations due to decimation of the deer herd.

That year, even as the department abandoned the so-far successful program, the Passamaquoddy Tribe instituted its own. Reservation lands had a larger deer herd with more year-round open water—namely larger rivers—and now the tribe aimed to protect it.

It was around this time, in Fowler Township on the Maine side of the St. Croix River, that Master Guide, Bill Gillespie was checking the area known as Rolling Tier—a place deer used to cross to a deeryard on the Canadian side of the river. He had been discovering mangled deer carcasses there through the winter months—an average of three kills per week. The previous year, while the ADC was in force, he'd been hard-pressed to find a single deer kill all winter. As soon as it was repealed, they began to show up.

Bill saw what appeared to be humps pushed up against shelf ice in the river. There were also the usual tree parts, grass, and debris carried by moving ice as it breaks up. With binoculars, Gillespie was startled to identify the shapes of eight deer carcasses—and more were arriving by the minute. In no time, the count had risen to thirteen. That was when he went for help.

By pick-poling a canoe across the shelf ice and into open water, Gillespie and some friends used ropes to extract the dead deer, one by one. The final count was twenty-one. Guides and Game Wardens from both the Tribal Government and the State of Maine came to investigate the slaughter. The worst of the findings: The deer retrieved, in all likelihood, made up only a fraction of the total killed.

There was no good way to candy-coat this tale to the press. Coyotes, working in their typical pack size of four to seven, were traveling on the periphery of the wintering deer herd. Already vulnerable from winter conditions and a finite food supply, the deer were pushed and stressed by the ever-present predators. Gillespie had witnessed, in previous winters, coyotes behaving like sheep dogs, herding the deer toward desperation until finally, they jumped into the river.

That's what had happened here. At Rolling Tier, the coyotes sprung their trap, cornering the weaker members of the herd, almost all does and yearlings, and then pressed them to the river's edge. With no place to go but out on unsafe ice, they were quickly caught in a morass of fast current with shelf ice hemming them in on both sides. The coyotes might later be able to retrieve some flesh, but very likely, more deer were washed downstream under the ice than were found that day. The carnage had probably been going on for weeks. "A deer caught in that water with coyotes on both sides would stay there and die of hypothermia rather than get out and be overtaken by coyotes," Gillespie told a newspaper reporter.

None of the deer showed signs of any other means of meeting their deaths than drowning. Most of the does were carrying one or more fetuses. If the deer found were only a part of the total, and the unborn fawns were factored in, it would rank among the worst game slaughters in Maine history, one that had nothing to do with poaching rings. The Rolling Tier Slaughter, in bloody color photographs, became a placard for what can happen when game management measures are withdrawn. Meanwhile, the tribe was proving the worth of the program on the Reservation.

The somber epilogue to Rolling Tier was given by Gillespie in his final comment to the reporter: "It would be typical coyote behavior for the coyotes to now follow the surviving migratory animals back to the spring fawning grounds. There, they will eventually take the lambs (fawns) from the does, and a good number of does as well."

My musings on that awful incident, brought on by a pack of wailing coyotes, had gotten me a good distance along my way to my friend's cabin. Then came a related memory, only this one brought a smile. It was the day I presented Drummond with *Now or Never*, a painting by Philip Goodwin. I had rescued the print from a junk shop in mid-coast Maine.

Like many of Philip Goodwin's outdoor works, this one depicts a premise, giving the viewer what amounts to a starting point for the imagination. The painting appears to ask us, "What's going to happen next?"

In *Now or Never*, it is twilight in the woodsy setting at the edge of a frozen lake, where two hunters are staying in a snow-covered log cabin. One of the men, outside chopping a log for firewood, has been interrupted by a commotion on the lake. He has called to the other man, who has emerged with what appears to be a Winchester Model 94 30.30, the time-honored, classic, open-sighted deer rifle. The scene, from the woolens the men are dressed in to the wide-webbed, beavertail snowshoes stuck in the snow, is emblematic of any historic Maine hunting camp.

The man wielding the ax is pointing out onto the snow-covered lake. There, we see a buck deer, well bedecked in headgear, running across the lake, right to left. Close on his tail are three quadrupeds, which could either be coyotes or wolves, but the painting's vintage tips the scale toward timber wolves. And there, we are left in the lurch, wondering which of the many outcomes will ensue. The man with the rifle needs to take one more step away from the cabin so that he can see what his friend is pointing at. Then, if he's a good enough slap-shooter, he may get a decent shot off, but time is of the essence.

The painting also posits what he's going to aim at. Will he go for the buck or perhaps for the lead wolf? Philip Goodwin, friend to Will Rogers and Theodore Roosevelt, and illustrator of Jack London's *Call of the Wild*, has expertly and imaginatively framed a conundrum, which is now ours to decipher. It is a painting that looks well beyond itself, a mark of Goodwin's genius.

That the work went from a dustbin in a tourist trap to being admired every day by a man actually living the life of many of Goodwin's subjects, in a cabin bearing a strong resemblance to the one depicted in *Now or Never*, seemed to me the most fitting tribute to the artist.

Drummond put the painting in a place of honor—above and behind the wood cookstove. There it receives the southwestern light from two windows, causing the colors to change hues through the course of the day, to Drummond's endless delight. "He's gonna shoot the buck," he once said to me while sipping tea and staring up at the picture. "Better he gets the deer than they do," he added, nodding toward the wolf pack. Another time, he contradicted this. "The other fella's pointin' toward the dogs 'steada the deer. He wants him to shoot the wolves." I could see that he spends a lot of time studying his one window into Philip Goodwin.

Finally, as I neared the clearing that always makes my heart joyful, I realized, after all my daydreaming, that the yowling and yelping had faded and my nervous trigger finger had relaxed. "Kiskesasik," I said out loud, testing the sound of the word here in Township Unknown. Learning from Mihku that the word meant "garden plot" made the place even more alluring to me now. That's what it was for Drummond and Moses—a garden plot. For them, Kiskesasik was there to be tended, managed, sustained, and enhanced if they—and it—were to have a future. Now, that future belongs to just one man, as far as I know, and he is over eighty years old.

A gleeful Drummond Humchuck was pretty much assured this time. For one thing, I had the sundry supplies he loves to admire and comment on as each one comes out of the pack basket. I also had news from the world—the kind he loves best. And, I had fish!

Before I even broke the tree line to Drummond's dooryard, my nostrils flared at a stench I knew only too well. I scanned the clearing and, sure enough, a bear hide was stretched out, drying near the game pole. That meant that the thick layer of fat right under that hide, the product of a summer's feasting on beechnuts and berries, was now boiling down in a cauldron, producing a smell that could make you love skunk musk.

Off behind the bearskin I saw the smoke of a smoldering fire. Drummond stood up on the far side of it, red willow pipe clenched in his teeth, and called out, "Ready, Chum?"

It meant that he could use some help moving the heavy cauldron of rendered fat from the fire to a workable spot just inside the woodshed. It also meant that Drummond knew, within the narrowest margin, my arrival time. He takes the greatest pleasure in how this confounds me, then carries on as though I'd never left from the last visit. Not having seen my friend for five months, as I walked toward him I assessed him from head to foot, looking for any sign of injury or infirmity, any toll taken by age. I took into account the stamina he'd mustered to deal with the bear. Unless he shot it where it stood—an extreme unlikelihood—he'd dragged it some distance to get it home. He'd then winched it up on the game pole before skinning and butchering this bear, no small task for the fittest outdoorsman. And that's not to mention the painstaking removal of every ounce of fat. This gives Drummond his bear grease for soap, his boot lubricant, and bear meat for the winter. It takes a fair share of vim to do all that alone, and now, from the way he was moving, I had to conclude that he was as nimble as the first day we met, almost eleven years ago.

When we shook hands, his vise-like grip was accompanied by an extra gleam in his eye. "Hear them coyotes, Chum?"

I said I had, and told him they were close for a time, too close for my comfort.

"Figured that's what held ya up."

Even though I'm well used to his telepathy by now, or whatever it is that cues his awareness of my approach, it still flusters me that I can't divine his method. As he watched these thoughts travel across my face, it only brightened the gleam in his eye.

I slipped out of the pack basket straps and set it down. Drummond eyeballed it the way a child admires a wrapped Christmas present. We lifted the heavy grease pot to a low cribwork just under the eaves of the woodshed, where Drummond could deal with it after it cooled. Thinking that those white perch were probably close to thawing by now, I suggested we keep the fire going. Drummond gave me a double take. "Good 'nuff," he said. We each grabbed a piece of split ash off the woodpile and set it on the coals.

"Let's take a load off," he said, leading the way inside. When he opened the door, the smell of raspberry tea rushed out. It was Drummond's version of the red carpet treatment—homemade tea ready to serve to a guest who had just trekked a long way to see him. While he busied himself with teapot and cups, I took the perch out of the pack basket. When Drummond turned around and saw them, his eyebrows almost touched his hat brim. "Whooowee! Puh-itch!" When I told him I'd brought a few potatoes too, he said, "Fish 'n' chips! We'll have fish 'n' chips Chum!" and I wondered just how that colloquialism might've traveled to Township Unknown.

As my tea cooled, I began our ritual of reaching into the pack basket and bringing up one item at a time. Never has a Q-tip received such adulation. Who else goes googly-eyed over clothespins, Cloverine, and Bag Balm? When he thought I'd reached the bottom and he had a veritable store scattered all around the basswood chair he was seated in, I had one more surprise. Kurt Cressey had recently asked me to field test a pack basket shelf set up on doweled feet. It provides a space in the bottom of the basket (or a picnic basket) for a pie or pastry, while protecting it from the dunnage above it. In my freezer at home, I'd found four date squares left over from the last shore lunch of the season. When I removed the basket shelf and pulled out those squares, I thought that Drummond's eyebrows would knock his hat off.

"Yessah!" That was high praise from Drummond Humchuck, a man who is anything but verbose.

When we settled down to our tea, I led off with the story of the near-fatal incident on West Grand Lake. I had taken pains with Kurt to get all the details, such as the length of the boat, the horsepower of the motor, the size of the dog, and so forth. I knew I'd be retelling it to Drummond, who would ask these questions if the details weren't included. Even so, Drummond asked about the line of sight from the camp where the fateful angel was staying to the spot on the lake where the metal boat flipped. "From the camp, the man with the binoculars would've been facing due north, looking uplake about two-and-a-half miles," I said.

"The dog coulda swum that," Drummond said. "They'll swim miles in ice water if they hafta." When the story came to its happy conclusion, my friend relit his pipe and studied those hemlock rafters. This was his process of converting the story to a mental movie. He asked a few more questions, mostly for editing purposes, I imagined, then viewed it all once more to his satisfaction.

Over the long winter, he would view it again and again, considering different angles that might've made for alternate endings. For example, a distraction of no greater consequence than a sneeze might have prevented the man in the camp from looking out just at the right moment. A different roll of the boat as it capsized might've caused the man or the boy to take a knock on the head, rendering one or both of them unconscious. With so complicated a play of parts and possibilities, it would be hard to view happy endings like this one as coincidence, or mere good luck. That would reduce its meaning. Too many things had to coalesce in perfect timing to make this particular ending possible, which meant that the boy and his father were supposed to survive. The survivors must then ask why. How their lives will be affected thenceforth, begins there.

But this one story had only whet Drummond's appetite, and now he was looking to me for more. He knew from past fall visits that my richest store of tales came after a full season of guiding. I had him securely over a barrel now and decided to enjoy it. Not knowing if I'd fired all my guns, or if he might get to stock another movie into his mental vault for the cold months to come, Drummond puffed his pipe back into action and waited. I took my time, sipping my tea and sizing up the cozy, inner world of Drummond's cabin. He fidgeted in his chair several times, then finally blurted, "You want me to throw another stick on that fire outside, Chum?" I waited a good long time to answer. Then, I gave a long sigh and said, "Sit still, Drum. I'll do it." His face was aglow like the aurora borealis.

The fire that had been used for rendering bear fat was now close to becoming the perfect cook fire. I inspected the contraption that we had removed the cauldron from—a cauldron big enough to serve soup to a train yard of hobos. It was a skidder chain welded into a stand with legs that came up to a ten-inch steel ring. The heavy pot sat on this ring, perfectly positioned over the fire. It was ingenious. Knowing there was no MIG welding business within three hours of Township Unknown, and no oxyacetylene dealers either, I had to assume that this was a gift from Mihku, who apparently had many talents. When the time came, I'd cook my perch in a cast iron spider set on this marvelous cooking stand. For now, I'd let the fire perfect itself while I spun my second yarn for Drummond, the one I'd been saving up since July.

Even though the incident I was about to relate had only occurred two-and-a-half months prior to my current visit with Drummond, its real beginnings reached all the way back to January 19, 1996. That was when the tank barge *North Cape*, along with its tug boat, *Scandia*, went aground at Moonstone Beach in South Kingston, Rhode Island. It happened because of a fire in the *Scandia's* engine room. The *North Cape* lost its cargo of 828,000 gallons of No. 2 fuel oil into Block Island Sound and the Trustom Pond National Wildlife Refuge. The catastrophe illustrated, with painful clarity, how interdependent the links of the food chain are in a biodiverse ecosystem. Besides the untold lobsters and other shellfish killed immediately by the spill, 250 square miles of the Sound were indefinitely closed off to fishing.

Then, as with all oil spills, there's the bird life. It turned out that this was prime wintering habitat for *Gavia immer*, the Common Loon, branded forever in the minds of Maine tourists as an emblem of the state's pristine rivers and lakes. By the most conservative estimates, 400 wintering loons were killed in the *North Cape* oil spill.

When the legal fallout settled, the US Fish and Wildlife Service (USFWS) would administer the funds paid out in damages by the responsible parties. The scale of the disaster to wintering birds was so massive at the site that the focus for redevelopment of loon populations shifted to their breeding habitats. In the Grand Lakes region of Maine, the USFWS helped the Downeast Lakes Land Trust (DLLT) and the New England Forestry Foundation (NEFF) purchase conservation easements considered to be prime areas for loon propagation. The next order of business was to establish a baseline of loon density, breeding activity, and survival rates along the 445 miles of shoreline acquired by these groups.

Beginning in 2001, an intern was hired for twelve weeks each summer to collect data for what came to be known locally as "the loon survey." Volunteer guides who were willing to work at approximately half their guide's rate assisted in the survey by ferrying the interns around to dozens of different bodies of water. Interns and guides carried 10X binoculars as they motored, paddled, and sometimes walked to far-flung nesting sites in the St. Croix, Machias, East Machias, and Dennys River watersheds.

Up till then, it was easy for all of us to take loons for granted as the perfect photo-op for sports, the lilting soundtrack to summer vacations, or the strikingly beautiful panhandler at the perch hole. Now, it was learned, Maine's 1,400 breeding pairs of loons needed help. Shoreline development, mercury in the water, drought, and other factors were causing a slow loss of population, and that was even before the *North Cape* spill.

With some exceptions, loons prefer to breed and raise chicks near lakes larger than sixty acres. Of the forty-six lakes that were under study in the Downeast Lakes region, nearly three-quarters of them are suitable for loon nesting. Since loons are clear-water predators that must be able to see prey in order to catch them, pristineness is yet another qualifier for habitat. Loons are even pickier when it comes to nesting sites. Lakes with wild, irregular shorelines interrupted by rock outcroppings, blowdowns, and tiny cove-lets are choice, as are lakes sprinkled with small islands. A typical nesting location might be the lee side of such an island, with a broad view. Another favorite is a floating hummock—a raft of moss and other vegetation, which allows protection from fluctuations in water levels.

Loons are members of the Gavidae family of rump-footed birds, ill-suited for walking on land. Bobcats, fishers, otters, and coyotes are lethal threats to onshore nests, which don't offer good visibility and underwater escape routes. Loons have even been known to take over a muskrat house or beaver lodge that has these attributes.

Once the chicks hatch, the shallows within close range of the nest provide a nursery where four- to six-inch perch and other forage can be easily caught. Survivorship is measured by the number of chicks that make it to September, divided by the number of chicks hatched in late spring.

In the second year of the loon survey, drought conditions were threatening reproduction. If water levels going into winter are low, followed by poor snowpack and low spring melt, loons find far fewer promising nesting sites. Breeding then drops dramatically. It was precisely this scenario that unfolded in 2002. Jay Beaudoin, Environmental Superintendent of then-Domtar Industries in Baileyville, Maine, headed up a program to artificially enhance breeding habitat.

"The problem for loons," Jay said at the time, "is that reproduction and birthing rates can be impacted by a six-inch fluctuation in water levels. They depend on the vegetative fringe, or emergent as well as submerged vegetation near the shoreline, for nesting material, refuge, and reproduction. An unexpected fluctuation of six inches or more of water level can either flood or leave loon nests high and dry. This year we were looking at high and dry."

Placement of nesting sites was therefore crucial. The usual sites chosen by loons would be endangered due to low water by summer, making the chicks vulnerable to high predation. Twelve nesting platforms were donated by Domtar and built by Jay's environmental engineering department. They were of cedar log construction, with a galvanized wire mesh in the middle, measuring four feet by four feet, mimicking the floating hummocks sometimes sought out by breeding pairs. Guides and volunteers harvested moss and wetland grasses to build nesting beds on these rafts before they were strategically placed in known loon nesting areas. The sites of the twelve platforms ranged from the St. Croix Flowage to Lewey and

Long Lakes, to West Grand Lake and Pocumcus Lake. The group effort helped to salvage what might've been a net loss in successfully breeding pairs in 2002.

In 2006, the Biodiversity Research Institute (BRI) based in Gorham, Maine, joined the loon survey, contributing standardized methods of gathering and measuring loon data. That year was the opposite of 2002, with high water and flooding during the peak of nesting season. In 2006, Maine Audubon reported the second lowest chick survival rate in its twenty-three years of study. The work to monitor, measure, and enhance territorial breeding pairs of loons still continues.

When veteran master guide Kim Vose set out from the landing at West Musquash Lake in Talmadge Township that July morning in 2008, he was happy to be with his favorite among the many fine loon survey interns he'd guided over the years. Up in the bow, Jessie Tompkins-Howard, an Adventure Recreation major at Washington County Community College, was already juggling data from dozens of nesting sites spread over an enormous portion of Washington County. She could tell you how the twins born on the beach at Mud Lake were doing. She knew whether the mother loon nesting in The Bog in Dyer Cove on West Grand Lake had one or two chicks this year; which of the Domtar-donated floating nests had been annexed by a breeding pair; how many shore nests versus island nests there were; and whether there had been any predations. Information like this comprised the loon survey currency Jessie dealt in daily.

Pretty and petite, the strawberry blonde barely made enough ballast in the bow of Kim's Grand Laker, but her sunny smile and bright wit made great company for any of the guides who worked with her. That morning, I had seen Kim and Jessie leaving from The Pine Tree Store parking lot as I headed to West Grand Lake with my sports for the day. When the wind came up in force that afternoon, causing us to seek shelter in the lee of Hardwood Island, I figured Kim and Jessie were out in the same gale on West Musquash, ten miles due north of us.

Because of the amount of area to cover and data to collect, loon survey days don't include a shore lunch. It's a packed lunch, often eaten on the fly. Kim and Jess worked their way around the shoreline in relative calm. There is a litter of small, loon-enticing islands positioned in the southern end of West Lake Bay. That part of the workday afforded protection from the big sweep of the northwest wind. As the day wound to a close and Jessie was up to date on loon activity, the long downwind run to the boat landing began.

Motoring with the wind, which served up a following sea, the day was warm with full sun highlighting the froth on the crests of the rollers. In such conditions, the Grand Laker rides the waves while the guide provides ruddering with the outboard. The temperature had risen enough so that Kim had taken his shirt off and draped it over the first thwart between the stern and the amidships seat. In the bow, Jessie rose and dipped with the peaks and troughs, lulling her into a pleasant drowse.

That peaceful interlude was about to shatter.

As the shadows lengthened and the wind continued to kick up, the first chill of late afternoon registered on Kim's back. His shirt was just far enough away that Kim had to rise ever-so-slightly from his seat to reach for it. When he did, he let go of the tiller of the eight-horsepower Johnson outboard for a split second.

In that same split second, a rogue gust of wind caught the canoe's bow, turning it one way, which turned the motor the other. Kim reached for the tiller that had just been there, but now wasn't. Poised precariously, and caught off-balance between a standing and sitting position, the momentum of the suddenly lurching canoe threw him over the side directly into the path of the still-running outboard.

The Johnson propeller found Kim's back, dug in, and rototilled until the blades fetched up, the effect of which was to violently jolt the outboard off the stern of the Grand Laker. It left two deep grooves where it had been clamped to the metal stern plate, but the propeller blades left more than that on Kim's back.

The scene took place in the time it takes a camera to flash. Jesse watched helplessly from the bow as the motor struck Kim, jumped off the canoe, and sank unceremoniously to the bottom of West

Musquash Lake. In seconds, she was blown far downwind of where Kim, still apparently conscious, was afloat. A red halo, like a circle marking the spot, widened around him.

As if struck by a lightning bolt, Jessie duck-walked her way to the stern of the canoe where the paddle was, balancing herself by holding the gunwales of the canoe on both sides. When she reached the paddle, she about-faced and turned the bow of the canoe into the wind.

The force of the northwest wind, in disguise up to then as a friendly escort, fought every ounce of Jessie's energy. She began to make headway in inches. Everything was loud and yet deafeningly quiet at the same time. How Jessie Tompkins-Howard summoned the strength in such an adverse sea to reach the seriously injured guide that day must join a long list of inexplicable wilderness mysteries. Even so, reaching him meant that only half the battle had been won.

Kim, in pain but unaware of how badly he was hurt, flailed his arms to grab the approaching canoe. He couldn't see that the water downwind of him was stained red with his blood. He and Jessie yelled back and forth, hatching the plan to get him into the canoe. It was the standard method of entry, known to them both, but difficult enough to execute in calm water, much less when the rescuer's weight was half that of the victim.

Kim hand-over-handed his way to the middle of the canoe, his feet dangling under him, his back shedding blood as each skin flap opened and shut as waves buffeted his back. Jessie maneuvered into the middle of the canoe, facing Kim. She braced her back against the gunwale opposite him, then placed her feet next to Kim's hands. Bending her knees, she leaned forward. On a count, Kim let go of the canoe and grabbed her hands. When she felt the grip tighten, she threw herself backward; and the pretty, petite, strawberry blonde was somehow able to yard a man nearly twice her size into the canoe like a gaffed halibut.

Pools of blood instantly formed on the floor between the cedar ribs of the Grand Laker. If Jessie lost her breath or felt her eyes well up at seeing the full extent of Kim's wounds, she concealed this behind the business at hand. She turned him, positioned his back against the middle thwart, placed a towel there, and ordered him to press his body against it, hard. Kim obeyed. She now took paddle in hand, righted the canoe in the downwind direction of the landing, and leaned into her work. Kim fell into twilight consciousness, seeing events as though they were oddly disconnected from him. Jessie, knowing she needed to keep Kim conscious, tried some self-deprecating humor. "We'd be at the landing already if I didn't paddle like a girl," she jibed.

Jessie paddled the Grand Laker the remaining mile and a half to the boat launch, where she helped Kim out of the canoe and into his truck's passenger seat. It was a forty-eight-mile ride to Calais Regional Hospital's emergency room, the first ten of which were over logging roads. They were even stopped and made to wait at a construction site. The saturated towel stayed wadded up behind Kim's back as he wavered between grasping the seriousness of his situation and thinking it was all a dream. After they arrived and Kim was admitted, Jessie stayed at the hospital until word came back that Kim, despite the loss of blood and a lot of pain and stitching, would survive.

I told Drummond what I believed he already knew—that one split second makes no blemish on a forty-year guiding career. Kim had always been a good guide, and would now be a better one. The fickle winds of calamity can blow on anyone at any time, and the guide who has been humbled by happenstance carries greater caution to his work than the untested and unscathed. Drummond nodded his agreement.

The news from West Musquash Lake traveled the word-of-mouth speedway to every guide in Grand Lake Stream and beyond. The very next morning after her West Lake ordeal, Jessie was in front of The Pine Tree Store waiting to be picked up by her guide for the day when I pulled up to meet my sports. Though we had never met, I approached her, introduced myself, and extended my hand.

"Jessie—you're my new hero."

"No, no," she blushed. "No, but thank you just the same. I'm not a hero."

"Well, I beg to differ, and I'm very proud to make your acquaintance."

A few weeks later, well on the road to a full recovery, Kim threw a barbeque in Jessie's honor. Friends, fellow guides, and family members attended to thank the young intern for saving Kim's life. Jessie, as taciturn and unassuming as ever, was graciously uncomfortable in the spotlight. Early the next morning, she was at her post in the bow of a Grand Laker taking pictures of the twin chicks on Mud Lake, hoping they'd be big enough by fall to make their migration south.

Drummond Humchuck must've said, "Ain't them puh-itch some good!" six or seven times before we were through. Then, he was in for another treat. We'd found out years before that we shared date squares as our favorite dessert. When we'd finished them, there wasn't a morsel left for mice.

The days were much shorter now than on my last visit, so I timed my departure with the sun's first tinge of orange, before it began its descent in earnest. Just before that happened, I got up my nerve for the question I'd been planning to ask my friend all day. I'd learned that a rich repertoire of music lay dormant in Drummond, only awaiting some catalyst to awaken it. This time, I decided to be that catalyst.

"You in the mood for whistling, Drum?" At this, the shadow that had begun to cross his face, as it always does when my leaving draws near, vanished.

"What tune?" he asked. I knew that by requesting one of my favorite melodies, I'd also be testing Drummond. Each time he whistled, something new was revealed. Each song was a window into his past, dating him, and pairing him up with times, people, and things he'd been influenced by during his long life. I asked him if he knew *The Water is Wide*.

Before I could explain myself, Drummond cocked his chin toward the rafters, and formed, with odd-looking contortions of his mouth, the first reed he'd already selected to interpret the Scottish folk ballad. I followed his performance, whispering the lyrics under my breath:

The water is wide; I can't cross o'er,
And neither have I wings to fly.
Give me a boat that can carry two,
And both shall row, my love and I.

There is a ship and she sails the sea
She's loaded deep, as deep can be;
But not as deep as the love I'm in,
And I know not how I sink or swim.

Love is gentle and love is kind,
The sweetest flower when first it's new.
But love grows old and waxes cold
And fades away like morning dew.

As usual, when he'd blown the last notes with extra vibrato for effect, the ones corresponding to the repetition of the chorus, "And both shall row, my love and I," we sat listening to those notes echoing out through the firs and spruce of Township Unknown. I was going to ask how he knew such a song. I was going to ask where he was when he first heard it. I was going to tell him how many different versions of it I'd heard. I was going to, until Drummond's performance made an absurdity of any such chatter. Instead, I waited with him the customary time for the music to wash over us, then stood, extending my hand.

"I can't tell you how much that meant to me Drum. Please be careful eelin'," I added. "And tell Mihku I'll catch up with him this winter." With that, I put my arms through the straps of my much lighter pack basket and strode onto the trail before turning around to wave. Drummond raised his pipe and sat down in his chair by the open door. When I found my pace, *The Water is Wide* was still resounding in those woods.

A Changing Landscape

As winter approached, keeping my movements closer to home, I settled in to read *The Poacher's Son* and its sequel, *Trespasser*, by Paul Doiron. One aspect of these very engaging crime fiction novels really caught my eye. An older couple is being given an ultimatum by a new investment company/landowner to either buy their beloved lease lot on a remote lakeshore, or lose it. It's not that retired game warden Charlie Stevens and his wife wouldn't try to buy the lot if they could. They can't afford it. The fictitious owner of Charlie's lease lot is demanding a price befitting glim-and-glitter vacation destinations. Their little piece of Eden is miles out on a logging road, deep in the willywacks. Charlie and his wife are at retirement age, and we are left feeling their pain, as it appears they'll be bullied off the place by an invisible investor group.

It was too close for comfort to my own situation, only in my case, there was nothing fictitious about it. Like Charlie Stevens in Doiron's novels, I had over thirty years invested into what used to be known in Maine lease lot language as a "primitive campsite." You didn't need to be rich to have one as long as you met the terms and conditions of the lease. I felt a kinship to those who came before me, since the place had served as guides' site, lunchground, layover/shelter, and hunting and fishing camp for over eighty-three years.

As the current lessee, I was but one in a long line who kept the place essentially the same for the better part of a century. Pop Moore and Earl Bonness, friends of mine when I was young, had built the structures on the lakeshore in 1929, when they were nineteen years old. They'd been visiting my thoughts a lot lately. Neither one could've made enough canoes, paddles, or axes, nor guided enough days in their lifetimes, to afford the price tag the new investor group had placed on the lot. And neither could I.

Back during the summer, when I was at the bottom of despair over this gathering storm, unable to sort out my jumble of confused thoughts, Agnes arrived. I got the call from a local lodge in mid-July to guide the eighty-three-year-old widow of a man I'd only guided once. The lodge owner told me she had asked for me. Agnes had not been part of her husband's fishing trips here throughout his adult life. When I guided him, he was in his late seventies and a little rickety on his feet. Up till then, he'd fished on his own. After he passed, Agnes decided on a pilgrimage to discover Grand Lake Stream, the mere mention of which always put a glint in her husband's eye. Now, she meant to see why.

In the sporting lodge the morning we met, she came out of the dining room with a handful of pamphlets and brochures on the conservation efforts going on throughout the region. I hoped they were going to get stowed in her cabin before we left, but instead she brought them along. Because of my own trouble with this topic, I began planning my distraction strategies.

Once we were in the canoe, the first thing Agnes did was to inquire about the latest conservation news. Agnes asked me about these projects, wondering whether a gift in her husband's name might be the perfect, crowning gesture of her pilgrimage here.

"Sure," I said, but right away, in my voice or on my face, Agnes detected the very hitch I was determined to hide.

She asked for details, and wanted to know how the projects were being received. She wanted assurance that it was something Milton would have approved of. It was only 8:30 in the morning, and I was swallowing hard. Every attempt I made to gently redirect the conversation, calling her attention to every duck, loon, or bullfrog, failed.

Finally, Agnes, who unlike me was very direct, sat up in her seat and said, "I can see you're conflicted. May I ask why?" I swallowed hard once more.

"I apologize. It's true. I try to avoid the topic. In my position, I should want everything conserved, shouldn't I? The more things remain the way they are, the better, right?" Pensively, Agnes watched a pretty stretch of shoreline pass. I followed her eyes and admired it, too, wondering for the thousandth time how I could have any objection to making sure everything stayed just this beautiful. And wondering, too, whether it was that, or some other objection that stuck in my craw.

"Who is the new landowner?" she asked, a question that used to be an easy one to answer.

"I don't know," I said.

Facing me from the bow of the canoe, Agnes trapped the butt section of her trolling rod between her knees, raised both hands into the air, and said, "You don't know?"

I made my best effort to explain that the days of family ownership of giant swaths of Maine woodlands, and paternalistic companies who stewarded the forest for generations, are mostly over now. Replacing them are consortiums of investors who are often known collectively by some generic name. In most cases, that name is followed by the abbreviation "LLC," or limited liability company. The LLC shields them not only from many kinds of liabilities, but also from the public, who may never know who the investor-landlords are who own all the land around them.

That, I told her, had happened here. I said, too, that there are no laws compelling an LLC to disclose the identities of its investors, a nice feature if you're profiting from lands destined for preservation. I said that since it flies under the flag of conservation, it can be very attractive to investors or investor groups who worry about their image. I explained that after a specified time, and after being thoroughly logged to reap value for the investors, the lands would be purchased by a land trust. It was win-win, since the investors would make money twice—first from the wood harvesting and second, from the sale to the local land trust, which could then boast a new acquisition to its other saved tracts. Agnes listened patiently, then studied more stretches of shoreline without saying a word. This went on so long, I was certain I'd offended her.

Finally, she sat straight up in her seat. "Saved from what?"

"Development," I said, mechanically.

"Yes . . ." she almost whispered, then neither of us spoke for another stretch of shoreline.

That morning, we lolled and trolled through different coves and streams, wandering into Tribal Reservation lands and back out again. Agnes preferred fishing this way, because, as, she told me, it "left her mind free to lollygag."

"It must have been exactly this way for the Indians," she said as we passed a stunning batch of glacial erratic rock formations on shore.

"What do you mean?" I asked, looking with her at those magnificent, eleven-thousand-year-old deposits.

"I'm talking about watching all the land around them be taken over by white men, big chunks at a time." Then, as if jouncing herself out of a daydream, she sat up in her seat even more, which I knew by now was my signal to pay attention. I was up to my old habit of guessing professions, picking up teacher notes from Agnes.

"Tell me this: As you understand it, after the invisible investors are through with the land, sell it to the land trust, and make their money, will an average, working person ever be able to have something—a cabin or fishing shack—on those lands?"

"No," I said.

"Then who do those belong to?" she asked, pointing to some camps along the lakeshore.

"To people who were already here, leasing the land before. They were offered a price to buy their leases."

Agnes started using her rod tip as a pointer now, raising and flicking it for emphasis, giving my teaching theory more credence.

"That will be quite the exclusive club," she said, sweeping the rod up in an arc. "If you were lucky enough to have been here already and can afford the price to stay, or can buy someone out who can't, you get to be in this club." This got two rod flicks, and now I was sure she'd been a teacher.

"But it will still *look* the way it does now," I said, repeating the conservation mantra that had been unable to unravel my own tangle of thoughts.

"Yes. I read that in the brochures. This is supposed to be the point that reconciles everything. That the land not owned by existing camp owners will be preserved, and open to visitors. We have to think of many of those visitors as admirers, don't we? Admirers, and dreamers who might've one day wished that they, too, could have something, however modest, on a lakeshore, too. And that's when they'll realize that they can participate in this lovely place a little less than the privileged few."

I was surprised by the sharp edge in this gentle woman's tone. We drifted through a narrows that lead back out of reservation territory into the open lake. Riffles made gentle slapping sounds against the sides of the canoe.

I stared at Agnes, probably for too long. I wondered if the eighty-three-year-old woman had any inkling that she was dynamiting a logjam. Up to this day, I'd wondered what this problem of mine was over something that sounded so good and yet caused me some unnamable grief.

Agnes took a deep breath as if to go on, but if there's one thing fish love to do, it's interrupt a conversation. The report from the rod tip startled Agnes so much that the butt section slipped out of her hands and went over the side, in response to a formidable pull from the other end. I had a split second to make a swoop with my right hand and came up with it, even though the canoe nearly upset in the process. I hit the kill switch on the outboard, then leaned forward, passing the butt section back to Agnes. "Oh my!" she said, now feeling the strength of whatever she had hooked.

"Reel, Agnes! Reel!" I heard a heavy splash behind me and saw Agnes's eyes widen. I turned around only in time to see the rings and bubbles. From this, and the arc of her rod, I knew this was a heavy fish.

"Oh my!" she called out again.

"Are you OK, Agnes? Can I help you?"

"I'm OK. I think—I think I can do this." She was in fact making progress, and now the second showing was so close to the canoe, I felt a few drops of water splash onto my neck.

"You must have it well-hooked," I cheered as Agnes steered the lunker in close. I half-stood in the stern of the canoe for a longer reach, if necessary. Very often, after one pass close to the canoe, a fish will bolt, a moment that vastly increases the likelihood of losing it. When I saw that pass coming, I swung the rubber mesh pole net in front of its path, lifted, and came up with Agnes's bass. It was the luckiest pass of the season, though I didn't mention that to Agnes.

She clapped, calling out, "Bravo! Bravo!"

I was grateful to the nineteen-inch, four-and-a-half pound smallmouth for helping us remember why we were here. I decided to lengthen that reprieve with lunch. We chose an island close by, one vulnerable to almost any wind, but on a calm day like this one, a Shangri-la. I knew the island because I knew the owners of the single camp on it, and only then did I realize my choice of lunchgrounds played right into the topic that had been floating with us all morning. Still flushed from the bass bout she'd just fought and won, the very fit and agile Agnes knelt down and splashed water on her face at the beach, then ambled slowly down the shore admiring the place.

"Who owns this island?" she called back to me as I readied the site. I had to swallow hard again. It was another Charlie Stevens story—the same mystery mix of investors owned this island, too. Agnes had distinguished herself as someone who wouldn't suffer even the kindest deception. I told her that these camp owners were close to her age and could lose the place. A sum of money, which clearly leveraged their sentimental attachment to it against them, had been asked, and it was of course a sum they could never afford. If they defaulted, it theoretically could be torn away, and with it, four generations of family history and heritage. When I'd finished, the closest thing to a frown I'd seen all day stole across Agnes's face.

"Agnes, we don't need to—"

"Maybe it's time we stopped saying *saved.*"

I was now sure of my private wager. "Agnes, are you by any chance a retired teacher?"

Her lined, pretty face opened into an infectious smile. "Is it that obvious?"

"Well, it's just that I see a lot of people, and I play this game of guessing their line of work."

Agnes laughed again. "You've gotten good at it, too. English Literature, twenty-nine years. Guilty as charged."

Now I imagined Agnes stalking the lecture hall like the conductor of a symphony, flicking a pointer for emphasis just the way she used the trolling rod I'd lent her. I was satisfied, thinking I'd steered her off a troubling topic, but she wasn't about to abandon her train of thought.

"These are such lovely words, aren't they?" she said, clearly enunciating each one. "*Save. Preserve. Trust.*" Agnes's tone carried the gravity of years. She seemed to be awaiting a response, perhaps from the armada of cloud formations she was staring at.

"Many good folks would agree that they are," I said. As the fire crackled and the tin coffee pot sputtered, I stabbed at the coals with my hookaroon as though there might be an answer hiding among them. Agnes came around and sat down beside me on the end of the picnic table seat.

"Look, I came up here to see the place my husband loved, and now I know why he loved it. To him, it was different than anyplace else." She paused long enough to watch an osprey take off from the top of a widowmaker on the opposite shore, then soar over the island. We both followed its flight between tree lines. There was something dangling from its talons.

"What we're talking about would've saddened my Milton, the same as it saddens you. It's time I told you a little about him . . .

"Milton did well for himself and we had a good life—the businessman who never went to college and his college professor wife who admired him more than anyone. A son of immigrants, he came from nothing. His was a poor, hard-working family, from a hardscrabble, eastern Massachusetts town. That never left him. Even when he owned his own tool and dye company and it became successful, and even with our combined incomes, we never moved out of the same little house, because he couldn't. He mowed the lawns around his business himself, not because he was cheap and didn't want to pay someone else to do it, but because he never wanted to think of those things as being beneath him. Milton never forgot who he was and where he came from—a rare trait among self-made men. I can almost imagine what he'd say if he were here, in this canoe with us." Agnes then paused, as though listening to what Milton was saying.

"He'd say if you own something, own up to it. A man like Milton could give no quarter to secret owners. Then, in a very few words, he'd explain what was happening here so that it was no longer confusing. He was good at that, much better than me—at pulling the wool away from people's eyes. He'd say that the land is changing hands twice; once for the profit of the invisible investors, and again for somebody's idea of what its future should be. For good measure, and to help sell the concept, they'll say that they're preserving the local way of life—I saw that in the brochure." Agnes stood up, gesturing back toward the camp on the island. ". . . Only these people won't be around to remind us what that way of life was before it got *saved*, will they?"

If Milton was good at pulling away wool, Agnes was his rival. She'd pulled away more wool in one morning than I'd been able to in two years. That afternoon in the canoe, feeling as if I'd known her much longer than I had, an old fog continued to lift thanks to Agnes. In return, I did some sharing of my own.

I told her after lunch about camp owners who'd written heartfelt *To Whom it May Concern* letters to the unknown investors. I'd read those letters. Some were like prayers. Others were pleas. Some came from people just like her husband, Milton.

The letters told of teams of horses dragging a building across the ice on skids. Then, local guides positioned it onshore where succeeding generations have preserved it for a hundred years. They told of camps having been built during the Great Depression on the proceeds of logging birch and maple destined to become bowling pins, camps that could then be used to guide sports in the days when nearly every able-bodied man in Grand Lake Stream was a guide.

"I have the word!" she interrupted. Only then did it dawn on me that all this time, Agnes had been thinking of a better word than the "lovely" ones used in the brochures.

"Gentrification!" she said, triumphantly. "It was the reason I asked earlier if an average working person would ever be allowed to do what those early guides did, and build something modest. We know now that they won't, but those lakeshore properties will still exist in the *saved, preserved* future—owned only by those who can afford them. That's what I meant when I said that most will get to enjoy this beautiful place a little less than the lucky few. That, my dear man, is gentrification. The old way of life is replaced, maybe not tomorrow, but eventually, and not by anyone like the people who dragged those buildings across the ice in the first place. No one ever believes that's what's actually happening." Agnes pulled a kerchief from her jacket pocket and gave it a flick toward her shoulder. "How'd I do, Milton?" Then she looked back at me, eyes glistening wet, and said, "I wish you'd have gotten to know him better."

Looking back on that July day during my winter mulling, I knew that Agnes and I talked more before going in. I knew that wherever our conversation wandered, I marveled at how my professor/sport was able to order an undifferentiated jumble of thoughts into something comprehensible. I knew that in the end, I told Agnes I hoped she would keep in touch and come back next season. I said I hoped I hadn't sullied her pilgrimage by taking up so much of our day talking about the big, sweeping changes that had occurred since Milton's passing. She said she had loved every minute of her day on the lakes and had no regrets at all. I believed her. The season had long since ended, and it was close to Christmas when Agnes's letter arrived. With her permission, I share some of it here:

> I must apologize to you for an offense you had no idea was being committed against you. It was hardly what you deserved after showing me the most wonderful day I've had since my Milton passed away. It was a lie by omission, the easiest of all to rationalize.
>
> You may remember that I cried that day, but briefly. It was when I was telling you what Milton would've said. That was my sin. It was not what Milton would've said. It was what he did say. It came right through me, almost word for word, after hearing you out that day in the canoe and on that island.
>
> No, Milton was not speaking to me from the grave. He had actually spoken those words from a podium at a town meeting here in Massachusetts three years before he died. At the time he spoke them, he had already received his diagnosis of non-Hodgkin's lymphoma.
>
> What you are faced with all the way up there on the Canadian border is what we were faced with here back then. There were beautiful, undeveloped lands and lakes surrounding our town, owned by the same few families since the 1800s. There were leases on that land that were older than anyone alive could remember. Milton's one extravagance during our fifty-seven-year marriage was to have taken over one of those leases when it was offered by an aging widow, who had retired from Milton's company and needed the money. There were wonderful walks, streams, ponds, and a quarry where Milton especially loved to go.
>
> When modern descendants of those old New England families began to sell off bits and pieces of the lands, the cry rose up from the town fathers that we were "endangered." If developers came in, they said, it could ruin the heritage and character of our town.
>
> A committee of volunteers was formed and that committee evolved into a land trust board of directors. Coincidentally, some board members owned land adjacent to the tracts that they said were endangering us. In other words, they had something of their own that needed saving, too.

I won't repeat the details of what happened, because you already know them. During our day together, I'm ashamed to say, I playacted. I knew what you were going to say before you said it. The questions I asked came from what had transpired here, and you merely confirmed for me that it was following a similar pattern.

Milton's voice was a candle in the wind. He was accused of everything from being self-serving, since we had one of the leases, to being in cahoots with developers poised and ready to pounce. But they had him all wrong. The idea of buying up all the land to save it put Milton's blue collar, populist fur up like nothing else could. There were people who agreed with him that the heritage and character of our town was not something you could bottle and save by controlling who owned what. They just didn't speak up. Milton refused to pay the exorbitant price placed on our cherished lease, but someone else did, and now their piece of the kingdom is secure. Milton bore no ill will against them. In fact, he bore no ill will against anyone, but you'd never know it from some of the savage things that were said about him after he made his speech.

So, did it save our town? Well, we're safely preserved and protected from whatever foreboding future was headed our way, except that the "us" and the "we" are almost gone now. Taxes drove most of the old, working-class residents away, and most of the people remaining perform service work for those affluent enough to have bought their way in. My little shoebox house looks pretty incongruous now, and I'm sure when I'm gone, it will go, too.

To Milton, your neck of the woods was different. I'm thankful it remained so as long as he knew it. He said he wished he'd discovered it earlier in his life. I know he fantasized that a younger Milton might've gone there, carved out something simple on a lakeshore, and found his own piece of heaven. I guess we both know it couldn't happen now. I don't mean to say that all conservation is bad. There are wonderful efforts that I support, and Milton did, too. It's just that there's an unacknowledged shadow side to some of them.

I'm sorry I deceived you. I just want you to know that there was someone else who went through what you're going through, and that there's at least one kindred spirit even if she's just an old lady. No matter what happens, don't forget, as Milton used to say, there are blessings all around you that you haven't counted yet.

Every so often a day comes along that stands apart from all the others. It arrives bearing gifts that seem undeserved. They are such a rare and pleasant surprise, these enchanted days of peace and lucidity, that over-scrutinizing them would be like pulling the wings off a swallowtail butterfly for a closer look at its beauty.

Agnes's letter came on one of those days, and I finished reading it feeling grateful to her.

I wrote back over the holidays. My response turned out to be a long overdue exercise in wrestling my misgivings to the mat. I knew that despite the claim that things would remain forever unchanged—a claim too bold for mortals—they of course wouldn't. It didn't take a college professor like Agnes to come to that conclusion. The signs were already afoot.

The newest landowners were presiding not only over a preserved vastness, but over vacancy. A ghost of its former self, the increasingly quiet town gave proof of times and trends greater than anyone's power to resist. Protecting the old way of life, the old economy, the traditions of a historic inland lakes and woodlands culture was not possible, not by preventing development, and not even by controlling who owned what.

Land, its uses, and ownership were all changing irreversibly, and that trend was big enough to eclipse both credit and blame. Thanks to Agnes, I was now less conflicted on this point. If there were to be a Maine wilderness at all for future generations, it would be in the form of kingdoms, refuges, parks, and trusts. Some would restrict access, some wouldn't. This future might be regrettable in some ways, but it was also unstoppable—as unstoppable as the shifting of other epochs in Maine's history.

There are aging leather sole stitchers still alive in Maine who watched their industry, an epicenter of shoe making, move to Asia. The Bangor Haymarket Square lumbering heyday, so beautifully depicted in many Tom Hennessey artworks, must have seemed like it would last forever, too. As if to symbolize the erasure of that epoch, Paul Bunyan's statue stands today on State Street in Bangor with a coliseum at his back, and a casino in front, blocking his view of that iconic Maine lumbering artery, the Penobscot River.

I felt indebted to Agnes, who'd arrived like that old Serenity Prayer about accepting the things we can't change. Agnes is not among the blessings I forget to count. I've saved the last passage of her letter to share here:

> *Milton saw how things would change, and was wise enough to know he couldn't stop it. But that's not where Milton stopped. He knew where he had to stand to be true to who he was, and to his own ideals. That's why he spoke up when he did. If he didn't do that, he wouldn't have been the Milton I loved, with the fierce, egalitarian spirit.*
>
> *In those final days before we lost our beloved lease, we spent such time there as Milton's strength would allow. On one of those last walks, he mused that the Native Americans had it right. Owning the land, he said, was an illusion anyway. That's what I was thinking the day we spent together.*

Two seasons later, I was able to write to Agnes and tell her that after a four-year stalemate with the new landowner, we were able to come to an agreement based on a much-reduced price for our "primitive campsite." Its long life as a guide's outpost and landing would be continued. Agnes wrote back that she was happy not only for her own part, but on behalf of Milton. We continue to correspond, her health is good, and she plans to come lollygag for another day soon.

BEYOND THE MAELSTROM

Guides who work the waters of their region every day for weeks and months on end can't process the steady stream of people and experiences at the time that they happen. They can do the jobs all right, but must reflect on them later. The guide is there in body and mind each day, paying full attention, but the brain is registering things to be contemplated further down the road, when there's time.

That time is winter. The first presentiment of it was already happening as I walked out the trail from Township Unknown after a late fall visit, arriving at my truck just after dark. One of the first frosts of fall was descending onto the slash piles in the logging yard where I'd parked. A chill like that can change everything.

In the days and weeks to follow, I mulled over my season, an exercise that seems important to me. Of course, I'd never forgotten how it started, with that one terrible evening on the Hatchery Pool. But many wonderful days came after that, and besides, I'd already developed an email relationship with Joe Verlicco. Joe was becoming a friend. I'd do my best to cheerlead his return to Grand Lake Stream, just as I believed Tyke would do if the situation had been reversed.

I knew that by now, my submarine commander sport, Caleb, had left the surface world to rejoin his crew. He could be anyplace, from the Ionian Sea off the coast of Albania to somewhere along the Pacific Rim, to running up under the Arctic ice sheet. Now that I knew him, it was fun to imagine just where he might be. I remembered, most of all, the intensity of Caleb's gaze over the lakes, and a man whose world darkens for six months at a time as he probes its depths.

The older I get, the more time I spend thinking about my senior sports. Forrest Lipscomb and two generations behind him came for their usual five-day trip, and of course we talked about Forrest's brother, Charlie. It warms my heart in February to think of Forrest coordinating schedules of family members in order to plan another installment in the fifty-year family tradition.

It's the same for the Moulton family, which now needs three guides as more family members have signed on to their annual trip. Over the winter, I was lucky enough to meet up with Henry on a stay in Boston. At eighty-eight, he was as spry as ever, recalling anecdotes from long before I was born. I must continually remind myself that Henry views me in a context of many guides over many decades. He tells me that while many things have changed since his father first set foot in Grand Lake Stream in 1913, many things haven't. I was saddened to hear, last summer, that Henry lost his beloved Betsy following a brief illness.

I knew, too, that for the first time in fourteen years, I would have to get used to not fishing with Arthur, my Mandolin Man. Would I take anyone else to the places we shared, where so many of his insights still live? The meaning of a place is so often owed to the person with whom you shared it. Rob and Rebecca were already booked for different dates throughout the next season, but when we fish nowadays, I pick them up at their own place in Grand Lake Stream. It's a second home, but I sometimes believe that in their heart of hearts, it's their first home. If ever I have some crazy fishing idea that might include bushwhacking, portaging, beaver-dam fording, or uncharted water, I always think of them.

I spent many a night lying awake with disturbing images of the helicopter war in Vietnam that John Jewett so vividly described. If that's what it was like for me after only three days of listening to John, what, I wondered, must it be like for him, or for his buddies from the 187th who have never stopped reliving them? I've rarely been so humbled and at the same time grateful for what someone, who with great patience and kindness, was able to share.

Such reflections are a welcome aspect of winter. When there's deep snow on the roof, when narrow paths are shoveled to the woodshed and to the garage, when you're hunkered down for long nights with the woodstove hissing, those images and those special moments are a balm to the spirit.

Settling into winter at the top of the year is a learned discipline. So much is curtailed, so much prevented by weather conditions, that a plan B must be always at the ready. Much of what winter dishes out is negotiable with snowshoes, skis, or snowmobiles. But sometimes, it is nothing short of a forced incarceration.

We were assailed from early January until April by an old-fashioned Maine winter. The lowest courses of spruce limbs were buried in deep snow by New Year's. Deer corralled themselves in cedar yards, where coyotes picked off the weak, the young, and the pregnant. Ridgepoles on older homes and camps sagged with snow weight. Then, in February, the cold came—relentless and nonnegotiable.

Cold can create a different world overnight. Even here at the forty-fifth latitude, not very northerly by Alaskan standards, it's possible to get into trouble without knowing how you got there. Thirty degrees Fahrenheit is unimpressive, but it can kill you. So can seventy, if it's water and you're in it long enough.

How well (and dangerously) the cold is delivered, regardless of dress, is a function of humidity. Ahead of a snowstorm, when the humidity is up but the temperature is only in the twenties, it will feel colder than five degrees does in zero humidity.

Moisture notwithstanding, five above zero doesn't feel much different than five below. As the mercury descends, however, there seem to be waypoints: unscientific categories of cold that tell us things are getting very different. From the mid-teens down to the mid-single numbers is one level. You can feel that change but can certainly cope, given sufficient layers of insulated clothing.

The next category on the way down might be in the five-below to fifteen-below range. You can't take chances in these temperatures. At the same time, out of the wind, it's entirely possible to be comfortable all day in breathing layers of polypropylene, polar fleece, Gore-Tex, and Thinsulate.

Somewhere in the vicinity of twenty-five below, things enter a *Twilight Zone* of cold. A histamine reaction will turn the nasal faucet on and trigger enough tears to undam the ducts. All of this immediately freezes on the face. Body moisture may be released this way to compensate for the shutdown of other body systems. Just as in extreme heat, the body, especially the bladder, conserves.

At these temperatures, it's as though we're all put into an early stage of hypothermia from which we can recover, provided warmth is on the way soon. In the meantime, speech slows down. The mouth loses some of its elasticity so that words are mispronounced enough to flunk a sobriety test. Lips don't close around consonants well when they're frozen. No one at this stage of cold can say words like "impropriety" very well.

Cold flue pipes draw more slowly, so fireplaces and woodstoves are slow to get going. A strike-anywhere match may not strike easily or at all, because any humidity was frozen into the match head. The same thing has happened to the wood in the woodshed. Though dry and under cover, it took up any moisture in the air and then froze. It may sizzle and pop for a long time before giving up any BTU's.

Outside, it feels as if the cold has weight, making everything more cumbersome. The slightest bit of wind in the woods can produce a deafening racket of explosive cracks and snaps. The trees are frozen pillars, having lost all their give. But in the absence of wind, there is no quiet on earth like cold quiet. This is when carotid arteries are not only felt, but heard.

Streams slow to a trickle because so much of their water has fetched up into ice. What's left babbles and gurgles along under the covering, like subterranean voices. A frozen waterfall reflecting sunlight is a sight worth seeing. Sometimes, water that froze while in motion is blue. The pressure ridges that form on the lakes, as hundred-acre sections push against each other, can appear to be blue, as well. But not always. At other times, they are indistinguishable from a lake covered with snow. Snowmobilers going sixty miles per hour have slammed into walls of ice six feet tall—pressure ridges— and died without ever knowing what they hit. These ridges looked exactly like everything else in front of them.

Hunkering down in winter may be a dying art. Even as I was pondering this in February, wondering if I, too, might be losing the knack for doing without the diversions that now fill our overly-entertained homes, a snowstorm of the century dropped by while I was at camp preparing for a weekend of fishing through the ice.

Storm Nemo, as they called it, came in like a con man, schmoozing us before cleaning our clock. A light, powdery flurry fell gently through the afternoon as the world gradually whitened and brightened. The real storm would set in overnight. The camp was warming as I brought in water, using five-gallon pails to fill a galvanized washtub I'd set up on blocks. I also filled the old stainless steel donut-making basin that I'd put on the wood stove for a supply of hot water. This pan came with the camp. I've seen the same basin in old film footage of woods camps, where homemade donuts were a staple. They were deep-fried and served to the crews hot during the midmorning break from sawing and hauling.

Finishing these tasks in the fast-fading light, I deemed it too late to put out ice fishing tip-ups, or traps as they're sometimes called, for salmon or togue (lake trout). It was not, however, too late for a cusk line.

This is the fish whose photo is least sought and therefore most conspicuously absent from the family fishing album. It may be the mouth, downturned and puckered for effective bottom feeding. It may be the whiskers, cat-like, catfish-like, and creepy. What, you wonder, is something so southern-looking, so exotic, doing in stratified glacial lakes at this latitude? And that's even before noticing that its body tapers and elongates exactly like the anatomy of an eel.

As fate and fine cuisine would have it, the ugliest creatures sometimes make the most delectable fare. We need only evoke oysters, lobsters, or squid to argue this point. The cusk is in this lineup, with species that don't look tempting, but are incredibly tasty. Like other misshapen, repellent beings, this one is rarely seen socializing; he is scarce with his high-profile fellow swimmers, salmon and trout. His haunts are nocturnal. He'll bite when nothing else is biting. He is not seen in summer. If you stay up late enough on a winter's night, and are persistent enough, you'll see his face coming up through the ice hole at the other end of a flashlight beam and wonder if J. R. R. Tolkien was a cusk fisherman. The creator of Gollum would appreciate this creature.

Not wanting to tend more than two lines (the law requires checking them once every hour), I drilled two holes and set traps in with baits just off bottom. The tip-up flag does not need to be sprung in order to signify that a cusk has taken the bait. Sometimes, he will merely engulf it and stay put. Avid, savvy cusk fishermen gently lift the line, with a feather touch, to feel for weight. Feeling it, they react with a sharp jerk to set the hook.

Back at camp later, when one of these underworld Pisceans stretched across the sink well after dark, I might've questioned my motives. The slime alone would be off-putting enough to the bravest fish eaters. It's not a pretty process, but once the deed was done with a razor-sharp fillet knife, the results were redemptive, so said my palate.

By then, the winds were gusting to Category One. I turned on the Panasonic to learn that the power back home had gone out. For many people, that would mean no heat, as well as no lights, no water, and no cooking. I glanced around the rustic camp at the Humphrey gas lights—more than enough to cook by, read by, even tie flies by—and felt a kinship to the ones who came before, living this way routinely. Here were all the amenities: light, heat, cookstove, hot water. Lacking a companion to help me crowd a cribbage board, I went to the corner bookshelf and pulled out the volume that had always seemed perfect for hunkering beneath a blizzard—the complete works of Edgar Allen Poe. One title jumped out. Tonight, "A Descent into the Maelstrom" had to be the right choice for a short story.

It wasn't short enough. The day's journey and chore work weighed down my eyelids several pages before the end. The wood stove whistled and hissed as I fell through the vortex with the narrator of Poe's story, making it to the part when he saw the indescribable beauty following the terror of the hurricane at sea and his swirling descent. That was my cue to fill the stove, douse the lights, and do some descending and hissing of my own.

Curious about the storm's progress, I aimed a flashlight beam outside. The snows were coming all right, not the way they did that afternoon, but in drifts now. Why, I wondered, had the sharp minds at Meteorology Central recruited Jules Vernes' *Twenty Thousand Leagues Under the Sea* to name this snowstorm Nemo? Recognizing the synchronicity of Poe's maelstrom and Captain Nemo's journey to the depths was the last spark fired by my weary synapses.

A couple of times during the night, I heard the "Whomp!" of snow sliding off the metal roof onto the ground on the other side of the wall beside my bed. At 2:40 a.m., after one of these, I refilled the stove, letting the dampers remain only a third open to keep the camp at a good sleeping temperature. From then on, it was a night of dreamscapes that included rolling seas, loud winds, and the appearance of a Jungian mermaid anima figure that seemed to be guiding me on some journey downward, or inward.

At 5 a.m. I switched on Maine Public Broadcasting and put the blue enamel coffee pot on full flame. Thirty-one inches had already fallen in Portland, but the storm was expected to rage all day in Downeast Maine. Well, I reasoned, that's why I built an ice shack. I kicked up the stove several notches, lit the gaslight over the bed, and let Poe's narrator finish telling his listener in the story—and me— how he escaped certain death. A barrel went by within his reach. He was able to grab it and float up and out, never to forget the heavenly images he'd seen.

By then, the coffee pot had completed its song and dance on the cookstove. I poured myself a big, steaming mug. As the camp warmed, I sipped and Edgar spun out the rest of his yarn. Looking up from the last word, I saw that dawn was breaking.

Catching and filtering those first shards of light were beautiful ice designs on the insides of the camp's single-paned windows. On the one next to me, I rubbed a circle with the warmth of my hand. The day's dawning had done nothing for visibility. What I could make out was bare ground closest to the camp, just outside the row of snow dumped from the roof. The wind was eddying right where I'd parked my snowmobile, leaving it completely clear! That was a chore I'd be spared before heading out to the shack.

It was still snowing sideways, as it most often does out here. Sideways snow creates an ocean of snow waves on dry land. Moguls and billows several feet deep and sometimes fifty yards long might have little or no snow between them. It can make snowmobile travel dicey and shank's mare close to impossible. Enter the snowshoes. Mine are of the bearpaw variety, though I do like the beavertail type for really deep snow. That's what there was between the camp's outhouse—about thirty yards away—and me, and it was calling. Without snowshoes, it might've been a close call to the finish line.

The storm volume outside reached a deafening decibel, but I was able to drown most of it out with the sizzle of venison sausage and the rest with the radio. I intended to be well-fortified for whatever energy stores it might take to get from the camp to the ice shack. For such a morning, only my lumberjack special would do: two eggs over medium, deer meat patties, home fries, raisin toast with strawberry jam, and hot coffee.

When all this was overpowered and the galley cleaned up, it was still only 7 o'clock, a good time to wet a line.

The wind was out of the east, as it usually is during Nor'easters here. This sculpted the aforementioned snow waves so that instead of blocking my route crossways to the shack, they lined up with it. In other words, there were lanes of shallow snow between high ridges, leading straight from the camp to my green camouflage shanty. I merely chose a lane and snowmobiled the half mile to the shack with less difficulty than if it were the Long Island Expressway.

Looking out the windows of a fishing shack, plugged into the middle of a lake during an unrelenting blizzard, reminded me again of Poe's character. One could almost believe that there was nothing else out there beyond the whiteout, or the maelstrom—that you were indeed the last person on earth. A speck in the vastness. A smudge on fifteen-thousand acres of snow. The propane heater was set on high, but cold air still blew in through cracks around the door. Through most of the morning, snow continued to eddy around the shack, leaving bare ice up close to the skis, and a growing, high wall of snow behind my home on the ice. When this wall reached a certain height, the shack, in its eddy, suddenly became easier to heat, warranting a switch to medium, and then eventually low, on the space heater. The cold air stopped coming in around the door. The shack had been surrounded, encased by tons of the best insulation Nature has.

Amid that fantasy of ultimate loneliness, which I let develop for my own amusement—amid the howling wind, blowing snow, and mounting drifts—something happened. It wasn't the roof caving in from snow weight on the six-by-eight structure. The wind was too strong to allow very much snow to build up topside. It wasn't the shack heater running out of propane—I'd attached a new, full one that I'd put on the tote sled and towed out here with me. It wasn't my fantasy of a snow Armageddon playing all the way out to full panic, either. It was something that snaps you back into reality faster than anything else can.

The fish started biting.

Just as if the barometer had plummeted to a magic number—just as if I'd won the biggest betting hand of my life at the Solunar Table—all of a sudden, under me, there were fish! While outside my shack there was a loud, swirling, spiraling blight upon any life form, inside, the action went into overdrive.

I had two holes inside the shack, both lined with five-gallon pails with the bottoms cut out. Over one, I'd placed a Polar tip-up. I'd rigged an Emerald shiner with a tiny split shot weight so that I could get it to the bottom. That's where the whitefish would be, if any chanced into the area. I sat slightly to the left of the other hole, jigging a leadfish lure with my right hand from a poplar jig stick I'd made myself.

No sooner had the flag on the Polar rig gone up and I was half way to my feet, than something almost yanked the jig stick out of my hand. I came up so hard, my knuckles rapped the shack's ceiling. The line piled up on the floor as I hand-over-handed, hoping not to lever the fish on the lower edge of the ice hole and lose it. So many go that way. I leave enough Maxima leader attached to the ice fishing line to let me know when to slow up and maneuver a fish to the mouth of the hole.

The moment came. A flash of white belly went left to right, tugging hard, too fast for me to gauge the fish's size. On the next pass, I saw only a shadow—the back of the fish. All this time, line was paying off of the Polar reel, which I was powerless to tend. I assumed a school of whitefish had arrived, and I had one on each line.

Fishing assumptions are like weather predictions. When you're wrong, you can always cite the vicissitudes of Nature. On the next pass, I got the fish's mouth pointing upward. When I hauled with both hands, a two-foot, five-pound togue was suddenly flopping on the floor, trying to get back down the hole. I blocked it with my body, disgorged the hook with a hemostat, opened the door, and pitched it outside, not without noticing that it possessed every attribute of dinner.

By then, the line on the Polar rig was almost to the knot—the end. Setting the hook was easy. In fact, the Emerald shiner was probably half digested by now. This, too, felt like a sizable fish, but it fought differently. More yanking—not the steady, downward pressure of the togue. It surprised both the fish and me when it fairly flew out of the hole as though when seeing light, it believed it to be the direction of its freedom. A twenty-inch landlocked salmon now lay at my feet. With due dispatch, I determined the hooking was not mortal and released the gorgeous specimen back down the hole. From its depths, this *Salmo salar* could dream of its trip to the outer space maelstrom. As fast as I rebaited and let down the line, the Polar flag went up again. It was a seventeen-and-a-half-inch whitefish, and this was only the beginning.

Like the proverbial tree falling in the forest, sounds that no one else heard rose from my green smudge on the snow for the rest of that stormy day. It was the special laughter that comes from crazy fishing luck, a laughter that, once hearing it, produces more. For some star-crossed reason, fish flocked to my two holes while snow drifted all around my meager shelter. Those two shafts of light beaming down to the depths were signaling fish from acres away to swim toward them. Many fell into my trap, suddenly pulled up through the tunnel to the other universe, the one that sent them insects in summer. Just as quickly, they were released back down the shaft, perhaps shaken, perhaps euphoric from escape like Poe's narrator.

The narrow arc scribed by the winter sun was never evident, thanks to Nemo. He apparently possessed the power to darken the day earlier than usual too. By then, his help from Titan was weakening. The angle of the falling snow would soon be 90 degrees instead of 30, a sure sign that the wind was dying. By the time I brought more water into camp, the snow had stopped, and Venus was visible over the southwestern horizon.

A thick bed of red-orange coals glowed when I opened the woodstove door. The camp, by no means cold, would soon be toasty, sending the aroma of trout hollandaise out through the stovepipe, enough to flare the nostrils of any wayfaring moose. In gas lamplight, I selected another product of Poe's boundless imagination, every now and then looking up from it to reminisce on the day's fishing experience, the sparest telling of which would smack of exaggeration. Nor would its full measure ever be known from any camp log entry. It was mine to dream on and nurture.

After dousing the gaslights, the night's final conscious brainwave activity was a reflection on hunkering of the kind I'd done this weekend. Maybe it *was* a dying art, and maybe I'd tested myself. Maybe I needed to know that I hadn't grown passively reliant on the amusements that came only through a 110-volt outlet. If ever I lost my willingness to cancel the distractions and background noise of connectivity, then that important road inward might be blocked, and something cherished, lost. To this secluded, backwoods outpost came the certainty that sometimes, the self required its own, undivided company to regenerate. As Poe demonstrated, just beyond the maelstrom, there is indescribable beauty.

MIHKU IN SPRING

Spring weather in Downeast Maine is often unsettled well into June. Rain, wind, and temperatures that may not be below freezing, but feel it, are common, and so is low-grade hypothermia. It will also happen that, tucked into that tumultuous period of the year, a day or two of perfect calm will appear. Then, like a teenager freed after house arrest, spring bursts forth as if to make up for lost time. Temperatures may soar into the sixties or even seventies.

I'd been nurturing an idea for the season's maiden voyage, only to have it scuttled day after day by the weather. I'd waited, busying myself with trapping bait, tying some trout flies, tuning up my paddle, and changing the gear oil in the outboard. Then, during the last week of April, it happened. When the sun rose, no wind rose with it. I checked NOAA and every other local forecast I could find. Everything agreed that this was the reprieve. The next day, the wind would pick up again.

As I drove the paved, then dirt, roads to a certain boat launch, I noticed the poplars were in full bloom. This meant that out in Township Unknown, Drummond would be harvesting the blossoms in order to make batches of bogwani for the coming year. The forsythia had jumped forward, too, and as I pulled up to the launch, I was sure I saw a couple of mayflies skittering across the surface of the water. If I could capture one in my hat, I'd try to copy the pattern back at the fly-tying vise when the weather reprieve was over.

Winter ice had moved and reconfigured the Roman garden of stump sculptures at "the mouth of Unknown Stream," as I'd come to call it. There were some tight squeezes negotiated with the outboard tilted up, using the paddle to deflect some of the floating gargoyles. Amongst them, a mayfly was perched atop a particular stump that looked like a coyote in a yelping stance. I brought my fine-meshed trout net gently down over it until the mayfly flew upward and into it. A model for my next fly-tying session was now on retainer.

The water temperature was much too frigid for good bassing on the fly rod. In fact, shale ice still clung to the shoreline under the alders. Four Common Mergansers boiled up when I rounded the first bend and started the motor. I knew I'd probably see them again, since they headed upstream.

I had two missions in mind. One was to try to rouse a trout or two from the quickwater just above Mihku's cabin. I'd tied some early season patterns like a Hare's Ear Nymph and a Woolly Worm to fish in the eddies formed by some of the large boulders in the stream. The other mission was to visit Mihku, following a hunch that he'd be visiting his cabin on this beautiful, warm, windless day.

Intermittently, on my way upstream, I cut the motor and paddled. It's difficult not to feel like an intruder as you make your way noisily through one of nature's sanctums. Without wind, and with the Johnson 9.9 horsepower motor off, the quiet was excruciating. Only my paddle strokes and the slight lapping of the downstream current on my hull breached the silence.

There are a dozen or so hairpin bends in the stream as it makes its way from the fast water above Mihku's cabin, all the way down to the Roman stump garden at the stream's mouth. These turns are so sharp, the river sometimes reverses directions for a short stretch before righting itself. As I began to nose around one of these turns, a splashing sound froze my paddle stroke in midair. Even so, the propulsion from my previous stroke was bringing the bow around the bend.

I leaned forward, craning my neck to see. The first thing I saw was a flow of ripples pushing out across the stream. The next was a head. A bull moose with a stubble of velvety antlers had entered the stream from a game path that came up through the black alders to the water's edge. He was now in deep water as I backpaddled in order to prevent hitting him with my bow. The bull eyeballed me without altering his stroke. I saw his destination—another game path that parted the pucker-brush. Obviously, he had made this crossing before.

When his hooves found a purchase, he seemed to grow out of the stream to an eye-popping height and majesty. Assuming he'd mosey down the trail, showing me his sentiments with his backside, I waited, suspended in the current by using feathering paddle strokes. I watched in awe as he turned side-to to me, dripping a deluge onto the bank of matted, dead grass. Presently, I heard some unidentifiable sound coming from his direction—a low, muffled grumble, and I wondered if I was about to see another moose step out from behind him. As the sound changed into muddled groans that almost sounded like words, I finally realized it was the bowels of the bull moose talking. The sounds were moving from the far end of his digestive tract toward his head. He seemed to be listening to them just as attentively as I was. It was an orchestra that was building up, like Beethoven's Ninth Symphony finale, to a crescendo that both the bull and I awaited, full of anticipation.

When the moment came, the bull lowered his chin so that his bell drooped below his brisket. The belch that had traveled so far, gathering force along the way, disappointed neither of us. Once the alders in front of him stopped rustling from the blast, once its echo faded off into reservation lands, the proud bull turned and looked straight at me. Was it a bid for acknowledgement? I hadn't moved a muscle—from long experience in close proximity to these sometimes irritable titans of the north woods. But, reading my cue, I gave a subtle nod. With that, the dripping wet bull, which had just ejected what must have been a very uncomfortable gas bubble, gave a glance down the game path, another back at me, then sauntered off at a leisurely gait.

Rounding the next turn, the four Mergansers flushed again, touching the stream with their wing tips until they were out of sight around the next bend. That would be the one where I'd feel the change in current under the canoe. The water was up from snowmelt and spring runoff anyway, which meant it took heavier work at the paddle to make upstream progress. Any break or interruption in my rhythm allowed the current to take over, turning me one way or the other.

I thought I was making good headway, with both concentration and stamina, until—"QUARK!"

The high water had fooled me. I thought the Black Sentinel's perch was farther along, but there he was, ancient and oily black, and on the job as usual. The trouble was, he startled me, and I lost rhythm. The current spun me around, and as it did, I peered up the embankment to see the huge bird atop a black spruce. That's when I saw a coil of wood smoke coming from the chimney of Mihku's cabin.

It was work to turn the Grand Laker back around, and even more to make progress upstream. After each stroke, I looked left until I saw Mihku, alerted by his guardian and standing beside the cabin. I gave a paddle wave between strokes and Mihku waved me in. If I could negotiate it, the opening to his paddleboat canal was about two canoe lengths away.

The stream now thrashed against the bow as though it were dead set against any further intrusion upriver. I managed to get just beyond the opening so that when I ruddered reverse strokes from the left side, my bow would hit shore. By this time, Mihku was there to meet me. I was impressed by the pulling power he was able to exert to get me out of the current and up into the canal. Once in, everything went quiet.

"Tahn Gok!" Mihku said, and I remembered the last time he'd greeted me with the same salutation when he'd snuck up on me from behind in this same canal.

"Tahn Gok!" I replied, as I stood and extended my hand. As I poled the Grand Laker the thirty yards or so that brought me around behind his camp, I explained how I'd wanted to come sooner but the winter had gotten the best of me with its one hundred and ten inches of snow, followed by a long mud season. Mihku said it was the same for him—a long winter holed up inside while the storms raged outside. I apologized for bringing only sandwiches. My intention had been to make it upstream a little farther and invite some trout to join us. Mihku smiled, saying he had a better idea. When I followed him up the hill, he pointed to the pelts of two muskrat hanging from the hemlock limb nearest the fire pit.

"Kiwhos," he said. Kiwhosuwey, or muskrat meat, was a spring treat long relished in the tribe. It was unavoidably losing favor with the young, who had little interest in the meat or the pelts, even though the market for the latter had actually grown and become more lucrative in recent years. Mihku told me it had been a good spring for trapping. "A nice steady snowmelt and runoff, and no sudden floodings," he said.

Without any trapping pressure, the population of kiwhos had mushroomed. I knew this from my own observations during the guiding season. While muskrats are most active at night, they're also visible in the daytime, going into or coming out of their lodges, which are built almost exclusively from aquatic plants. Occasionally, I'll see the opening to a den on the stream bank. This will be above the waterline, and somewhere there will be an exit, most likely underwater. One of the least known characteristics of "rats," as they are sometimes called by trappers, is that they can swim backwards.

Mihku explained that his stretching frames at home were all used up with pelts already on them drying, and that he could've used more. He expected a good return on them when he met up with his trading contact from Montreal. Since it had also been a good eeling harvest the previous fall, he had gone into winter pretty flush financially. "Got stir-crazy a few times," he laughed. "The wife was ready to trade me in for a bigger TV."

The fact that there are members of the tribe still living very close to the old ways is mostly hidden from public view. These are quiet lives, concerned with tradition, sustenance, and meanings more endangered than any fish or game. It's only because my work takes me to such out-of-the-way places that I encounter people like Mihku, and even then, it seems like something more fated than accidental. There are others living and working as Mihku does. Tribal guides still offer traditional moose hunts to clients with the right combination of grit and forbearance to sleep out by night, and by day silently cruise narrow waterways in a canoe. The ancestors of Mihku's ancestors hunted just this way.

It was inevitable that our conversation would turn to those things that mattered most to us. The subject of our mutual friend, as yet unmentioned, hovered in front of the fire with us as if Drummond was there in person. We may have been playing a game of who would speak of him first. It turned out to be me. I said I'd made my usual winter trek into Kiskesasik, or Township Unknown, only to find him hale and busy. Mihku had not seen him since their eel-and-provisions swap the previous fall. He, too, found Drummond to be as fit as ever as he admired all the items Mihku had brought him.

We fell silent for a time as I attempted to fight back the urge to express a smoldering worry of mine. I wondered if Mihku had it, too. Finally, I clumsily blurted out that eventually one of us would find him dead out there. And what then? Would there even be anyone to tell?

Mihku's expression didn't change. His eyes met mine as if to say, "Yes?" If there was a point to be made, Mihku was still waiting to hear it. In turn, he saw this puzzle me and, after a long moment, said, "Our friend chose his fate long ago."

The Black Sentinel left its perch and swept over the small clearing where we sat. The beat of its wings produced a tumult in the upper boughs of the hemlocks, a whirring and whooshing sound unique to the larger raptors. When it was quiet again, what Mihku had just said rested comfortably on my mind.

I saw how Mihku carried something of Drummond in him: some uncanny calm, or resolve—some aura of acceptance as if there was nothing in his life either to prove or repudiate. Yes, I'm sure he, too, thought that one of us would find Drummond one day. But it was the life, and therefore the death, Drummond chose. The sorrow we would feel with Drummond's passing would be solely our own. We would do all the missing and mourning; doing so on our friend's behalf would be a mistaken interpretation of his life.

Just as we were finishing our splendid muskrat lunch, I glanced at Mihku's cabin and mentioned that my own place on West Grand Lake was very similar in design and construction. That, of course, led to explaining how I might lose it. Mihku had heard and read all about what was going on next door to the reservation. Every Indian, he said, pays close attention to these things, as if it's born into them to do so. There had been too much suffering and loss in the history of the tribes not to take notice when big changes came to the land around them.

He then spoke of a "mark of sadness," which he said was evident on every Indian face if you stopped to look. It's in all the paintings and photographs of Native people, he said, dating back centuries. It was there, he admitted, in his own face, and I'm certain he saw me searching for it. "No shame," he said, laughing. I didn't know if he meant there was no shame in my looking for it, or no shame in his having this mark.

The remains of the kiwhos lay scattered on our tin plates on a great, flat rock off to one side of the fire pit. I'd made guide's coffee. After pouring two cups, Mihku went on to say that the sadness he was speaking of was not there originally, before there was anyone to take photographs or paint likenesses. It was not there before Black Robe arrived with his news of a fiery forge awaiting unsaved souls. It was not there in the tribe's own mythology, remnants of which are still alive today in various songs, chants, and recitations.

On the contrary, the original Native outlook and customary disposition, he said, was positive, open, and accepting. It was, according to Mihku, this very trait that made them prey to people who would corral them into pens and cages before either eradicating them or removing them from their homeland. It was this "great displacement" of the original Americans that etched the mark, he said, not only on Passamaquoddy faces, but on the faces of all Native people.

"But now there's the reservation," I said. I was referring to the Maine Indian Claims Settlement Act of 1980, which had returned lands to Maine's Native peoples along with payments of around $81 million.

"Yes," Mihku smiled. And then he went silent. I'd learned from years of working with tribal guides that a better way to hear if there was more was to wait, rather than coax. In the Native way, the silences were natural, and during them, there were things going on all around us. The current where the fast water smoothed out gurgled softly. Wood thrushes trilled out in the woods, and our waning cook fire hissed and popped. When this soundtrack had played for some sufficient interlude, Mihku continued.

He told me that I could see, if I wished, my own relationship to my guide's site as a reenactment of what the tribes lived through long before either of us was born. Ownership, originally, was a foreign concept to them. The real privilege, he said, had never been ownership, but stewardship. He was right—that was the privilege I had enjoyed for so many years. Now, the choices were ownership— or forfeiture.

That was the depth and breadth of the problem, though I hadn't known how to say it so simply, not before hearing from Agnes, and now Mihku. Agnes had said, "It must have been exactly this way for the Indians," and now, here was Mihku explaining what she meant. The news that I must be an owner or one day lose my beloved charge produced the very reaction Mihku was talking about—an abiding sorrow brought on by displacement.

We sat a long time, refilling our tin cups, letting more refrains from stream and forest play through the campsite. I had the distinct feeling, once more, that while our voices remained silent, our thoughts were conversing.

Mihku and I cleaned up as a team, just as if we did this together every day. He walked me down to the canal, but not before I stopped once more to admire the paddle pen and the roller assembly he'd made for launching it.

As Mihku was about to shove my canoe out into the current, I asked him if he minded if I brought sports up the stream now and again when the winds were up.

"Keytol-al!" he called out to me as the current spun my bow around. "Of course! We don't own the river. We can't!" he called after me.

The swift current sent me downstream so fast that the "QUARK" that predictably sounded was like a delayed exclamation point on Mihku's words. I raised my paddle to Mihku before going around the first bend. I could feel his eyes on me as I drifted out of sight.

RETURNING

Spring arrived like an invasion. Suddenly, all six roads in town were fringed with thick growths of wide-bladed weeds obscuring the littered ditches. Fern tops and fiddleheads greened the forest floor, concealing the brown, rotted detritus, matted from snow weight. Recently skeletal yard maples swelled into bouquets of red and green buds and blossoms, as if an edict had been received to be fruitful and multiply. The first Phoebe came calling the second week of April, ten days before the ice went out. Robins were already chirping, even during the occasional spring snow squalls.

By May 1, everything was lush, though some days the temperature never left the forties. Salmon fishermen are least popular among spring's fair weather ambassadors. They lobby for wet, raw, blustery days—salmon weather—while the other group pickets the post office and The Pine Tree Store demanding sunny, salubrious days of easy living. The fishing hangs in this balance.

Making my rounds, crossing the traffic bridge over the stream, I noticed, each day, a few more fishermen lashing the pools. When someone's rod was doubled, I stopped to follow the fray to a conclusion. Through windows left partly open at night, I could hear the changes in stream flow, following the inevitable adjustments to the gates at the dam with the spring rains.

As May progressed, I loved the lilac-perfumed mornings and the peep-frog symphonies at dusk. Everything was alive and making noise about it, including me. After a long winter of relative isolation, I probably talked more than listened on those first few jobs before my guiding stride kicked in. The company and the conversation were so welcome, I'm sure I presented the symptoms of someone who needed to cut down on caffeine.

Then, some demented scorekeeper apparently determined that I'd had too many contented days in a row. In an instant, one drizzly evening, my languorous mood was shattered by nothing more than a voice. One voice—one syllable. It came from the stream, like so many voices do at that time of year, but it carried a tone, or inflection, or likeness to another voice I'd once heard, fatefully, a year earlier. This time, there was no hesitation. It was an immediate, headlong charge toward the water, heart in my throat, breath suspended.

Bounding down the hill, the Hatchery Pool came into view. I made out two forms just below the sharp bend in the stream. Two forms! Just like before. But at the last instant, I pulled up short— just before leaping from the grassy bank. I stopped because a splash caught my eye and a voice caught my ear. "Hey!" it said. Then, as I stood there in glazed consciousness, the salmon jumped once more, and the lucky angler shouted, "Hey!" again. "Hey!" not "Help!"

My sudden, breathless appearance at the stream's edge drew the attention of the two fishermen to me. They looked at me strangely, though no less strangely than I looked at them. I was there with no rod. My distress and confusion must have been obvious. Did I need help? Was I OK? No. Yes. I babbled my replies and backed away.

When the stupor subsided enough to allow humiliation to replace it, I was most of the way back up the hill, trying to get my tachycardia under control. I'd fully expected another calamity awaiting me when I reached the river. In fact, I wondered if this would now be my permanent reaction to unexpected noises from the water. Instead, it was a landlocked salmon on one end of a line, and a jubilant fisherman on the other.

Twilight fell, and there were more voices coming up from the river. From the sound of it, the fishing was good. I tried transporting myself to Fenway Park by tuning in the ball game. It was the fourth inning and there was no score between the Toronto Blue Jays and the Boston Red Sox, but the cadence of the calls and the drone of the fans worked to calm me. I was being lulled into the first presentiments of sleep when a knock at the door startled me to my feet.

I switched on the yellow light bulb outside the cabin and looked through the blinds, but the wader-clad man who stood there had the hood up on his rain slicker, obscuring his face. Feeling no threat from a fellow fisherman, I opened the door.

When I stepped back to let the sport enter, he dropped his hood, and I stood face to face with Joe Verlicco! The split second of recognition was followed by both of us falling into a bear hug. Then we shook hands, for a long time.

"You're back! You're back, Joe!" I effused, and only then noticed another man standing outdoors in the yellow haze of the light and mist. I moved to let him in. He was another friend of Joe's from Quincy.

"Yeah, I thought about it all winter, and decided I had to come back. I had to, but I can't be on that stream without thinking of Tyke. Without thinking about that night. How at the last minute, I changed my mind and came up to the Hatchery Pool where Tyke was. It was why I got to be with him in the last seconds. Like it was meant to be. I also wanted to thank you for coming over to my cabin that night. It meant a lot to me. It still does."

I turned the radio off, and we talked of the fishing, my guiding season so far, and of Joe's family back home. He said he hoped to bring his wife up in September. May and September had always been the two months Joe and Tyke chose for their trips.

"It'll be tough," Joe said. "I expect it will be tough for a long time. I hope I can keep coming." Eventually, Joe and his friend said they'd like to get back to their cabin, get out of their waders, and settle in for the night.

When Joe was about to take the last step down the stoop, he turned around and said, "You know, we'll always be connected, you and I, because of that night, because of what happened."

"I know, Joe." Right then, I thought about telling him what had happened an hour earlier—how, when I'd heard a voice calling out from the stream, I thought I was about to relive that nightmarish event of a year ago. Instead, I let it pass, and watched both men grab the fly rods they'd leaned up against the side of the cabin and stroll off into the darkness.

Seeing Joe outside my door, wader-clad, with a fly rod in his hand, I knew from that day forward that he'd forever fish with the memory of his friend with him. Perhaps he'd realized that Tyke had died doing what he loved most, and that, after all, wasn't so bad an option.

Forrest Lipscomb had responded the same way as Joe, years before, after his brother, Charlie's ashes were committed to Kennebasis. Charlie had returned, faithfully, for decades, and now Forrest and his family do the same.

Henry Moulton, too, reinstated a family tradition of returning long after his friend and guide, Harley Fitch was gone. Now, family members two generations along are feeling the same magnetic pull that Francis Moulton had known a century earlier.

I knew there was something special about those quiet coves and river shores for Arthur, the Mandolin Man, when he wouldn't speak for long periods at a time. And Agnes came to discover for herself the magnetism that had drawn her husband for so many years before his passing.

This powerful force, the need to return, is why Ray Plewacki, now ninety-three, started putting change in a cigar box the day after he gets home from Nova Scotia each year. By the time the next year's trip rolls around, it's mostly paid for. I'd like to think that every deposit is a reminder that no matter what is going on in his life, there is always the thought of that hopeful cast over pristine water carrying him forward.

There is an oft-repeated story of a US Army Airborne soldier named Jack Hemingway, who was dropped behind enemy lines during the Normandy invasion of World War II. He was the only one who risked carrying a sectioned, bamboo fly rod along with the rest of his gear. During one of the few respites between the horrors of his unit's advance into the French interior, he saw a promising stream. It was his only chance to limber his cane fly rod, tie on a fly, and cast a pool before the bloody mayhem resumed.

As he fished, two German soldiers emerged on the far bank, fully armed. Both Old Glory and the Airborne patches were in full view on Jack Hemingway's sleeves. He marked the enemy soldiers, but never interrupted his casting. Instead of shouldering their weapons and drawing a bead, the Germans stood motionless, watching the fly line scribe its graceful figures over the angler's head, then lay out perfectly straight across the riffles.

Moments stretched into minutes, and then—a rise that all three saw. The soldier marked the spot, eased his line back in a retrieve, then landed his fly on target before the circle of ripples had dissipated. The splash and froth of the strike held all three spellbound. When it was over, and the hook removed, there were no waves or salutes. Neither were shots fired. Only a quiet retreat, deemed the best demonstration of reverence for a moment of truce produced by the simplest act among men.

ACKNOWLEDGMENTS

Working on this book introduced me to the idea of good debt. Receiving the gift of openness from people who trust you feels like good debt. It docsn't ask to be repaid, only to be reciprocated with equal openness.

That's what I've tried to do. The retelling of what has been so intimately shared should be as straight and true as the keel of my canoe. I've no doubt fallen short of that standard; I only wish to be on record as having tried to paddle that line as truly as I could.

I must thank those who bestowed this good debt, as a group. Their names are all here, except in those noted instances where wishes were honored with a pseudonym or first name only.

Barbara Barr, my friend and editor-at-large, from her Impeccably Edited studio in La Jolla, California, is somehow able to guide a writer down that shadowy path between subjectivity and objectivity, between the literary and the mechanical, between what's nice to write and what's nicc to read. I Iow she does that is as much a mystery to me as any alluded to in this book.

My Skyhorse editor, Cory Allyn, and I both share an admiration for what has to be one of the best writer's guides ever written: Stephen King's *On Writing*. We therefore had an easy time of it, working together toward clarity, brevity, and keeping the reader utmost in mind. Thanks Cory.

Native influences were bound to find their way into *Wide and Deep*. Working since 2002 for the History and Preservation Office of the Passamaquoddy tribe has brought the tribal culture into my life, and therefore into my work. Guiding with Passamaquoddy guides gives me an older lens through which to experience the woods and waters of our region. Donald Soctomah, Ray and David Sockabasin, and Wayne Newell have all had a hand in opening my eyes to Native wisdom, traditions, angst, and savvy.

Clearly, I wasn't the only listener in these pages. Sandra Lloyd, Craig Fowler, Agnes, Drummond, and others were gracious and patient as I spilled beans of my own. Outside of these pages, it was Shelley, as always, whose listening, reading, weighing, and considering determined so much of the way forward. When there was no oxygen left in the room, she piped it in. When thinking was playing bully to feeling, she pleaded for the underdog.

Finally, I've noticed that the one person left out of nearly every acknowledgments section is the reader. The reader—the endgame, the whole point—goes unmentioned in the end. Reader—you were there in spirit and on my mind for the whole project. For that, and for the forbearance to wade these waters with me, I'm sending along heartfelt thanks.